アドベンチャー
日本語上級

FURTHER ADVENTURES IN JAPANESE

AN ADVANCED COURSE, SUITABLE FOR AP* PREPARATION

HIROMI PETERSON, NAOMI HIRANO-OMIZO & JUNKO ADY

Illustrated by Michael Muronaka

Cheng & Tsui Company

Boston

*AP is a registered trademark of the College Board, which was not involved in the production of, and does not endorse, this product.

16 15 14 13 12 11 10 09   2 3 4 5 6 7 8 9 10

Field Test Edition 2009

Published by
Cheng & Tsui Company, Inc.
25 West Street
Boston, MA 02111-1213 USA
Fax (617) 426-3669
www.cheng-tsui.com
"Bringing Asia to the World"™

ISBN 978-0-88727-7047

Illustrations by Michael Muronaka

The *Adventures in Japanese* series includes textbooks, workbooks, teacher's handbooks, audio CDs, software, and hiragana/katakana workbooks. Visit **www.cheng-tsui.com** for more information.

Printed in the United States of America

FURTHER ADVENTURES IN JAPANESE TEXT
CONTENTS

DOWNLOADS

Users of this book have access to free, downloadable audio recordings that correspond to the listening sections, and an electronic flashcard program for studying the AP *kanji*. To download the audio files, you simply need to register your product key on our website.

Your Product Key: **2U4A-RYBA**

Instructions for Downloading Audio Recordings and Electronic Flashcards:
1. Visit the Cheng & Tsui Download Center at http://www.cheng-tsui.com/downloads and follow the instructions for creating a Cheng-Tsui.com user account.
2. Register your product key.
3. Download the files.
4. For technical support, please contact support@cheng-tsui.com or call 1-800-554-1963.

TO THE STUDENT AND THE TEACHER

Welcome to *Further Adventures in Japanese!* When discussions of an Advanced Placement Japanese Language and Culture exam began, we received many inquiries from current *Adventures in Japanese* text users if another text addressing advanced placement needs would be produced. We felt the responsibility to respond to these requests and began work on a text that would be firmly based on the Japanese National Standards and on the ACTFL Proficiency and Performance guidelines. In this text, we expect students of Japanese to further sharpen their communicative skills in listening, reading, writing and speaking. We want students to be able to function successfully in daily interactions at an advanced level and in culturally appropriate ways.

The goals of this field test version of our AP textbook are multifold. First, we would like to produce, at the end, a student who is skilled at communicating in Japanese at a multi-paragraph level. The student should be able to listen and comprehend, read, write (by typing) and speak at a paragraph level, and be able to connect these paragraphs into a more cohesive whole when it is required. Second, we want to prepare students to successfully take the Advanced Placement Japanese exam. We began writing this text by developing a list of required AP *kanji* and a list of commonly used *kanji* compound words. We then combined the 21 themes designated by the College Board as AP topics into seven lessons and created sample practice exams for each lesson. The students are introduced to the lessons, then practice new and review material, and take exams in the AP format so that they will be able to approach the actual AP exams with confidence. Our ultimate goal, however, is to develop students who not only gain skill in communicating in Japanese, but can think deeply and critically about cultural values and attitudes; in this way, they can better manage the challenges of becoming responsible, compassionate and thoughtful stewards of a more sustainable global community. By preparing for the exams using this text, we are hopeful that students will be able to reach our loftiest goals with support from their teachers.

In the following paragraphs, we discuss some of the features of this volume.

Kanji

The total amount of *kanji* on the recommended AP list is 410. The total amount of *kanji* found in AIJ Volumes 1-4 and in this text is 461 characters. In AIJ Volume 1, students learn 17 new *kanji*; in AIJ Volume 2, they learn 98; in AIJ 3 Volume 3, they learn 121; and in AIJ Volume 4, they learn 121. In this text, students learn an additional 121 new *kanji*. Cumulatively, by the end of Volume 1, students have learned 17 new *kanji*; upon completion of Volume 2, they know 121; at the end of Volume 3, they have 219; and on completing Volume 4, they know 340 *kanji*. After finishing this volume, students will have learned a total of 461 *kanji*. The AIJ texts introduce 51 *kanji* beyond those on the AP *kanji* list. We have compiled a list of commonly used *kanji* compounds with all of the *kanji* required for the AP exam. We have also prepared electronic *kanji* flashcards, available online at http://www.cheng-tsui.com/downloads, so students may study the *kanji* at their own pace.

Topics

According to the College Board, the AP Japanese exam will test Japanese language and culture using 21 selected topics. This text provides practice on all 21 topics. In order that all of the topics can reasonably be covered in a year, however, we have combined two to four related topics and consolidated them into seven lessons. The instructor may select any lesson, or part of a lesson, and may present them in any sequence, according to the needs of his or her class. The lessons and the topics are:

Lesson 1: Self, Family and Friends, Daily Life, Leisure, Hobbies and Sports
Lesson 2: Home and Community, Cities, Towns and Villages, Nature and Environment
Lesson 3: School and Education, Clothing, Communication and Media, Technology
Lesson 4: Work and Career, Rites of Life, Festivals and Annual Events
Lesson 5: Transportation, Weather and Climate
Lesson 6: Food, Shopping, Body and Health
Lesson 7: Travel, Japan and the World

Tasks

Each lesson begins with two or three tasks, which indicate the objectives of the lesson. The tasks may be used for conversation practice and/or an OPI (Oral Proficiency Interview) exam at the end of the term.

Culture

Cultural information broadens students' perspective of the language and promotes a deeper cultural understanding of Japan in the context of the cultures of the world. Cultural topics are provided to serve as a jumping-off point for students to conduct extended research and further enrich their independent learning.

New *kanji*

Each lesson introduces 17 to 19 new *kanji*, additional readings for previously learned *kanji,* and some *kanji* to be learned for recognition. Students are not required to write *kanji* by hand for the AP exam. They must be able to type *kanji* with accuracy and speed. In authentic situations, however, there are still times when writing *kanji* by hand is necessary, so we do recommend that students practice learning to write as many *kanji* as possible.

New vocabulary

Approximately 60 new vocabulary items are introduced in each lesson. These vocabulary items allow students to communicate at a more advanced level in all of the topics they study.

Grammar

The grammar taught in volumes 1-4 of *Adventures in Japanese* provides ample means for students to communicate successfully in most situations. While a few new grammatical forms are introduced in this volume, students are provided with more opportunities to practice grammar learned at earlier levels. This practice allows them to communicate with greater accuracy, ease and fluency. The concise treatment of grammar in this text also provides comparisons among similar grammatical forms and more practice so that students can make distinctions in usage among these similar forms.

Activities

Activities in each lesson enable students to practice their reading, speaking and writing skills, aiming at a paragraph level at minimum. The contents are related to the topics in the lesson. At the end of each section, there are also pre- or post-activities for the listening and reading AP sample tests. At the end of each lesson, you will find a set of sample tests designed in the AP exam format. Each set of sample tests includes one listening test with five multiple choice questions, one reading test with five multiple choice questions, a Text Chat test, a comparison/contrast test, a cultural posting test, a conversation test, a return telephone call test, a school announcement test, a story narration test and a cultural perspective presentation test. Of these, three tests (marked in the text with a CD graphic) are accompanied by audio files available for download from http://www.cheng-tsui.com/downloads. For more sample tests, please refer to *Strive for a 5: AP Japanese Practice Tests*. We urge teachers to carefully follow the instructions, including the time requirements, to provide an authentic test-taking situation for students.

Scripts and Answers

For your reference, you will find the scripts for the listening section, the conversation section (speaking) and the return telephone call section (speaking) following all of the lessons. They are also recorded on the audio files available online. So that you can check your own answers after completing the exercises, you will also find the correct answers to the multiple choice listening and reading questions at the end of the text.

Rubrics and Recommendations

The College Board provides rubrics for the assessment of each section of the AP exam. Students and teachers should be aware of the standards by which students are evaluated for each portion of the exam and the relative weights of each section of the exam. Finally, you will find a brief section which provides students and teachers with advice and recommendations on how to approach each test, based on our pilot testing of our own materials in our classrooms. We noted common errors and patterns of errors made by our students as they took the sample exams and share with you some of suggestions we have made to our students to improve their responses. We believe however, that individual teachers who use this text will find that this list of recommendations are just a start, and we welcome teachers' additional feedback to expand or revise this section.

Audio Recordings
Three audio files per lesson are available for download at http://www.cheng-tsui.com/downloads. They are the files for the listening, conversation, and return telephone call sections of the sample tests. For the listening section, students should take notes while listening, then answer the multiple choice questions. For the conversation and return telephone call sections, we suggest that student record their speaking within 20 seconds as they listen to the questions. Also available to download are the AP *kanji* flashcards for students to use as *kanji* practice on their own time.

   Finally, we close by requesting comments, suggestions and feedback from all users of this textbook. This particular version is our first attempt at responding to a need for AP Japanese exam preparation. It is ultimately an attempt to raise the bar of the proficiency of all students of Japanese as well as an attempt to broaden the minds and hearts of its student users. Since it is still a field test version, we will be happy to hear from you through the publisher about your ideas on how this text can be improved. Please contact us with any comments or suggestions at editor@cheng-tsui.com. Thank you for choosing this textbook.

がんばりましょう！

ACKNOWLEDGMENTS

The authors of this volume of *Further Adventures in Japanese* thank the following individuals for their contributions to this textbook. Their support is much appreciated.

- Michael Muronaka for the cartoon and icon illustrations.
- Keiko Kurose for reviewing the AP kanji list and flash cards and for sending some material from Japan.
- Natsumi Watanabe, a one-year exchange student from Japan, for writing a paragraph and the accompanying mulitple-choice questions.
- Ken Noguchi for giving permission to use his book titled 「あきらめないこと、それが冒険だ」 for creating reading material on "Environment."
- Masahiro Sasaki, older brother of Sadako Sasaki, for sharing his speech on Sadako that he presented at Stuyvesant High School in New York after the 9/11 memorial service held in 2007.
- Satomi Wise for creating reading material and accompanying games.
- Norie Masamitsu for proofreading the story of her father Mr. Soichiro Honda.
- Rika Onchi and her students at Yuuhigaoka High School in Osaka for creating listening material on "School uniform debate."
- Miki Matsuura and Shion Matsuura for their photo contribution.
- Jeff Ady for recording and editing the audio files.
- Misa Uyehara, Hiroki Shuto, Reona Ono, Jeff Ady for their voice recordings.
- The parents of Rainbow School in Honolulu, Hawaii for their voice recording.
- Gina Hara for proofreading the multiple choice listening and reading questions.

Hiromi Peterson, Naomi Hirano-Omizo, and Junko Ady

 AP漢字

 After studying this book, you are expected to be able to read, type, and know the meaning of the following *kanji*.

【タスク1：AP *Kanji*】

Master 410 AP *kanji*. You should be able to read and know the meanings of the *kanji* compounds for each AP *kanji*, and be able to type the *kanji* compounds properly.

【タスク2：AIJ Extra *Kanji*】

Master 51 extra *kanji* which are covered in the AIJ 1〜4 textbooks, but not in the AP *kanji* list. (The total *kanji* you will master at the end of this textbook will be 461!)

Abbreviations used in the list:

AP #　　= The number of the AP *kanji*
漢字　　= AP *Kanji*
　　　　　(The bolded *kanji* are introduced in the AIJ 5.)
AIJ-L.　= AIJ Level and Lesson which the *kanji* was introduced
AIJ #　　= The number of the AIJ *kanji*
訓読み = *Kun* (Japanese) reading
音読み = *On* (Chinese) reading
　　　　　(The order of the AP *kanji* listed is by あいうえお order of the *On* readings.)
意味　　= Meanings of the *kanji*
熟語　　= Compound *kanji* words with the *kanji*
X　　　 = no reading

AP#	漢字	AIJ-L	AIJ#	訓読み	音読み	意味	熟語
1	悪	IV-1	230	わる (い)	あく	bad	悪い〔わるい〕is bad 悪人〔あくにん〕a bad person
2	安	II-9	76	やす (い)	あん	cheap, peaceful	安い本〔やすいほん〕a cheap book 安物〔やすもの〕cheap things 大安売り〔おおやすうり〕big bargain sale 安田〔やすだ〕さん Yasuda-san 安心〔あんしん〕する be relieved 安全〔あんぜん〕safe 安藤〔あんどう〕さん Ando-san
3	暗	V-6	433	くら (い)	あん	dark	暗い〔くらい〕is dark 暗室〔あんしつ〕dark room 明暗〔めいあん〕light and dark
4	以	IV-4	267	X	い	to the ～ of	以上〔いじょう〕more than ～ 以下〔いか〕less than ～ 以前〔いぜん〕before ～ 以後〔いご〕after ～ 以内〔いない〕within ～ 以外〔いがい〕except ～ 以来〔いらい〕since ～
5	意	IV-6	287	X	い	meaning, mind	意味〔いみ〕meaning 意見〔いけん〕opinion 意外〔いがい〕unexpected; surprising
6	医	IV-2	239	X	い	medical	医者〔いしゃ〕doctor 医学〔いがく〕medical study 医学部〔いがくぶ〕medical department
7	育	IV-2	244	そだ (つ/ てる)	いく	to raise (a child or pet)	育つ〔そだつ〕someone grows 育てる〔そだてる〕raise (someone) 体育〔たいいく〕physical education 教育〔きょういく〕education
8	一	I-13	1	ひと	いち	one	一つ〔ひとつ〕one [general counter] 一人〔ひとり〕one person 一日〔ついたち〕first day of the month 一日〔いちにち〕one day 一月〔いちがつ〕January 一万〔いちまん〕ten thousand

漢字

2

AP#	漢字	AIJ-L	AIJ#	訓読み	音読み	意味	熟語
9	員	IV-1	221	X	いん	member	社員〔しゃいん〕company employee 会員〔かいいん〕group member 銀行員〔ぎんこういん〕banker 駅員〔えきいん〕station employee 店員〔てんいん〕store clerk
10	引	V-6	432	ひ（く）	いん	to pull	ドアを引く〔ひく〕pull (=open) the door 引き算〔ひきざん〕subtraction 辞書を引く〔じしょをひく〕 look up in the dictionary 引き出し〔ひきだし〕drawer
11	飲	III-3	152	の（む）	いん	to drink	水を飲む〔みずをのむ〕to drink water 飲み水〔のみみず〕drinking water 飲酒運転〔いんしゅうんてん〕drunken driving 飲料水〔いんりょうすい〕drinking water
12	院	IV-2	238	X	いん	institute	病院〔びょういん〕hospital 大学院〔だいがくいん〕graduate school 院長〔いんちょう〕a head of a hospital
13	右	II-13	95	みぎ	う/ゆう	right (side)	右手〔みぎて〕right hand 右足〔みぎあし〕right foot 右側〔みぎがわ〕right side 左右〔さゆう〕left and right
14	雨	II-11	87	あめ	う	rain	大雨〔おおあめ〕heavy rain 雨天〔うてん〕rainy weather 小雨〔こさめ〕drizzle 梅雨〔つゆ〕rainy season
15	運	IV-4	271	はこ（ぶ）	うん	to carry. luck	荷物を運ぶ〔にもつをはこぶ〕to carry luggage 運転〔うんてん〕driving 運動〔うんどう〕sports; exercises 運がいい〔うんがいい〕lucky 運が悪い〔うんがわるい〕unlucky
16	映	III-6	170	うつ（す）	えい	to project	映画〔えいが〕movie 映画館〔えいがかん〕movie theater 上映時間〔じょうえいじかん〕running time of a movie 映し出す〔うつしだす〕to project

漢字

AP#	漢字	AIJ-L	AIJ#	訓読み	音読み	意味	熟語
17	泳	V-1	355	およ（ぐ）	えい	to swim	泳ぐ〔およぐ〕to swim 水泳〔すいえい〕swimming 遠泳〔えんえい〕long-distance swimming
18	英	III-4	158	X	えい	British, brave	英国〔えいこく〕England 英語〔えいご〕English 英会話〔えいかいわ〕English conversation
19	駅	III-9	210	X	えき	station	駅〔えき〕(railway) station 駅名〔えきめい〕station name 上野駅〔うえのえき〕Ueno Station 乗車駅〔じょうしゃえき〕boarding station
20	円	III-9	219	まる	えん	circle, yen	百円〔ひゃくえん〕100 yen 一万円〔いちまんえん〕10,000 yen 十万円〔じゅうまんえん〕100,000 yen 百万円〔ひゃくまんえん〕1,000,000 yen 円山公園〔まるやまこうえん〕Maruyama Park
21	園	IV-6	281	その	えん	garden	公園〔こうえん〕park 上野公園〔うえのこうえん〕Ueno Park 動物園〔どうぶつえん〕zoo 園長〔えんちょう〕kindergarten principal 遊園地〔ゆうえんち〕amusement park 園田〔そのだ〕さん Sonoda-san
22	遠	V-3	389	とお（い）	えん	far	遠い〔とおい〕far 遠回り〔とおまわり〕detour 遠足〔えんそく〕hike; outing 遠泳〔えんえい〕long-distance swimming
23	横	V-5	419	よこ	おう	side	横山〔よこやま〕さん Yokoyama-san 横浜〔よこはま〕Yokohama 横綱〔よこづな〕sumo grand champion 横断歩道〔おうだんほどう〕pedestrian crossing
24	屋	II-15	121	や	おく	store, roof	花屋〔はなや〕flower shop 魚屋〔さかなや〕fish market 薬屋〔くすりや〕pharmacy 屋根〔やね〕roof 屋上〔おくじょう〕rooftop 屋外〔おくがい〕outdoors

漢字

AP#	漢字	AIJ-L.	AIJ#	訓読み	音読み	意味	熟語
25	温	V-2	361	あたた (かい)	おん	warm	温かい水〔あたたかいみず〕warm water 温度〔おんど〕temperature 気温〔きおん〕temperature (atmospheric) 体温〔たいおん〕body temperature 水温〔すいおん〕water temperature
26	音	III-3	154	おと	おん	sound	雨の音〔あめのおと〕sound of rain 音楽〔おんがく〕music 音楽家〔おんがくか〕musician 高音〔こうおん〕high-pitched tone 雑音〔ざつおん〕static noise
27	下	II-3	27	した	か/げ	under	山下〔やました〕さん Yamashita-san 以下〔いか〕less than 下手〔へた〕unskillful
28	化	III-2	136	ば(ける)	か	to change	文化〔ぶんか〕culture 化学〔かがく〕chemistry 変化〔へんか〕する (something) changes お化け〔おばけ〕ghost 文字化け〔もじばけ〕unintelligible characters; gibberish
29	何	II-3	31	なに/なん	か	what	何時〔なんじ〕What time? 何人〔なんにん〕How many people? 何人〔なにじん〕What nationality? 何回〔なんかい〕How many times? 何日〔なんにち〕What day of the month? 何時間も〔なんじかんも〕many hours 何度も〔なんども〕many times
30	夏	III-3	147	なつ	か	summer	暑い夏〔あついなつ〕hot summer 夏休み〔なつやすみ〕summer vacation 真夏〔まなつ〕mid-summer 初夏〔しょか〕early summer 春夏秋冬〔しゅんかしゅうとう〕spring, summer, autumn and winter
31	家	II-7	67	いえ	か/け	house, person	大きい家〔おおきいいえ〕a big house 家族〔かぞく〕family 家内〔かない〕(own) wife 家庭〔かてい〕family; household 画家〔がか〕painter (artist) 小説家〔しょうせつか〕novelist 田中家〔たなかけ〕Tanaka family

AP#	漢字	AIJ-L.	AIJ#	訓読み	音読み	意味	熟語
32	科	V-4	398	X	か	subject	科目〔かもく〕(school) subject 社会科〔しゃかいか〕social studies 科学〔かがく〕science
33	歌	III-6	172	うた	か	song	歌を歌う〔うたをうたう〕to sing a song 校歌〔こうか〕school song 歌手〔かしゅ〕singer
34	火	I-13	13	ひ	か	fire	花火〔はなび〕fireworks 火曜日〔かようび〕Tuesday 火事〔かじ〕fire, conflagration
35	花	III-2	137	はな	か	flower	花子〔はなこ〕さん Hanako-san 花屋〔はなや〕flower shop 花火〔はなび〕fireworks 生け花〔いけばな〕flower arrangement
36	荷	V-7	449	に	か	luggage	荷物〔にもつ〕luggage; baggage 重荷〔おもに〕heavy burden
37	画	III-6	171	X	が/ かく	picture, stroke	映画館〔えいがかん〕movie theater 日本画〔にほんが〕Japanese painting 洋画〔ようが〕Western paintings/movie 画家〔がか〕painter (artist) 漫画〔まんが〕comic, cartoon 画数〔かくすう〕number of strokes
38	会	II-11	91	あ(う)	かい	to meet	会う〔あう〕to meet 教会〔きょうかい〕church 会に出る〔かいにでる〕to attend a meeting 会長〔かいちょう〕president (of an organization) 会場〔かいじょう〕meeting place 司会〔しかい〕master of ceremonies
39	回	III-4	168	まわ(る)	かい	-time(s)	右に回す〔みぎにまわす〕to turn to the right 遠回り〔とおまわり〕detour 回り道〔まわりみち〕detour 何回〔なんかい〕How many times? 今回〔こんかい〕this time 回転寿司〔かいてんずし〕conveyor belt sushi

漢字

6

AP#	漢字	AIJ-L.	AIJ#	訓読み	音読み	意味	熟語
40	海	III-2	138	うみ	かい	sea/ocean /beach	広い海〔ひろいうみ〕spacious ocean 海鳥〔うみどり〕sea bird 海の家〔うみのいえ〕beach house 日本海〔にほんかい〕Sea of Japan 海水〔かいすい〕ocean water 海軍〔かいぐん〕navy 地中海〔ちちゅうかい〕Mediterranean Sea 海産物〔かいさんぶつ〕marine products
41	界	IV-3	254	X	かい	boundary	世界〔せかい〕world
42	皆	V-1	346	みな/ みんな	かい	everyone	皆さん〔みなさん〕everyone [polite, address form] 皆〔みんな〕everyone 皆川〔みながわ〕さん Minagawa-san
43	絵	IV-6	282	え	かい	painting	絵を描く〔えをかく〕to paint a picture 絵文字〔えもじ〕pictograph 絵画〔かいが〕picture
44	開	III-7	193	あ(ける)/ あ(く)/ ひら(く)	かい	to open	戸を開ける〔とをあける〕to open a door 戸が開く〔とがあく〕door opens 花が開く〔はながひらく〕flowers open 開場時間〔かいじょうじかん〕opening time 開会式〔かいかいしき〕opening ceremony
45	階	V-6	442	X	かい/ がい	floor	階段〔かいだん〕stairs 三階〔さんがい〕3rd floor 地下二階〔ちかにかい〕basement 2nd floor
46	外	II-3	33	そと	がい/ げ	outside	家の外〔いえのそと〕outside of the house 外国語〔がいこくご〕foreign language 外国人〔がい(こく)じん〕foreigner 外出〔がいしゅつ〕する to go out 海外旅行〔かいがいりょこう〕travel abroad 外来語〔がいらいご〕word of foreign origin 市外電話〔しがいでんわ〕long-distance call 外泊〔がいはく〕する to spend a night away from home 外食〔がいしょく〕eating out 外車〔がいしゃ〕foreign car 外見〔がいけん〕appearance 外交〔がいこう〕diplomacy 外科〔げか〕surgical department

漢字

AP#	漢字	AIJ-L.	AIJ#	訓読み	音読み	意味	熟語
47	学	II-4	38	まな(ぶ)	がく	to learn	学ぶ〔まなぶ〕to study/learn (in depth) 学校〔がっこう〕school 学期〔がっき〕semester 学生〔がくせい〕student (college) 学長〔がくちょう〕university president 学者〔がくしゃ〕scholar 大学院〔だいがくいん〕graduate school 工学部〔こうがくぶ〕school of engineering 言語学〔げんごがく〕linguistics 男女共学〔だんじょきょうがく〕coed 修学旅行〔しゅうがくりょこう〕excursion 学士号〔がくしごう〕bachelor's degree
48	楽	III-3	155	たの(しい)	がく/らく	enjoyable	楽しい〔たのしい〕enjoyable 音楽〔おんがく〕music 楽器〔がっき〕musical instrument 楽な椅子〔らくないす〕comfortable chair
49	活	IV-3	263	X	かつ	active, live	生活〔せいかつ〕living 活動〔かつどう〕activity 部活〔ぶかつ〕club activity
50	寒	IV-4	275	さむ(い)	かん	cold	寒い風〔さむいかぜ〕cold wind 寒冷前線〔かんれいぜんせん〕cold front
51	漢	III-1	122	X	かん	Chinese	漢字〔かんじ〕Chinese characters 漢方薬〔かんぽうやく〕Chinese medicine 漢和辞典〔かんわじてん〕Chinese character-Japanese dictionary
52	間	II-7	64	あいだ/ま	かん	interval, space	夏の間〔なつのあいだ〕during the summer 客間〔きゃくま〕guest room 洋間〔ようま〕Western style room 床の間〔とこのま〕alcove 上間〔うえま〕さん Uema-san 時間〔じかん〕time 何時間〔なんじかん〕How many hours?
53	関	IV-8	324	せき	かん	barrier	大関〔おおぜき〕second highest ranked sumo wrestler 関東〔かんとう〕Kanto area [region of eastern Honshu including Tokyo] 関西〔かんさい〕Kansai area [region of western Honshu including Osaka and Kyoto] 関係〔かんけい〕relationship 玄関〔げんかん〕entrance way; foyer

漢字

AP#	漢字	AIJ-L.	AIJ#	訓読み	音読み	意味	熟語
54	館	IV-4	279	X	かん	building	図書館〔としょかん〕library 体育館〔たいいくかん〕gymnasium 映画館〔えいがかん〕movie theater 美術館〔びじゅつかん〕art gallery/museum 博物館〔はくぶつかん〕museum 水族館〔すいぞくかん〕aquarium 館内〔かんない〕in the building 開館〔かいかん〕opening of a building 閉館〔へいかん〕closing of a building 館長〔かんちょう〕superintendent
55	顔	IV-7	298	かお	がん	face	顔を洗う〔かおをあらう〕to wash one's face 美顔〔びがん〕クリーム facial beauty cream 洗顔石鹸〔せんがんせっけん〕facial soap
56	願	V-3	379	ねが(う)	がん	wish	お願いします〔おねがいします〕Please. [request]
57	期	V-2	372	X	き	term	学期〔がっき〕semester 秋学期〔あきがっき〕fall semester 春学期〔はるがっき〕spring semester 一学期〔いちがっき〕first semester 期末試験〔きまつしけん〕semester exam
58	機	V-5	422	X	き	machine	機械〔きかい〕machine 飛行機〔ひこうき〕airplane 機長〔きちょう〕pilot 洗濯機〔せんたくき〕washing machine 機会〔きかい〕opportunity
59	帰	II-10	81	かえ(る)	き	to return	家に帰る〔いえにかえる〕return home 帰宅時間〔きたくじかん〕time one returns home 帰国子女〔きこくしじょ〕child who has returned to his/her own country
60	気	II-11	90	X	き	spirit	元気〔げんき〕healthy 天気〔てんき〕weather 天気予報〔てんきよほう〕weather forecast 気温〔きおん〕temperature 気分〔きぶん〕がいい to feel good; to be in good spirits 合気道〔あいきどう〕aikido 空気〔くうき〕air 電気〔でんき〕electricity 人気〔にんき〕がある is popular 気持ちが悪い〔きもちがわるい〕to feel sick

9

漢字

AP#	漢字	AIJ-L.	AIJ#	訓読み	音読み	意味	熟語
61	記	V-1	350	X	き	to mark	日記〔にっき〕diary 伝記〔でんき〕biography 記号〔きごう〕symbol 記事〔きじ〕article, news story 記録〔きろく〕record; archive
62	起	III-6	181	おき（る）	き	to wake up	起きる〔おきる〕to wake up 早寝早起き〔はやねはやおき〕sleep early, get up early 起立〔きりつ〕Stand. 起床時間〔きしょうじかん〕rising time
63	休	II-15	115	やす（む）	きゅう	to rest	夏休み〔なつやすみ〕summer vacation 冬休み〔ふゆやすみ〕winter vacation 春休み〔はるやすみ〕spring vacation 休み時間〔やすみじかん〕recess 休日〔きゅうじつ〕day off 定休日〔ていきゅうび〕regular day off
64	急	V-5	414	いそ（ぐ）	きゅう	to hurry	急がば回れ〔いそがばまわれ〕less haste, more speed 急行〔きゅうこう〕express 特急〔とっきゅう〕limited express 急用〔きゅうよう〕urgent business 救急車〔きゅうきゅうしゃ〕ambulance
65	泣	IV-4	276	な（く）	きゅう	to cry	泣く〔なく〕to cry 泣き虫〔なきむし〕crybaby 号泣〔ごうきゅう〕する to cry aloud
66	究	V-4	399	X	きゅう	to investigate	研究〔けんきゅう〕research
67	牛	II-10	78	うし	ぎゅう	cow	子牛〔こうし〕baby cow 牛の肉〔うしのにく〕cow meat 牛肉〔ぎゅうにく〕beef 牛乳〔ぎゅうにゅう〕milk (cow's) 和牛〔わぎゅう〕Japanese beef steer 神戸牛〔こうべぎゅう〕Kobe beef 牛丼〔ぎゅうどん〕beef *donburi*
68	去	III-1	131	さ（る）	きょ, こ	to leave	去年〔きょねん〕last year 死去〔しきょ〕death 過去〔かこ〕the past

AP#	漢字	AIJ-L.	AIJ#	訓読み	音読み	意味	熟語
69	魚	II-14	107	さかな	ぎょ	fish	魚料理〔さかなりょうり〕fish cooking 魚屋〔さかなや〕fish store 魚釣り〔さかなつり〕fishing 人魚〔にんぎょ〕mermaid 金魚〔きんぎょ〕goldfish
70	京	III-9	209	X	きょう	capital	東京〔とうきょう〕Tokyo 京都〔きょうと〕Kyoto 京子〔きょうこ〕さん Kyoko-san
71	強	III-4	167	つよ (い)	きょう	strong	強い力〔つよいちから〕strong power 勉強〔べんきょう〕study 強風〔きょうふう〕strong wind 強力〔きょうりょく〕なチーム strong team
72	教	III-2	140	おし (える)	きょう	to teach	教える〔おしえる〕to teach 教室〔きょうしつ〕classroom 教科書〔きょうかしょ〕textbook 教育〔きょういく〕education 教師〔きょうし〕teacher 教授〔きょうじゅ〕professor
73	橋	V-5	420	はし	きょう	bridge	橋を渡る〔はしをわたる〕to cross a bridge 橋本〔はしもと〕さん Hashimoto-san 日本橋〔にほんばし〕Nihonbashi 歩道橋〔ほどうきょう〕pedestrian bridge
74	業	IV-1	228	X	ぎょう	work, business	卒業〔そつぎょう〕graduation 授業〔じゅぎょう〕class 工業〔こうぎょう〕(manufacturing) industry 商業〔しょうぎょう〕business 開業〔かいぎょう〕opening of business
75	局	V-1	349	X	きょく	office	郵便局〔ゆうびんきょく〕post office 放送局〔ほうそうきょく〕broadcast station 薬局〔やっきょく〕drug store
76	近	II-13	103	ちか (い)	きん/こん	near	近い店〔ちかいみせ〕nearby shop 国近〔くにちか〕さん Kunichika-san 近藤〔こんどう〕さん Kondo-san 近所〔きんじょ〕neighborhood
77	金	I-15	16	かね	きん	gold, money	お金〔おかね〕money 金曜日〔きんようび〕Friday 貯金する〔ちょきんする〕to save money

漢字

AP#	漢字	AIJ-L.	AIJ#	訓読み	音読み	意味	熟語
78	九	I-14	9	ここの	きゅう/く	nine	九つ〔ここのつ〕nine (general counter) 九日〔ここのか〕the 9th day of the month; 9 days 九人〔きゅうにん〕nine people 九月〔くがつ〕September
79	空	IV-4	273	そら/から/あ(き)	くう	sky	青空〔あおぞら〕blue sky 空気〔くうき〕air 空港〔くうこう〕airport 日本航空〔にほんこうくう〕Japan Air Lines 航空会社〔こうくうがいしゃ〕airline company 空手〔からて〕karate 空き缶〔あきかん〕empty can
80	係	V-7	460	かか(り)	けい	in charge	係りの人〔かかりのひと〕a person in charge 関係〔かんけい〕relationship
81	兄	III-1	126	あに/にい	けい/きょう	older brother	兄〔あに〕(own) older brother お兄さん〔おにいさん〕older brother 父兄会〔ふけいかい〕PTA 兄弟〔きょうだい〕siblings
82	形	V-5	413	かたち	けい	shape	色と形〔いろとかたち〕color and shape 三角形〔さんかくけい〕triangle
83	経	V-4	394	X	けい	to pass through	経済〔けいざい〕economics 経営〔けいえい〕management 経営者〔けいえいしゃ〕manager
84	計	V-4	396	はか(る)	けい	to measure	計算〔けいさん〕する to calculate 計画〔けいかく〕a plan 時計〔とけい〕clock
85	決	IV-9	339	き(める)	けつ	to decide	決める〔きめる〕to decide 決まる〔きまる〕to be decided 決心する〔けっしんする〕to decide 解決する〔かいけつする〕to solve
86	結	V-4	401	むす(ぶ)	けつ	to tie	結婚〔けっこん〕marriage

AP#	漢字	AIJ-L.	AIJ#	訓読み	音読み	意味	熟語
87	月	I-15	11	つき	げつ/がつ	moon, month	月が出ている〔つきがでている〕The moon is out. お月見〔おつきみ〕moon viewing 三日月〔みかづき〕crescent moon 九月〔くがつ〕September 三カ月〔さんかげつ〕three months 満月〔まんげつ〕full moon 月末〔げつまつ〕end of the month 月謝〔げっしゃ〕monthly tuition fee
88	犬	II-15	119	いぬ	けん	dog	小さい犬〔ちいさいいぬ〕a small dog 秋田犬〔あきたけん〕Akita dog (breed)
89	見	II-4	40	み（る）	けん	to see, to look, to watch	見つける〔みつける〕to find お花見〔おはなみ〕cherry blossom viewing 見物〔けんぶつ〕sightseeing 見学〔けんがく〕study by observation 意見〔いけん〕opinion
90	験	V-1	344	X	けん	testing	試験〔しけん〕exam 経験〔けいけん〕experience 体験〔たいけん〕personal experience 実験〔じっけん〕experiment
91	元	III-3	151	もと	げん/がん	origin	元田〔もとだ〕さん Motoda-san 元気〔げんき〕healthy 元旦〔がんたん〕the first day of the year
92	現	V-7	459	X	げん	to appear	表現〔ひょうげん〕expression 現実〔げんじつ〕reality 現在〔げんざい〕present, nowadays 現代〔げんだい〕modern
93	言	II-7	60	い（う）	げん	to say	言う〔いう〕to say 言語〔げんご〕language 言語学〔げんごがく〕linguistics 方言〔ほうげん〕dialect
94	個	V-3	386	X	こ	individual	一個〔いっこ〕one (general counter) 個人の問題〔こじんのもんだい〕personal problem 個人〔こじん〕タクシー privately owned taxi
95	古	II-14	110	ふる（い）	こ	old	古い本〔ふるいほん〕an old book 古本屋〔ふるほんや〕second hand bookstore 古新聞〔ふるしんぶん〕old newspaper 中古車〔ちゅうこしゃ〕second hand car

漢字

AP#	漢字	AIJ-L.	AIJ#	訓読み	音読み	意味	熟語
96	五	I-13	5	いつ(つ)	ご	five	五日〔いつか〕the 5th day of the month; five days 五つ〔いつつ〕five (general counter) 五月〔ごがつ〕May 五分の一〔ごぶんのいち〕1/5
97	午	III-2	143	X	ご	noon	午前〔ごぜん〕a.m. 午後〔ごご〕p.m. 正午〔しょうご〕noon
98	後	III-2	142	うし(ろ)/ あと	ご	after	後で〔あとで〕later 車の後ろ〔くるまのうしろ〕behind the car 午後〔ごご〕p.m. 前後〔ぜんご〕front and back
99	語	II-7	61	かた(る)	ご	to talk	物語〔ものがたり〕story 日本語〔にほんご〕Japanese language 外国語〔がいこくご〕foreign language 語学〔ごがく〕language study 言語学〔げんごがく〕linguistics
100	公	III-2	134	おおや(け)	こう	public	公立〔こうりつ〕public (institution) 公園〔こうえん〕park ハチ公〔ハチこう〕Hachiko (a statue of a dog) 公害〔こうがい〕pollution 公衆便所〔こうしゅうべんじょ〕public toilet
101	口	II-2	18	くち/ ぐち	こう	mouth	大きい口〔おおきいくち〕a big mouth 入口〔いりぐち〕entrance 出口〔でぐち〕exit 改札口〔かいさつぐち〕ticket gate 人口〔じんこう〕population
102	向	V-2	358	む(く)/ む(ける)/ む(かう)/ む(こう)	こう	to face	向井〔むかい〕さん Mukai-san 向こう〔むこう〕other side; beyond 向かい〔むかい〕other side (of) 若者向け〔わかものむけ〕for young people 方向〔ほうこう〕direction
103	好	II-6	57	す(き)/ よし	こう	like	好きな本〔すきなほん〕a book (I) like 大好き〔だいすき〕like very much 三好〔みよし〕さん Miyoshi-san 好子〔よしこ〕さん Yoshiko-san 好物〔こうぶつ〕favorite food

AP#	漢字	AIJ-L.	AIJ#	訓読み	音読み	意味	熟語
104	工	V-2	366	X	こう	industrial	工業〔こうぎょう〕 (manufacturing) industry 工学部〔こうがくぶ〕 department of technology/engineering 工芸品〔こうげいひん〕 handicraft 工場〔こうじょう〕 factory 工事中〔こうじちゅう〕 under construction
105	広	III-7	189	ひろ (い)	こう	wide	広い庭〔ひろいにわ〕 a spacious garden 広島〔ひろしま〕 Hiroshima 広本〔ひろもと〕 さん Hiromoto-san 広大〔こうだい〕 なキャンパス huge campus
106	校	II-4	39	X	こう	school	学校〔がっこう〕 school 小学校〔しょうがっこう〕 elementary school 中学校〔ちゅうがっこう〕 middle school 高校〔こうこう〕 high school 校長先生〔こうちょうせんせい〕 principal 校歌〔こうか〕 school song
107	港	IV-8	315	みなと	こう	harbor	港の船〔みなとのふね〕 a boat in the harbor 港町〔みなとまち〕 harbor town 空港〔くうこう〕 airport 成田空港〔なりたくうこう〕 Narita Airport 関西空港〔かんさいくうこう〕 Kansai Airport
108	考	IV-7	303	かんが (える)	こう	to think	いい考え〔かんがえ〕 a good idea 参考書〔さんこうしょ〕 reference book
109	行	II-4	34	い (く)/ ゆ (く)/ おこな (う)	こう/ ぎょう	to go	海へ行く〔うみへいく〕 go to the beach 急行〔きゅうこう〕 express (train) 東京行き〔とうきょうゆき〕 bound for Tokyo 親孝行〔おやこうこう〕 filial piety 年中行事〔ねんちゅうぎょうじ〕 annual event
110	降	IV-2	245	ふ (る)/ お (りる)	こう	to fall, to get off	雨が降る〔あめがふる〕 It rains. 電車を降りる〔でんしゃをおりる〕 get off the train 降り口〔おりぐち〕 an exit (from the train) 降水量〔こうすいりょう〕 precipitation
111	高	II-9	77	たか (い)	こう	tall/ expensive	背が高い〔せがたかい〕 tall (height) 高田〔たかた〕 さん Takata-san 高校〔こうこう〕 high school 女子高校〔じょしこうこう〕 girl's high school 男子校〔だんしこう〕 boy's school 高校生〔こうこうせい〕 high school student 最高〔さいこう〕 supreme

AP#	漢字	AIJ-L.	AIJ#	訓読み	音読み	意味	熟語
112	号	V-7	461	X	ごう	#	ロボット第一号〔だいいちごう〕Robot No. 1 ひかり５６号〔ごじゅうろくごう〕Hikari No. 6 [shinkansen] ６号車〔ろくごうしゃ〕Car No. 6 号外〔ごうがい〕newspaper extra 信号〔しんごう〕traffic light
113	合	IV-3	259	あ(う)	ごう	to match	待合所〔まちあいしょ〕waiting area 話し合い〔はなしあい〕discussion/conference 合格〔ごうかく〕passing an exam
114	国	II-9	75	くに	こく	country	美しい国〔うつくしいくに〕a beautiful country 国々〔くにぐに〕countries 中国〔ちゅうごく〕China 韓国〔かんこく〕Korea 外国〔がいこく〕foreign country 国内〔こくない〕domestic 全国大会〔ぜんこくたいかい〕national athletic meet 四国〔しこく〕Shikoku island 国語〔こくご〕national language
115	黒	III-6	175	くろ	こく	black	黒い犬〔くろいいぬ〕a black dog 黒猫〔くろねこ〕a black cat 黒字〔くろじ〕in the black (balanced budget) 目黒〔めぐろ〕(city in Tokyo) 黒人〔こくじん〕black person
116	今	II-2	22	いま	こん	now	今、何時？〔いまなんじ〕What time is it now? 今井〔いまい〕さん Imai-san 今川〔いまがわ〕さん Imagawa-san 今日〔きょう〕today 今週〔こんしゅう〕this week 今月〔こんげつ〕this month 今年〔ことし〕this year 今朝〔けさ〕this morning
117	困	IV-2	246	こま(る)	こん	to be troubled	困っている〔こまっている〕troubled 困難〔こんなん〕difficulty 貧困〔ひんこん〕poverty
118	婚	V-4	402	X	こん	marriage	結婚〔けっこん〕marriage 婚約〔こんやく〕engagement 新婚旅行〔しんこんりょこう〕honeymoon 離婚〔りこん〕divorce 再婚〔さいこん〕する to marry again 初婚〔しょこん〕first marriage 晩婚〔ばんこん〕late marriage

漢字

AP#	漢字	AIJ-L.	AIJ#	訓読み	音読み	意味	熟語
119	左	II-13	96	ひだり	さ	left	左目〔ひだりめ〕left eye 左手〔ひだりて〕left hand 左側〔ひだりがわ〕left side 左利き〔ひだりきき〕left-hander 左右〔さゆう〕left and right
120	最	IV-6	288	もっと(も)	さい	most	最も安い〔もっともやすい〕cheapest 最高〔さいこう〕highest, the most 最近〔さいきん〕recent 最長〔さいちょう〕longest 最小〔さいしょう〕smallest 最大〔さいだい〕biggest 最古〔さいこ〕oldest 最新〔さいしん〕newest 最前線〔さいぜんせん〕foremost line
121	歳	V-1	348	とし	さい/ せい	age; - years old	百歳〔ひゃくさい〕hundred years old 何歳〔なんさい〕how old? 御歳暮〔おせいぼ〕year-end present
122	祭	V-2	360	まつり	さい	festival	桜祭り〔さくらまつり〕Cherry Blossom Festival 祭日〔さいじつ〕national holiday 文化祭〔ぶんかさい〕cultural festival 学園祭〔がくえんさい〕school festival
123	際	V-7	451	きわ/ ぎわ	さい	edge	山際〔やまぎわ〕さん Yamagiwa-san 国際〔こくさい〕international 国際空港〔こくさいくうこう〕international airport 国際問題〔こくさいもんだい〕international problem
124	作	II-14	105	つく(る)	さく	to make	作る〔つくる〕to make 作り方〔つくりかた〕how to make 作文〔さくぶん〕composition 作家〔さっか〕novelist 作詞〔さくし〕lyrics 作曲〔さっきょく〕musical composition 作品〔さくひん〕work, production 作田〔さくだ〕さん Sakuda-san 作物〔さくもつ〕crops
125	昨	V-1	345	X	さく	last preceding	昨日〔きのう／さくじつ〕yesterday 昨年〔さくねん〕last year 昨夜〔さくや〕last night 昨今〔さっこん〕nowadays

漢字

AP#	漢字	AIJ-L.	AIJ#	訓読み	音読み	意味	熟語
126	雑	V-7	458	X	ざつ	miscellaneous	雑誌〔ざっし〕magazine 複雑〔ふくざつ〕complicated 雑音〔ざつおん〕noise 雑学〔ざつがく〕miscellaneous knowledge
127	三	I-13	3	み/ み (つ)/ みっ (つ)	さん	three	三つ〔みっつ〕three (general counter) 三人〔さんにん〕three people 三日〔みっか〕the 3rd day of the month, three days 三日月〔みかづき〕crescent moon 三月〔さんがつ〕March 三カ月〔さんかげつ〕three months 三年〔さんねん〕three years 三万円〔さんまんえん〕thirty thousand yen
128	山	II-5	44	やま	さん	mountain	山本〔やまもと〕さん Yamamoto-san 富士山〔ふじやま/ふじさん〕Mt. Fuji 山々〔やまやま〕mountains 山登り〔やまのぼり〕mountain climbing
129	残	V-6	436	のこ (す)/ のこ (る)	ざん	to leave	残り物〔のこりもの〕leftovers 残念〔ざんねん〕disappointing 残業〔ざんぎょう〕overtime work 残暑〔ざんしょ〕lingering summer heat
130	仕	III-1	133	つか (える)	し	to serve	仕事〔しごと〕job 運転の仕方〔うんてんのしかた〕how to drive 仕方〔しかた〕がない it cannot be helped 仕上げる〔しあげる〕to complete
131	使	III-4	165	つか (う)	し	to use	使う〔つかう〕to use 使用料〔しようりょう〕rent; hire 大使〔たいし〕ambassador 大使館〔たいしかん〕embassy
132	四	I-13	4	よ/ よ (つ)/ よっ (つ)/ よん	し	four	四つ〔よっつ〕four (general counter) 四人〔よにん〕four people 四日〔よっか〕the 4th day of the month; four days 四月〔しがつ〕April 四季〔しき〕four seasons
133	始	III-4	163	はじ (める)/ はじ (まる)	し	to begin	始まる〔はじまる〕(something) begins 始める〔はじめる〕begin (something) 始業式〔しぎょうしき〕opening ceremony (of the school term) 開始〔かいし〕する to start

漢字　　　　　　　　　　18

AP#	漢字	AIJ-L.	AIJ#	訓読み	音読み	意味	熟語
134	姉	III-1	124	あね/ ねえ	し	older sister	お姉さん〔おねえさん〕older sister 上の姉〔うえのあね〕elder of 2 older sisters 下の姉〔したのあね〕younger of 2 older sisters 姉妹〔しまい〕sisters
135	子	II-4	36	こ	し	child	子供〔こども〕child(ren) 花子〔はなこ〕さん Hanako-san 女子〔じょし〕girl 男子〔だんし〕boy 電子〔でんし〕レンジ microwave oven 子孫〔しそん〕descendants
136	市	IV-4	266	いち	し	city	魚市場〔さかないちば〕fish market 京都市〔きょうとし〕Kyoto city 市長〔しちょう〕mayor 市内〔しない〕(within a) city 市外電話〔しがいでんわ〕long-distance call 市川〔いちかわ〕さん Ichikawa-san
137	思	II-15	114	おも(う)	し	to think	思い出〔おもいで〕memory 思い出す〔おもいだす〕to recall, remember 思考力〔しこうりょく〕ability to think
138	指	V-6	441	ゆび	し	finger	指輪〔ゆびわ〕ring 親指〔おやゆび〕thumb 中指〔なかゆび〕middle finger 薬指〔くすりゆび〕ring finger 小指〔こゆび〕little finger 指定席〔していせき〕reserved seat 指圧〔しあつ〕finger pressure massage
139	止	IV-3	260	と(まる)/ と(める)	し	to stop	止まれ！〔とまれ！〕Stop! 中止〔ちゅうし〕する to cancel 通行止め〔つうこうどめ〕No thoroughfare.
140	私	II-2	24	わたし	し	I/private	私の本〔わたしのほん〕my book 私立〔しりつ／わたくしりつ〕private (establishment)
141	紙	III-3	157	かみ	し	paper	手紙〔てがみ〕letter 折り紙〔おりがみ〕origami (paper folding) 色紙〔いろがみ〕colored paper 色紙〔しきし〕square drawing paper 新聞紙〔しんぶんし〕newsprint (paper)
142	試	V-1	343	ため(す)	し	to try	試合〔しあい〕game (sports) 試験〔しけん〕exam

漢字

AP#	漢字	AIJ-L.	AIJ#	訓読み	音読み	意味	熟語
143	事	II-10	86	こと/ ごと	し/ じ	matter	どんな事〔こと〕what kind of matter? 仕事〔しごと〕job 工事中〔こうじちゅう〕under construction 事務所〔じむしょ〕office 年中行事〔ねんじゅうぎょうじ〕annual event 州知事〔しゅうちじ〕governor
144	字	III-1	123	X	じ	character	字を書く〔じをかく〕to write characters きれいな字〔じ〕beautiful handwriting 漢字〔かんじ〕Chinese character 字画〔じかく〕number of strokes in a character 数字〔すうじ〕numeral
145	寺	II-7	62	てら/ でら	じ	temple	お寺〔てら〕temple 寺田〔てらだ〕さん Terada-san 本願寺〔ほんがんじ〕Hongwanji Temple
146	持	II-10	83	も (つ)	じ	to hold	持ち物〔もちもの〕one's property お持ち帰り〔おもちかえり〕takeout (food)
147	時	II-7	63	とき/ と	じ	time	その時〔とき〕at that time 時々〔ときどき〕sometimes 時計〔とけい〕clock; watch 九時〔くじ〕nine o'clock 時間〔じかん〕time 時差〔じさ〕time difference
148	次	IV-3	256	つぎ	じ	next	次の日〔つぎのひ〕next day 次郎〔じろう〕さん Jiro
149	治	V-1	357	なお (る)/ なお (す)	じ/ ち	to treat	治る〔なおる〕to be cured 政治〔せいじ〕politics 治療〔ちりょう〕treatment
150	自	II-15	118	X	じ	self	自分〔じぶん〕oneself 自信〔じしん〕confidence 自動車〔じどうしゃ〕car 自転車〔じてんしゃ〕bicycle 自動改札口〔じどうかいさつぐち〕ticket gate 自動販売機〔じどうはんばいき〕vending machine
151	辞	V-6	431	X	じ	word	辞書を引く〔じしょをひく〕to look up a word in a dictionary 辞職〔じしょく〕する to resign 祝辞〔しゅくじ〕congratulatory address

漢字   20

AP#	漢字	AIJ-L.	AIJ#	訓読み	音読み	意味	熟語
152	式	V-4	403	X	しき	ceremony	卒業式〔そつぎょうしき〕graduation ceremony 始業式〔しぎょうしき〕opening ceremony (of a school term) 結婚式場〔けっこんしきじょう〕wedding ceremony hall 式服〔しきふく〕ceremonial dress お葬式〔そうしき〕funeral 開会式〔かいかいしき〕opening ceremony (of a meeting) 終了式〔しゅうりょうしき〕closing ceremony (of a meeting)
153	七	I-14	7	なな	しち	seven	七つ〔ななつ〕seven (general counter) 七日〔なのか〕the 7th day of the month; seven days 七月〔しちがつ〕July 七味〔しちみ〕seven spice mixture 七夕〔たなばた〕Star Festival (July 7th)
154	失	V-4	407	うしな(う)	しつ	to lose	子供を失う〔こどもをうしなう〕to lose a child 失業〔しつぎょう〕unemployment 失業者〔しつぎょうしゃ〕unemployed person 失望〔しつぼう〕する to be disappointed 失明〔しつめい〕する to lose one's eyesight
155	室	III-2	141	X	しつ	room	教室〔きょうしつ〕classroom 図書室〔としょしつ〕library room 茶室〔ちゃしつ〕tea room
156	実	V-3	387	み	じつ	truth	実は〔じつは〕as a matter of fact, by the way 現実〔げんじつ〕reality 事実〔じじつ〕fact, truth 実話〔じつわ〕true story 実力〔じつりょく〕true ability 木の実〔このみ〕nut
157	写	V-5	427	うつ(す)	しゃ	to copy	写す〔うつす〕to copy 写真〔しゃしん〕photo 写生〔しゃせい〕する to sketch 複写〔ふくしゃ〕する to copy
158	社	IV-1	220	X	しゃ/じゃ	company	社会〔しゃかい〕society 社長〔しゃちょう〕company president 社員〔しゃいん〕company employee 会社〔かいしゃ〕company 神社〔じんじゃ〕shrine

漢字

AP#	漢字	AIJ-L.	AIJ#	訓読み	音読み	意味	熟語
159	者	IV-2	240	もの	しゃ/じゃ	person	怠け者〔なまけもの〕lazy person 若者〔わかもの〕young person 学者〔がくしゃ〕scholar 医者〔いしゃ〕doctor 患者〔かんじゃ〕patient
160	車	II-4	37	くるま	しゃ	car	車に乗る〔くるまにのる〕to ride a car 電車〔でんしゃ〕electric car 自動車〔じどうしゃ〕automobile 中古車〔ちゅうこしゃ〕used car 新車〔しんしゃ〕new car 外車〔がいしゃ〕foreign car 空車〔くうしゃ〕empty car 車内〔しゃない〕inside a carriage 駐車場〔ちゅうしゃじょう〕parking lot
161	若	IV-9	335	わか(い)	じゃく	young	若者〔わかもの〕young person 若さ〔わかさ〕youth
162	主	III-7	191	おも	しゅ	main	主に〔おもに〕mainly 主人〔しゅじん〕(own) husband; master 主食〔しゅしょく〕staple (main) food 主役〔しゅやく〕main character
163	取	IV-1	226	と(る)	しゅ	to take	日本語を取る〔にほんごをとる〕to take Japanese 取引〔とりひき〕business; dealings
164	手	II-6	52	て	しゅ	hand, person	右手〔みぎて〕right hand 左手〔ひだりて〕left hand 手前〔てまえ〕this side (of) 勝手〔かって〕selfish; arbitrary 上手〔じょうず〕skillful 下手〔へた〕unskillful 選手〔せんしゅ〕(sports) player; athlete 運転手〔うんてんしゅ〕driver 歌手〔かしゅ〕singer 手話〔しゅわ〕sign language 拍手〔はくしゅ〕する to applaud; to clap (for) 握手〔あくしゅ〕する to shake hands
165	酒	V-5	417	さけ	しゅ	alcohol	酒を飲む〔さけをのむ〕to drink alcohol 日本酒〔にほんしゅ〕Japanese rice wine 洋酒〔ようしゅ〕Western liquor ぶどう酒〔ぶどうしゅ〕wine 飲酒運転〔いんしゅうんてん〕drunken driving

AP#	漢字	AIJ-L.	AIJ#	訓読み	音読み	意味	熟語
166	受	IV-9	326	う (ける)	じゅ	to receive	試験を受ける〔しけんをうける〕to take an exam 受け取る〔うけとる〕to receive 受験〔じゅけん〕する to take an entrance exam 受験地獄〔じゅけんじごく〕examination hell
167	授	V-4	397	さず (かる)	じゅ	to receive	子供を授かる〔こどもをさずかる〕to be gifted with a child 授業〔じゅぎょう〕class 授業料〔じゅぎょうりょう〕tuition 教授〔きょうじゅ〕professor 助教授〔じょきょうじゅ〕associate professor
168	州	IV-3	253	X	しゅう	state	本州〔ほんしゅう〕main island of Japan 九州〔きゅうしゅう〕Kyuushuu Island 州知事〔しゅうちじ〕governor 州立大学〔しゅうりつだいがく〕state university
169	秋	III-3	148	あき	しゅう	autumn	秋学期〔あきがっき〕fall semester 秋風〔あきかぜ〕autumn breeze 晩秋〔ばんしゅう〕late fall 秋山〔あきやま〕さん Akiyama-san 秋分の日〔しゅうぶんのひ〕Autumnal Equinox Day (holiday-Sept. 23 or 24)
170	終	III-4	164	お (わる)	しゅう	to end	終わる〔おわる〕(something) ends 終了式〔しゅうりょうしき〕closing ceremony 終電〔しゅうでん〕last train
171	習	IV-6	290	なら (う)	しゅう	to learn	習う〔ならう〕to learn 習い事〔ならいごと〕lesson; practice 学習〔がくしゅう〕learning 練習〔れんしゅう〕practice 習字〔しゅうじ〕calligraphy
172	週	III-4	169	X	しゅう	week	今週〔こんしゅう〕this week 来週〔らいしゅう〕next week 先週〔せんしゅう〕last week 毎週〔まいしゅう〕every week 週末〔しゅうまつ〕weekend 一週間〔いっしゅうかん〕one week
173	集	IV-9	338	あつ (まる)/ あつ (める)	しゅう	to gather, collect	集める〔あつめる〕to collect (something) 集まる〔あつまる〕(something/someone) gathers 集会〔しゅうかい〕meeting 集合時間〔しゅうごうじかん〕meeting time

漢字

AP#	漢字	AIJ-L.	AIJ#	訓読み	音読み	意味	熟語
174	住	III-7	192	す(む)	じゅう	to live	住む〔すむ〕to reside 住所〔じゅうしょ〕address 住人〔じゅうにん〕resident 住田〔すみだ〕さん Sumida-san 三井住友銀行〔みついすみともぎんこう〕Mitsui-Sumitomo Bank
175	十	I-14	10	とお	じゅう	ten	十日〔とおか〕the 10th of the month; ten days 二十日〔はつか〕the 20th of the month 十人十色〔じゅうにんといろ〕Ten people, ten colors. 十万円〔じゅうまん〕hundred thousand yen 十分〔じゅうぶん〕enough
176	重	III-8	206	おも(い)	じゅう	heavy	重い〔おもい〕heavy 体重〔たいじゅう〕(body) weight
177	宿	V-2	370	やど	しゅく	inn	宿題〔しゅくだい〕homework 原宿〔はらじゅく〕Harajuku 新宿〔しんじゅく〕Shinjuku 宿屋〔やどや〕inn 宿泊〔しゅくはく〕する to take lodging (at); to stay over (at)
178	出	II-5	45	で(る)/ だ(す)	しゅつ	to go out	家を出る〔いえをでる〕to leave home 出口〔でぐち〕exit 日の出〔ひので〕sunrise 宿題を出す〔しゅくだいをだす〕to turn in homework 出来る〔できる〕can do 出発〔しゅっぱつ〕する to depart 外出〔がいしゅつ〕going out 出身〔しゅっしん〕place of origin 出席〔しゅっせき〕attendance 出世〔しゅっせ〕promotion; successful career
179	術	V-3	384	X	じゅつ	art	美術〔びじゅつ〕fine arts 芸術〔げいじゅつ〕art 手術〔しゅじゅつ〕surgery 忍術〔にんじゅつ〕fighting art of the ninja
180	春	III-3	146	はる	しゅん	spring	春の花〔はるのはな〕spring flower 春分の日〔しゅんぶんのひ〕Vernal Equinox Day (holiday-March 20 or 21) 青春〔せいしゅん〕youth 思春期〔ししゅんき〕adolescence 春夏秋冬〔しゅんかしゅうとう〕spring, summer, autumn and winter

AP#	漢字	AIJ-L.	AIJ#	訓読み	音読み	意味	熟語
181	初	V-1	341	はじ (め)/ はつ	しょ	beginning	最初〔さいしょ〕 beginning; first 初日〔しょにち〕 the first day 初〔はじ〕めまして　How do you do? 初夏〔しょか〕 early summer
182	所	II-13	102	ところ	しょ	place	どんな所〔ところ〕 What kind of place? 田所〔たどころ〕さん Tadokoro-san 台所〔だいどころ〕 kitchen 場所〔ばしょ〕 place 住所〔じゅうしょ〕 address
183	暑	IV-4	274	あつ (い)	しょ	hot	暑い夏〔あついなつ〕 hot summer 暑中見舞い〔しょちゅうみまい〕 summer greeting card 残暑〔ざんしょ〕 lingering summer heat
184	書	II-5	51	か (く)	しょ	to write	書く〔かく〕 to write 辞書〔じしょ〕 dictionary 参考書〔さんこうしょ〕 reference book 書道〔しょどう〕 calligraphy
185	女	II-6	56	おんな	じょ	female	女の人〔おんなのひと〕 woman 女子〔じょし〕 girl 女性〔じょせい〕 female 男女共学〔だんじょきょうがく〕 coed 彼女〔かのじょ〕 she, her
186	商	V-4	395	あきな (い)	しょう	commer-cial	商業〔しょうぎょう〕 commerce 商売〔しょうばい〕 business 商品〔しょうひん〕 goods 商品券〔しょうひんけん〕 gift certificate
187	小	II-3	29	ちい (さい)/ お/ こ	しょう	small	小さい〔ちいさい〕 small 小学校〔しょうがっこう〕 elementary school 小学生〔しょうがくせい〕 elementary student 小人〔こども〕 child 小川〔おがわ〕さん Ogawa-san 小山〔こやま〕さん Koyama-san 小型〔こがた〕 small size
188	少	II-14	109	すく (ない)/ すこ (し)	しょう	few	少ない〔すくない〕 few 少し〔すこし〕 a little 少々〔しょうしょう〕 just a minute 少年〔しょうねん〕 juvenile 少女〔しょうじょ〕 little girl 少人数〔しょうにんずう〕 small group (of people) 多少〔たしょう〕 more or less

漢字

AP#	漢字	AIJ-L.	AIJ#	訓読み	音読み	意味	熟語
189	笑	IV-4	277	わら (う)	しょう	to smile, laugh	笑う〔わらう〕to smile, laugh
190	上	II-3	26	あが (る)/ うえ/ かみ	じょう	top	上がる〔あがる〕to go up 上原〔うえはら〕さん Uehara-san 川上〔かわかみ〕さん Kawakami-san 上手〔じょうず〕skillful 上下関係〔じょうげかんけい〕vertical relationship 上品〔じょうひん〕elegant
191	乗	III-9	211	の (る)	じょう	to ride	乗物〔のりもの〕vehicle 乗り場〔のりば〕place for boarding vehicles 乗車券〔じょうしゃけん〕passenger ticket
192	場	IV-9	330	ば	じょう	place	場所〔ばしょ〕location 入場券〔にゅうじょうけん〕admission ticket 会場〔かいじょう〕meeting place
193	色	III-8	197	いろ	しき	color	黄色〔きいろ〕yellow 色紙〔いろがみ〕colored paper 色紙〔しきし〕square drawing paper
194	食	II-4	42	た (べる)	しょく	to eat	食べ物〔たべもの〕food 食事〔しょくじ〕meal 朝食〔ちょうしょく〕breakfast 昼食〔ちゅうしょく〕lunch 夕食〔ゆうしょく〕dinner 夜食〔やしょく〕night meal 食後〔しょくご〕after meal 食券〔しょっけん〕meal ticket
195	信	IV-9	340	しん (じる)	しん	to trust	信じる〔しんじる〕to believe, trust 自信〔じしん〕confidence 信用〔しんよう〕trust 赤信号〔あかしんごう〕red light
196	寝	III-6	182	ね (る)	しん	to sleep	早寝早起き〔はやねはやおき〕Early to bed, early to rise. 寝室〔しんしつ〕bedroom 寝具〔しんぐ〕bedding
197	心	II-15	113	こころ	しん	heart	いい心〔こころ〕good heart 安心〔あんしん〕する to be relieved 心配〔しんぱい〕する to worry 中心〔ちゅうしん〕center

AP#	漢字	AIJ-L.	AIJ#	訓読み	音読み	意味	熟語
198	新	II-14	111	あたら（しい）	しん	new	新しい〔あたらしい〕new 新聞〔しんぶん〕newspaper 新学期〔しんがっき〕new semester 新人〔しんじん〕new face 新入生〔しんにゅうせい〕first-year student 新入社員〔しんにゅうしゃいん〕freshman employee
199	森	III-4	161	もり	しん	forest	緑の森〔みどりのもり〕green forest 森川〔もりかわ〕さん Morikawa-san 森林〔しんりん〕forest 青森〔あおもり〕Aomori (prefecture)
200	神	IV-7	296	かみ/ かん	しん	God	神様〔かみさま〕god 神田〔かんだ〕さん Kanda-san 神社〔じんじゃ〕shrine 神道〔しんとう〕Shintoism
201	親	IV-2	236	おや	しん	parent	父親〔ちちおや〕father 母親〔ははおや〕mother 両親〔りょうしん〕parents 親戚〔しんせき〕relatives 親切〔しんせつ〕kind
202	身	V-2	369	み	しん	body	身長〔しんちょう〕(person's) height 中身〔なかみ〕contents 心身〔しんしん〕mind and body
203	進	V-3	377	すす（む）	しん	to advance	進め！〔すすめ〕Advance! 前進〔ぜんしん〕advancement 行進〔こうしん〕parade 進学〔しんがく〕する to go on to college 進化〔しんか〕evolution
204	人	II-2	20	ひと	じん/ にん	person	人々〔ひとびと〕people 日本人〔にほんじん〕Japanese person 人口〔じんこう〕population 何人〔なんにん〕how many people? 何人〔なにじん〕what nationality? 一人〔ひとり〕one person 二人〔ふたり〕two people
205	図	III-9	214	はか（る）	ず/ と	chart	図書館〔としょかん〕library 地図〔ちず〕map 図画〔ずが〕drawing

漢字

AP#	漢字	AIJ-L.	AIJ#	訓読み	音読み	意味	熟語
206	水	I-15	14	みず	すい	water	水を飲む〔みずをのむ〕to drink water 水曜日〔すいようび〕Wednesday 海水〔かいすい〕ocean water 水泳〔すいえい〕swimming
207	数	V-2	374	かず/ かぞ(え る)	すう	number, to count	数を数える〔かずをかぞえる〕to count the amount 生徒数〔せいとすう〕number of students 数字〔すうじ〕numeral 数学〔すうがく〕mathematics 算数〔さんすう〕arithmetic
208	世	IV-2	235	よ	せ	world	世の中〔よのなか〕society, world 世界〔せかい〕world 二世〔にせい〕second generation ２１世紀〔にじゅういっせいき〕21st century
209	制	V-3	375	X	せい	system	制服〔せいふく〕uniform 制度〔せいど〕system 制作〔せいさく〕する to produce
210	成	V-7	450	な(る)/ なり	せい	to become	成田空港〔なりたくうこう〕Narita Airport 平成時代〔へいせいじだい〕Heisei Period 成人の日〔せいじんのひ〕Coming of Age Day 成功〔せいこう〕success 成績〔せいせき〕results; score
211	晴	IV-8	316	は(れ)	せい	clear sky	晴れのち曇り〔はれのちくもり〕clear later cloudy 秋晴れ〔あきばれ〕clear autumn weather 晴天〔せいてん〕fine weather
212	正	II-7	66	ただ(し い)	せい/ しょう	correct	正しい〔ただしい〕correct 正座〔せいざ〕する to sit properly お正月〔おしょうがつ〕New Year's Day 正直〔しょうじき〕honest
213	生	II-5	47	う(まれ る)/ なま	せい/ じょう	to be born	生まれる〔うまれる〕to be born 誕生日〔たんじょうび〕birthday 学生〔がくせい〕student (college) 生徒〔せいと〕pupil 生たまご〔なまたまご〕raw egg
214	西	III-7	184	にし	せい	west	大西〔おおにし〕さん Onishi-san 西海岸〔にしかいがん〕West Coast 西洋〔せいよう〕the West

AP#	漢字	AIJ-L.	AIJ#	訓読み	音読み	意味	熟語
215	青	III-8	199	あお	せい	blue	青色〔あおいろ〕blue color 青空〔あおぞら〕blue sky 青木〔あおき〕さん Aoki-san 青森〔あおもり〕Aomori 青信号〔あおしんごう〕green light 青春〔せいしゅん〕youth
216	静	IV-6	294	しず(か)	せい	quiet	静かな庭〔しずかなにわ〕quiet garden 静岡〔しずおか〕Shizuoka
217	昔	V-2	368	むかし	せき	long ago	昔話〔むかしばなし〕folk tale 昔々〔むかしむかし〕once upon a time
218	石	IV-6	280	いし	せき	rock, stone	大きい石〔おおきいいし〕a big stone 石川〔いしかわ〕さん Ishikawa-san 石田〔いしだ〕さん Ishida-san 石庭〔せきてい〕rock garden 宝石〔ほうせき〕jewel
219	赤	III-8	198	あか	せき	red	赤色〔あかいろ〕red color 赤ちゃん〔あかちゃん〕baby 赤字〔あかじ〕deficit 赤信号〔あかしんごう〕red light 赤飯〔せきはん〕red bean mochi rice 赤道〔せきどう〕equatorial line
220	切	IV-6	289	き(る)	せつ	to cut	紙を切る〔かみをきる〕to cut paper 切手〔きって〕(postage) stamp 大切〔たいせつ〕important 親切〔しんせつ〕kind
221	接	V-3	381	X	せつ	to connect	直接〔ちょくせつ〕direct 間接〔かんせつ〕indirect 面接〔めんせつ〕interview 面接室〔めんせつしつ〕interview room
222	節	V-4	X	ふし/ -ぶし	せつ	node, joint	節目〔ふしめ〕turning point 季節〔きせつ〕season 節分〔せつぶん〕Bean Throwing Celebration 関節〔かんせつ〕joints (knee, elbow) 節句〔せっく〕seasonal festival 節約〔せつやく〕する to economize
223	説	V-7	453	と(く)	せつ	to explain	説明〔せつめい〕explanation 小説〔しょうせつ〕novel 解説者〔かいせつしゃ〕commentator

漢字

AP#	漢字	AIJ-L.	AIJ#	訓読み	音読み	意味	熟語
224	雪	III-3	150	ゆき	せつ	snow	雪が降る〔ゆきがふる〕to snow 大雪〔おおゆき〕heavy snow 雪祭り〔ゆきまつり〕Snow Festival 雪山〔ゆきやま〕snow covered mountain 雪像〔せつぞう〕snow statue
225	先	II-5	46	さき	せん	first	お先に〔おさきに〕Excuse me for going/doing something first. 先生〔せんせい〕teacher 先月〔せんげつ〕last month 先週〔せんしゅう〕last week 先日〔せんじつ〕the other day
226	千	II-9	71	ち	せん	thousand	千円〔せんえん〕one thousand yen 三千〔さんぜん〕three thousand 千代田区〔ちよだく〕Chiyoda Ward (Tokyo)
227	専	V-4	400	X	せん	exclusive	専攻〔せんこう〕major (college) 専門店〔せんもんてん〕specialty store 専業主婦〔せんぎょうしゅふ〕housewife [full-time]
228	川	II-5	43	かわ	せん	river	大井川〔おおいがわ〕Ooi River 川上〔かわかみ〕upper reaches of a river 川下〔かわしも〕downstream 川本〔かわもと〕さん Kawamoto-san 小川〔おがわ〕さん Ogawa-san
229	洗	IV-4	265	あら(う)	せん	to wash	洗う〔あらう〕to wash 洗濯機〔せんたくき〕washing machine 洗面所〔せんめんじょ〕washroom 洗顔石鹸〔せんがんせっけん〕facial soap
230	線	V-5	423	X	せん	line	線を引く〔せんをひく〕to draw a line 山手線〔やまのてせん〕Yamanote Line 新幹線〔しんかんせん〕bullet train 下線〔かせん〕underline 白線〔はくせん〕white line
231	選	V-7	457	えら(ぶ)	せん	to choose	選ぶ〔えらぶ〕to choose, select 選手〔せんしゅ〕athlete 選挙〔せんきょ〕election
232	前	II-13	100	まえ	ぜん	before, front	寝る前〔ねるまえ〕before sleeping 病院の前〔びょういんのまえ〕front of the hospital 前川〔まえかわ〕さん Maekawa-san 午前〔ごぜん〕a.m. 前後〔ぜんご〕front and back

漢字

30

AP#	漢字	AIJ-L.	AIJ#	訓読み	音読み	意味	熟語
233	然	IV-6	286	X	ぜん	be as is	自然〔しぜん〕nature 全然〔ぜんぜん〕(not) at all 突然〔とつぜん〕suddenly
234	全	IV-1	232	まった（く）	ぜん	whole	全部〔ぜんぶ〕all 全体〔ぜんたい〕whole 全然〔ぜんぜん〕(not) at all 全国〔ぜんこく〕national 全員〔ぜんいん〕everyone
235	組	V-3	385	くみ/ ぐみ	そ	group	赤組〔あかぐみ〕red team テレビ番組〔ばんぐみ〕TV program 一年一組〔いちねんいちくみ〕1st year class, Group #1
236	早	II-15	117	はや（い）	そう	early	早寝早起き〔はやねはやおき〕early to bed, early to rise 早川〔はやかわ〕さん Hayakawa-san 早春〔そうしゅん〕early spring 早朝〔そうちょう〕early morning 早退〔そうたい〕leave early
237	相	V-3	378	あい	そう	mutually	相手〔あいて〕partner, other party 相談〔そうだん〕する to consult 相撲〔すもう〕sumo wrestler
238	走	III-6	180	はし（る）	そう	to run	走る〔はしる〕to run 走者〔そうしゃ〕runner 暴走族〔ぼうそうぞく〕delinquent drivers
239	送	IV-3	264	おく（る）	そう	to send	送る〔おくる〕to send 郵送〔ゆうそう〕する to send by mail 送料〔そうりょう〕postage 運送会社〔うんそうがいしゃ〕shipping company 送別会〔そうべつかい〕farewell party
240	贈	V-4	406	おく（る）	ぞう	to present	贈り物〔おくりもの〕gift 贈答品〔ぞうとうひん〕gift item
241	側	V-5	416	かわ	そく	side	右側〔みぎがわ〕right side 左側〔ひだりがわ〕left side 向かい側〔むかいがわ〕other side

漢字

AP#	漢字	AIJ-L.	AIJ#	訓読み	音読み	意味	熟語
242	足	III-6	178	あし/た(りる)	そく	foot, enough	右足〔みぎあし〕right foot 左足〔ひだりあし〕left foot 手足〔てあし〕hands and feet 足りない〔たりない〕not enough 不足〔ふそく〕shortage
243	速	V-2	364	はや(い)	そく	fast	速い車〔はやいくるま〕fast car 速度〔そくど〕speed 早速〔さっそく〕immediately
244	族	IV-2	248	X	ぞく	group	家族〔かぞく〕family 親族〔しんぞく〕relatives 暴走族〔ぼうそうぞく〕delinquent drivers
245	続	IV-6	291	つづ(く)	ぞく	to continue	続く〔つづく〕to continue 続ける〔つづける〕to continue (something) 連続〔れんぞく〕ドラマ serial drama
246	卒	IV-1	227	X	そつ	to graduate	卒業〔そつぎょう〕graduation 大学卒〔だいがくそつ〕college graduate 高校卒〔こうこうそつ〕high school graduate
247	村	IV-3	250	むら	そん	villate	村山〔むらやま〕さん Murayama-san 村人〔むらびと〕villager 村長〔そんちょう〕village chief
248	多	II-14	108	おお(い)	た	many	多くの人〔おおくのひと〕many people 多分〔たぶん〕probably 多少〔たしょう〕more or less
249	太	II-15	120	ふと(る)	た/たい	fat	太る〔ふとる〕to gain weight 太平洋〔たいへいよう〕Pacific Ocean 太陽〔たいよう〕sun 太郎〔たろう〕さん Taro-san
250	打	V-7	452	う(つ)	だ	to hit	ボールを打つ〔うつ〕to hit a ball 打者〔だしゃ〕batter (baseball) 打率〔だりつ〕batting average 打撃〔だげき〕batting (baseball)
251	体	III-3	153	からだ	たい	body	強い体〔つよいからだ〕strong body 体育〔たいいく〕physical education 体操〔たいそう〕physical exercises 体育館〔たいいくかん〕gym 全体〔ぜんたい〕whole 体重〔たいじゅう〕(body) weight 体力〔たいりょく〕physical strength

漢字

AP#	漢字	AIJ-L.	AIJ#	訓読み	音読み	意味	熟語
252	対	V-3	391	X	たい	vs.	A 対〔たい〕B A versus B 5 対 3〔ごたいさん〕5 to 3 対戦相手〔たいせんあいて〕competition opponent
253	待	II-10	82	ま (つ)	たい	to wait	待つ〔まつ〕to wait 待合室〔まちあいしつ〕waiting room 招待〔しょうたい〕する to invite
254	貸	V-6	446	か (す)	たい	to lend	お金を貸す〔おかねをかす〕to lend money 貸家〔かしや〕rental home
255	台	III-4	162	X	たい/だい	step	一台の車〔いちだいのくるま〕one car 台湾〔たいわん〕Taiwan 台所〔だいどころ〕kitchen 台風〔たいふう〕typhoon
256	大	II-3	28	おお (きい)	だい	big	大きい家〔おおきいいえ〕a big house 大人〔おとな〕adult 大学〔だいがく〕college 大学院〔だいがくいん〕graduate school 大学生〔だいがくせい〕college student 東大〔とうだい〕Tokyo University 大事〔だいじ〕important 大丈夫〔だいじょうぶ〕all right
257	第	IV-3	255	X	だい	ordinal	第一日〔だいいちにち〕the first day 第一〔だいいち〕first 第二月曜日〔だいにげつようび〕second Monday
258	題	IV-9	334	X	だい	title	題〔だい〕title 題名〔だいめい〕title name 宿題〔しゅくだい〕homework 問題〔もんだい〕problem 話題〔わだい〕topic 課題〔かだい〕theme; task
259	達	IV-2	249	X	たち	plural, skilled	友達〔ともだち〕friend 人達〔ひとたち〕people 速達〔そくたつ〕special delivery 配達〔はいたつ〕する to deliver 配達人〔はいたつにん〕delivery person 料理の達人〔りょうりのたつじん〕iron chef

AP#	漢字	AIJ-L.	AIJ#	訓読み	音読み	意味	熟語
260	単	V-1	342	X	たん	single	単語〔たんご〕vocabulary 簡単〔かんたん〕simple 単位〔たんい〕credit
261	短	V-6	439	みじか（い）	たん	short	短い本〔みじかいほん〕a short book 短所〔たんしょ〕weak point 最短〔さいたん〕shortest distance 短文〔たんぶん〕short sentence
262	男	II-6	59	おとこ	だん	male	男の子〔おとこのこ〕boy 男子〔だんし〕boy 男性〔だんせい〕male 男女共学〔だんじょきょうがく〕coed
263	知	III-2	145	し（る）	ち	to know	知らない〔しらない〕do not know 知人〔ちじん〕friend, acquaintance 知事〔ちじ〕governor
264	地	III-9	212	X	ち/ じ	land, ground	地下〔ちか〕basement 地下鉄〔ちかてつ〕subway 地震〔じしん〕earthquake 土地〔とち〕land 地球〔ちきゅう〕earth 地方〔ちほう〕area; locality
265	池	IV-9	327	いけ	ち	pond	池の中〔いけのなか〕inside the pond 池田〔いけだ〕さん Ikeda-san 電池〔でんち〕battery
266	置	V-2	359	お（く）	ち	to put	チップを置く〔おく〕to leave a tip 位置〔いち〕location
267	遅	V-1	353	おく（れる） /おそ（い）	ち	to be late	遅れる〔おくれる〕to be late 遅い〔おそい〕late 遅刻〔ちこく〕tardiness
268	茶	III-6	176	X	ちゃ	tea	茶色〔ちゃいろ〕brown color 茶道〔さどう/ちゃどう〕tea ceremony 緑茶〔りょくちゃ〕green tea 抹茶〔まっちゃ〕green tea for ceremony お茶漬け〔おちゃづけ〕rice with tea poured on

漢字

AP#	漢字	AIJ-L.	AIJ#	訓読み	音読み	意味	熟語
269	着	III-2	144	き(る)/つ(く)	ちゃく	to wear, arrive	着物〔きもの〕kimono 下着〔したぎ〕underwear 着る〔きる〕to wear [above the waist] 着く〔つく〕to arrive 東京着〔とうきょうちゃく〕to arrive in Tokyo 到着〔とうちゃく〕arrival 着信〔ちゃくしん〕arrival of mail
270	中	II-3	32	なか	ちゅう	inside	中村〔なかむら〕さん Nakamura-san 夜中〔よなか〕midnight 中学生〔ちゅうがくせい〕middle school student 中国〔ちゅうごく〕China 中止〔ちゅうし〕する to cancel 一日中〔いちにちじゅう〕all day long 勉強中〔べんきょうちゅう〕while studying
271	昼	III-1	129	ひる	ちゅう	noon	昼ご飯〔ひるごはん〕lunch 昼寝〔ひるね〕nap 昼食〔ちゅうしょく〕lunch
272	注	V-6	435	そそ(ぐ)	ちゅう	to pour	注意〔ちゅうい〕する to be careful 注文〔ちゅうもん〕する to order 特注〔とくちゅう〕special order
273	朝	III-1	128	あさ	ちょう	morning	朝ご飯〔あさごはん〕breakfast 朝食〔ちょうしょく〕breakfast 今朝〔けさ〕this morning 早朝〔そうちょう〕early morning
274	町	IV-3	251	まち	ちょう	town	町田〔まちだ〕さん Machida-san 町長〔ちょうちょう〕town chief 町内会〔ちょうないかい〕neighborhood association
275	調	V-5	418	しら(べる)	ちょう	to check	調べる〔しらべる〕to check, search 調子〔ちょうし〕がいい in good condition 調和〔ちょうわ〕harmony

漢字

AP#	漢字	AIJ-L.	AIJ#	訓読み	音読み	意味	熟語
276	長	III-6	179	なが(い)	ちょう	long, head	長い間〔ながいあいだ〕for a long time 長崎〔ながさき〕Nagasaki 長島〔ながしま〕さん Nagashima-san 社長〔しゃちょう〕company president 会長〔かいちょう〕president (of a society) 市長〔しちょう〕mayor 長所〔ちょうしょ〕good point
277	鳥	III-8	196	とり	ちょう	bird	青い鳥〔あおいとり〕a blue bird 小鳥〔ことり〕a small bird 焼き鳥〔やきとり〕grilled skewered chicken 鳥肉〔とりにく〕chicken 鳥類〔ちょうるい〕Aves
278	痛	IV-6	293	いた(い)	つう	painful	痛い〔いたい〕painful 頭痛〔ずつう〕headache 腹痛〔ふくつう〕stomach ache 痛み止め〔いたみどめ〕painkiller
279	通	IV-8	320	とお(る)/ かよ(う)	つう	to go through, to commute	通る〔とおる〕to go through 大通り〔おおどおり〕avenue 通う〔かよう〕to commute 交通〔こうつう〕transportation 通学〔つうがく〕commuting to school 通行人〔つうこうにん〕pedestrian 通行止め〔つうこうどめ〕Road closure. 通路〔つうろ〕pathway 通知表〔つうちひょう〕report card
280	低	V-5	412	ひく(い)	てい	low	背が低い〔せがひくい〕short (height) 最低〔さいてい〕worst 低気圧〔ていきあつ〕low (atmospheric) pressure; bad temper
281	定	V-6	437	さだ(める)	てい	fixed	指定席〔していせき〕reserved seat 予定〔よてい〕plans 日程表〔にっていひょう〕itinerary 定期券〔ていきけん〕commuter pass 定休日〔ていきゅうび〕day off
282	庭	IV-4	268	にわ	てい	garden	美しい庭〔うつくしいにわ〕beautiful garden 石庭〔せきてい〕rock garden 日本庭園〔にほんていえん〕Japanese garden 家庭〔かてい〕family, home, household 家庭科〔かていか〕home economics

AP#	漢字	AIJ-L.	AIJ#	訓読み	音読み	意味	熟語
283	弟	III-1	127	おとうと	てい/ だい/ で	younger brother	弟〔おとうと〕younger brother 兄弟〔きょうだい〕siblings 弟子〔でし〕disciple
284	的	IV-6	295	まと	てき	- like, target	日本的〔にほんてき〕typically Japanese 印象的〔いんしょうてき〕impressive 目的〔もくてき〕purpose
285	天	II-11	89	あま	てん	heaven	天気〔てんき〕weather 天国〔てんごく〕heaven 天才〔てんさい〕genius 天の川〔あまのかわ〕Milky Way 天ぷら〔てんぷら〕tempura
286	店	IV-1	222	みせ	てん	store	お店〔おみせ〕store 店長〔てんちょう〕shop manager 店員〔てんいん〕salesperson, clerk 本店〔ほんてん〕head office 開店〔かいてん〕opening of a shop 閉店〔へいてん〕closing of a shop
287	転	V-1	351	ころ(がる)	てん	to roll	運転〔うんてん〕する to drive 運転手〔うんてんしゅ〕driver 自転車〔じてんしゃ〕bicycle 回転寿し〔かいてんずし〕conveyor belt sushi
288	点	V-2	373	X	てん	point	十点〔じゅってん〕10 points 悪い点〔わるいてん〕bad score 満点〔まんてん〕perfect score
289	伝	V-2	367	つた(える)	でん	to convey	伝える〔つたえる〕to convey, report 手伝う〔てつだう〕to help 伝言〔でんごん〕verbal message 自伝〔じでん〕autobiography 伝統的〔でんとうてき〕traditional
290	田	II-6	58	た	でん	rice field	田中〔たなか〕さん Tanaka-san 田舎〔いなか〕countryside
291	電	II-11	88	X	でん	electricity	電話〔でんわ〕telephone 電車〔でんしゃ〕electric car 電気〔でんき〕electricity 電力〔でんりょく〕electric power 電子〔でんし〕レンジ microwave oven
292	登	V-7	448	のぼ(る)	と/ とう	to climb	登る〔のぼる〕to climb 登山〔とざん〕mountain climbing 登場人物〔とうじょうじんぶつ〕 characters (in a play or novel)

漢字

AP#	漢字	AIJ-L.	AIJ#	訓読み	音読み	意味	熟語
293	都	IV-4	272	みやこ	と	capital	都会〔とかい〕city; metropolis 京都〔きょうと〕Kyoto 東京都〔とうきょうと〕Tokyo Metropolitan area 都合〔つごう〕がいい convenient
294	度	IV-6	284	X	ど	- time(s)	もう一度〔いちど〕one more time 温度〔おんど〕temperature 態度〔たいど〕attitude
295	土	I-15	17	つち	ど/ と	soil	土田〔つちだ〕さん Tsuchida-san 土曜日〔どようび〕Saturday 土地〔とち〕land 本土〔ほんど〕mainland
296	冬	III-3	149	ふゆ	とう	winter	冬休み〔ふゆやすみ〕winter vacation 冬服〔ふゆふく〕winter clothing 真冬〔まふゆ〕midwinter 冬至〔とうじ〕winter solstice
297	島	IV-1	224	しま	とう	island	広島〔ひろしま〕Hiroshima 島田〔しまだ〕さん Shimada-san 島々〔しまじま〕islands 半島〔はんとう〕peninsula
298	東	III-7	183	ひがし	とう	east	東山〔ひがしやま〕さん Higashiyama-san 東西南北〔とうざいなんぼく〕east, west, south and north 東京〔とうきょう〕Tokyo 東大〔とうだい〕Tokyo University 関東〔かんとう〕Kanto area [region of eastern Honshu including Tokyo]
299	答	V-2	371	こた(える)	とう	answer	答え〔こたえ〕answer 解答〔かいとう〕answer; solution
300	頭	IV-7	299	あたま	とう/ ず	head	頭がいい〔あたまがいい〕smart 頭痛〔ずつう〕headache 一頭の馬〔いっとうのうま〕one horse
301	働	III-9	218	はたら(く)	どう	to work	働く〔はたらく〕to work 働き者〔はたらきもの〕hard worker 労働時間〔ろうどうじかん〕working hours 労働者〔ろうどうしゃ〕laborer; worker

漢字

AP#	漢字	AIJ-L.	AIJ#	訓読み	音読み	意味	熟語
302	動	III-9	217	うご（く）	どう	to move	動く〔うごく〕to move 自動車〔じどうしゃ〕automobile 運動〔うんどう〕exercise; sports 運動場〔うんどうじょう〕athletic field 動物〔どうぶつ〕animal 動物園〔どうぶつえん〕zoo 動詞〔どうし〕verb 動画〔どうが〕moving image
303	同	IV-1	229	おな（じ）	どう	same	同じ〔おなじ〕same 同点〔どうてん〕tie (score) 同時〔どうじ〕simultaneous 同意〔どうい〕consent 同情〔どうじょう〕する to sympathize
304	道	III-9	215	みち	どう	road, way	道〔みち〕road 道子〔みちこ〕さん 道路〔どうろ〕road 横断歩道〔おうだんほどう〕pedestrian crossing 書道〔しょどう〕calligraphy 茶道〔さどう/ちゃどう〕tea ceremony 柔道〔じゅうどう〕judo 剣道〔けんどう〕kendo [way of the sword] 合気道〔あいきどう〕aikido 道場〔どうじょう〕dojo; hall used for martial arts 北海道〔ほっかいどう〕Hokkaido 道徳〔どうとく〕morals
305	特	IV-8	325	X	とく	special	特に〔とくに〕especially 特急〔とっきゅう〕limited express 特別〔とくべつ〕special 特大〔とくだい〕extra big 特注〔とくちゅう〕special order
306	読	II-11	94	よ（む）	どく	to read	本を読む〔ほんをよむ〕read a book 読み物〔よみもの〕reading material 読売新聞〔よみうりしんぶん〕Yomiuri Newspaper 読書〔どくしょ〕reading 音読〔おんどく〕reading aloud

AP#	漢字	AIJ-L.	AIJ#	訓読み	音読み	意味	熟語
307	内	III-7	190	うち	ない	inside	山内〔やまうち〕さん Yamauchi-san 内田〔うちだ〕さん Uchida-san 内村〔うちむら〕さん Uchimura-san 家内〔かない〕(own) wife 家庭内暴力〔かていないぼうりょく〕domestic violence 内緒〔ないしょ〕secret; confidential
308	南	III-9	208	みなみ	なん	south	南口〔みなみぐち〕south gate 南田〔みなみだ〕さん Minamida-san 南極〔なんきょく〕South Pole 東南〔とうなん〕アジア Southeast Asia 南山大学〔なんざんだいがく〕Nanzan University
309	難	V-1	354	むずか(しい)/ -がた(い)	なん	difficult	難しい〔むずかしい〕difficult 有難う〔ありがとう〕Thank you. 難問〔なんもん〕difficult question
310	二	I-13	2	ふた	に	two	二つ〔ふたつ〕two (general counter) 二人〔ふたり〕two (people) 二日〔ふつか〕the second day of the month 二月〔にがつ〕February 二週間〔にしゅうかん〕two weeks 二年〔にねん〕two years
311	肉	II-14	106	X	にく	meat	牛肉〔ぎゅうにく〕beef 豚肉〔ぶたにく〕pork 筋肉〔きんにく〕muscles
312	日	I-15	11	ひ/か	にち/ じつ	day	何日〔なんにち〕what day?; how many days? 一日〔ついたち〕the 1st day of the month; two days 一日〔いちにち〕one day 二日〔ふつか〕the 2nd day of the month 日曜日〔にちようび〕Sunday 定休日〔ていきゅうび〕regular day off 祭日〔さいじつ〕national holiday, festival day 祝日〔しゅくじつ〕holiday 日の丸〔ひのまる〕(name of) the Japanese flag お日様〔おひさま〕Sun

AP#	漢字	AIJ-L.	AIJ#	訓読み	音読み	意味	熟語
313	入	II-13	97	はい(る)/ い(れる)	にゅう	to enter	入る〔はいる〕to enter 入れる〔いれる〕to put in 入口〔いりぐち〕entrance 入学式〔にゅうがくしき〕school entrance ceremony 入場券〔にゅうじょうけん〕admission ticket 入会〔にゅうかい〕する to join a group 入部〔にゅうぶ〕する to join a club 入試〔にゅうし〕entrance exam
314	熱	V-2	364	あつ(い)	ねつ	hot, fever	熱いお茶〔あついおちゃ〕hot tea 高い熱〔たかいねつ〕high fever 熱海〔あたみ〕Atami (place name)
315	年	II-2	23	とし	ねん	year	今年〔ことし〕this year 去年〔きょねん〕last year 来年〔らいねん〕next year 毎年〔まいねん〕every year 年を取っている〔としをとっている〕elderly お年寄り〔おとしより〕the elderly ２０２０年〔にせんにじゅうねん〕the year 2020 ３年生〔さんねんせい〕3rd grade student 年中行事〔ねんちゅうぎょうじ〕annual event お年玉〔おとしだま〕New Year's monetary gift 年末〔ねんまつ〕end of the year 中年〔ちゅうねん〕middle age 少年〔しょうねん〕boys; juveniles
316	背	V-5	411	せ	はい	back	背中〔せなか〕back (of one's body) 背が高い〔せがたかい〕tall (height)
317	配	V-5	426	くば(る)	はい/ぱい	to deliver	配る〔くばる〕to deliver; distribute 心配〔しんぱい〕する to worry 配達人〔はいたつにん〕delivery person
318	買	II-15	116	か(う)	ばい	to buy	買う〔かう〕to buy 買物〔かいもの〕shopping
319	売	II-11	93	う(る)	ばい	to sell	安売り〔やすうり〕sale 売店〔ばいてん〕shop, stand 商売〔しょうばい〕trade, business 券売機〔けんばいき〕ticket vending machine

漢字

AP#	漢字	AIJ-L.	AIJ#	訓読み	音読み	意味	熟語
320	白	II-9	69	しろ	ばい/はく	white	白い〔しろい〕white 白人〔はくじん〕Caucasian 白紙〔はくし〕blank paper 紅白歌合戦〔こうはくうたがっせん〕Red & White Song Festival
321	八	I-14	8	やっ/よう	はち	eight	八つ〔やっつ〕eight (general counter) 八日〔ようか〕the 8th day of the month; 8 days 八月〔はちがつ〕August 八人〔はちにん〕eight people 八百屋〔やおや〕greengrocery
322	発	IV-8	322	X	はつ	to depart	発音〔はつおん〕pronunciation 出発〔しゅっぱつ〕departure 東京発〔とうきょうはつ〕Tokyo departure 発車〔はっしゃ〕departure of a vehicle 発表〔はっぴょう〕する to present verbally; to announce 発達〔はったつ〕development 発明〔はつめい〕invention 発見〔はっけん〕discovery
323	半	II-10	79	X	はん	half	半分〔はんぶん〕half 五時半〔ごじはん〕5:30
324	反	V-3	390	X	はん	against	反対〔はんたい〕する to oppose 駐車違反〔ちゅうしゃいはん〕parking violation
325	飯	III-6	177	めし	はん	cooked rice	ご飯〔ごはん〕rice (cooked) 朝ご飯〔あさごはん〕breakfast 昼ご飯〔ひるごはん〕lunch 炊飯器〔すいはんき〕rice cooker 焼き飯〔やきめし〕fried rice
326	晩	III-6	173	X	ばん	evening	晩ご飯〔ばんごはん〕dinner 今晩〔こんばん〕tonight
327	番	II-10	85	X	ばん	number	一番〔いちばん〕best, first, No. 1 番号〔ばんごう〕number 番地〔ばんち〕house number 順番〔じゅんばん〕order; sequence 交番〔こうばん〕police box テレビ番組〔ばんぐみ〕TV program
328	非	V-4	409	X	ひ	non -	非常口〔ひじょうぐち〕emergency exit 非常に〔ひじょうに〕extremely; very

漢字

AP#	漢字	AIJ-L.	AIJ#	訓読み	音読み	意味	熟語
329	飛	V-5	421	と (ぶ)	ひ	to fly, jump	空を飛ぶ〔そらをとぶ〕to fly in the air 飛行機〔ひこうき〕airplane 飛行時間〔ひこうじかん〕flight time (length) 飛行場〔ひこうじょう〕airport
330	美	III-7	188	うつく (しい)	び	beautiful	美しい〔うつくしい〕beautiful 美人〔びじん〕beautiful woman 美術〔びじゅつ〕fine art 美術館〔びじゅつかん〕art museum 美容院〔びようい ん〕beauty salon
331	鼻	V-6	430	はな	び	nose	高い鼻〔たかいはな〕long nose
332	必	V-3	382	かなら (ず)	ひつ	necessary	必ず〔かならず〕surely; definitely 必要〔ひつよう〕necessary 必勝〔ひっしょう〕certain victory 必須科目〔ひっすかもく〕required subjects
333	百	II-9	70	X	ひゃく	hundred	百円〔ひゃくえん〕100 yen 三百〔さんびゃく〕300 八百〔はっぴゃく〕800 八百屋〔やおや〕greengrocer
334	氷	V-2	365	こおり	ひょう	ice	氷〔こおり〕ice かき氷〔かきごおり〕shaved ice; snow cone 氷河〔ひょうが〕glacier
335	表	V-4	410	おもて	ひょう	front, chart	家の表〔いえのおもて〕front of the house 表を作る〔ひょうをつくる〕make a chart 発表〔はっぴょう〕する to present (orally); announce 表現〔ひょうげん〕する to express
336	病	IV-2	237	やま (い)	びょう	illness	病は気から〔やまいはきから〕Illness starts from the spirit. 病気〔びょうき〕illness 病院〔びょういん〕hospital 病名〔びょうめい〕name of a disease 病人〔びょうにん〕sick person 心臓病〔しんぞうびょう〕heart disease
337	品	V-6	434	しな	ひん	item	品物〔しなもの〕goods 品川駅〔しながわえき〕Shinagawa Station 化粧品〔けしょうひん〕cosmetics 商品券〔しょうひんけん〕gift certificate 食品〔しょくひん〕commodity 上品な人〔じょうひんなひと〕elegant person

漢字

AP#	漢字	AIJ-L.	AIJ#	訓読み	音読み	意味	熟語
338	不	IV-3	262	X	ふ/ぶ	non -	不便〔ふべん〕inconvenient 不公平〔ふこうへい〕unfair 不道徳〔ふどうとく〕immoral 不安〔ふあん〕uneasy 不幸〔ふこう〕unhappy 不平〔ふへい〕complaint 睡眠不足〔すいみんぶそく〕lack of sleep
339	付	V-6	447	つ（く）	ふ	attach	付近〔ふきん〕neighborhood: vicinity みそ汁付き〔みそしるつき〕with miso soup 気付く〔きづく〕to notice 付き合う〔つきあう〕to associate with 添付〔てんぷ〕attachment
340	夫	V-7	456	おっと	ふ/ ふう	man/ (own) husband	夫婦〔ふうふ〕married couple ケネディー夫人〔ふじん〕Mrs. Kennedy 私の夫〔わたしのおっと〕my husband
341	婦	V-6	443	X	ふ	married woman	主婦〔しゅふ〕housewife 婦人〔ふじん〕woman 婦人服〔ふじんふく〕woman's clothing
342	父	II-5	48	ちち/ とう	ふ	father	お父さん〔おとうさん〕(someone's) father 父親〔ちちおや〕father 祖父〔そふ〕(own) grandfather 父母〔ふぼ〕(own) parents 父兄会〔ふけいかい〕parents' association 父方〔ちちかた〕father's side of the family 神父〔しんぷ〕Catholic priest
343	部	III-7	187	へ	ぶ	part	全部〔ぜんぶ〕all 一部〔いちぶ〕one part 部分〔ぶぶん〕portion 部員〔ぶいん〕member 部活〔ぶかつ〕club activity 部屋〔へや〕room 子供部屋〔こどもべや〕child's room
344	風	III-8	201	かぜ	ふう	wind	風〔かぜ〕wind 風邪〔かぜ〕a cold 強風〔きょうふう〕strong wind 台風〔たいふう〕typhoon 風力〔ふうりょく〕wind power 和風〔わふう〕Japanese style 洋風〔ようふう〕Western style

AP#	漢字	AIJ-L.	AIJ#	訓読み	音読み	意味	熟語
345	服	IV-8	314	X	ふく	cloth	制服〔せいふく〕school uniform 洋服〔ようふく〕Western-style clothes 和服〔わふく〕Japanese clothes 服装〔ふくそう〕clothing 呉服〔ごふく〕dry goods
346	払	V-5	429	はら(う)	ふつ	to pay	払う〔はらう〕to pay
347	物	II-13	98	もの	ぶつ/ もつ	thing (tangible)	食物〔たべもの〕food 飲物〔のみもの〕drinks 着物〔きもの〕kimono [traditional Japanese wear] 買物〔かいもの〕shopping 乗物〔のりもの〕vehicle 荷物〔にもつ〕luggage, baggage 洗濯物〔せんたくもの〕laundry 物語〔ものがたり〕tale, story 動物〔どうぶつ〕animal 動物園〔どうぶつえん〕zoo 植物〔しょくぶつ〕plants 物理〔ぶつり〕physics 生物〔せいぶつ〕biology
348	分	II-7	65	わ(かる)/ わ(ける)	ふん/ ぶん	to understand, to divide	分かる〔わかる〕to understand 一分〔いっぷん〕one minute 半分〔はんぶん〕half 四分の一〔よんぶんのいち〕1/4 多分〔たぶん〕probably 十分〔じゅうぶん〕enough ゴミを分ける〔わける〕to sort rubbish
349	文	III-2	135	ふみ	ぶん/ も	sentence	作文〔さくぶん〕composition 文字〔もじ〕character, letter (of alphabet) 文化〔ぶんか〕culture 文化の日〔ぶんかのひ〕Culture Day (holiday: Nov. 3) 文化祭〔ぶんかさい〕Cultural Festival 文学〔ぶんがく〕literature 英文学〔えいぶんがく〕British literature
350	聞	II-6	55	き(く)	ぶん	to listen	聞く〔きく〕to listen; to ask 新聞〔しんぶん〕newspaper

漢字

AP#	漢字	AIJ-L.	AIJ#	訓読み	音読み	意味	熟語
351	平	IV-3	261	たい(ら)/ ひら	へい/ びょう	flat, peace	平ら〔たいら〕flat 平田〔ひらた〕さん Hirata-san 平和〔へいわ〕peace 平日〔へいじつ〕weekday 平気〔へいき〕calm; unconcerned; indifferent 平安時代〔へいあんじだい〕Heian Period (794-1185) 平成時代〔へいせいじだい〕Heisei Period (1989-present) 平家物語〔へいけものがたり〕Tale of the Heike 平等〔びょうどう〕equal
352	別	V-6	440	わか(れる)	べつ	to separate	別れる〔わかれる〕to separate 特別〔とくべつ〕special 別々〔べつべつ〕separate 別居〔べっきょ〕する to live separately 別室〔べっしつ〕separate room 差別〔さべつ〕discrimination
353	変	IV-7	305	か(わる)/ か(える)	へん	to change	変える〔かえる〕to change (something) 変わる〔かわる〕(something) changes 大変〔たいへん〕terrible; hard; very 変化〔へんか〕change, conjugation
354	便	V-5	424	たよ(り)	べん/ びん	convenient	便利〔べんり〕convenient 不便〔ふべん〕inconvenient 便所〔べんじょ〕toilet 郵便局〔ゆうびんきょく〕post office ジャル8便〔はちびん〕JAL Flight #8
355	勉	III-4	166	つと(める)	べん	to study	勉強〔べんきょう〕study
356	歩	III-9	216	ある(く)	ほ/ ぽ	to walk	歩く〔あるく〕to walk 散歩〔さんぽ〕a walk, stroll 横断歩道〔おうだんほどう〕pedestrian crossing 歩行者〔ほこうしゃ〕pedestrian
357	母	II-5	49	はは/ かあ	ぼ	mother	母〔はは〕(own) mother お母さん〔おかあさん〕(someone's) mother 祖母〔そぼ〕(own) grandmother 父母〔ふぼ〕(own) parents

漢字

AP#	漢字	AIJ-L.	AIJ#	訓読み	音読み	意味	熟語
358	方	II-9	73	かた/ がた	ほう	person [polite], way of doing, side	あの方〔かた〕that person over there 夕方〔ゆうがた〕twilight; dusk 食べ方〔たべかた〕how to eat どちらの方〔ほう〕which one (of two)? 方言〔ほうげん〕dialect 地方〔ちほう〕district 方角〔ほうがく〕direction; compass point
359	法	V-4	393	X	ほう	law	法律〔ほうりつ〕law 文法〔ぶんぽう〕grammar 方法〔ほうほう〕method
360	忘	IV-2	243	わす(れる)	ぼう	to forget	忘れる〔わすれる〕to forget 忘れ物〔わすれもの〕forgotten item 忘年会〔ぼうねんかい〕year-end party
361	忙	V-5	415	いそが(しい)	ぼう	busy	忙しい〔いそがしい〕busy 多忙〔たぼう〕very busy
362	北	III-9	207	きた	ほく	north	北〔きた〕north 北村〔きたむら〕さん Kitamura-san 北の湖〔きたのうみ〕Kitanoumi (sumo wrestler's name) 北海道〔ほっかいどう〕Hokkaido 北大〔ほくだい〕Hokkaido University 東北大学〔とうほくだいがく〕Tohoku University (in Sendai) 南北問題〔なんぼくもんだい〕North-South problem
363	本	II-2	21	もと	ほん/ ぼん	origin, book	本を読む〔ほんをよむ〕to read a book 日本語〔にほんご〕Japanese language 本日〔ほんじつ〕today 一本〔いっぽん〕one (long objects) 三本〔さんぼん〕three (long objects) 山本〔やまもと〕さん Yamamoto-san
364	妹	III-1	125	いもうと	まい	younger sister	妹〔いもうと〕(own) younger sister 姉妹〔しまい〕sisters
365	枚	V-1	352	X	まい	- sheet(s)	一枚〔いちまい〕one sheet

漢字

AP#	漢字	AIJ-L.	AIJ#	訓読み	音読み	意味	熟語
366	毎	II-5	50	X	まい	every	毎日〔まいにち〕every day 毎週〔まいしゅう〕every week 毎月〔まいつき〕every month 毎年〔まいねん/まいとし〕every year 毎朝〔まいあさ〕every morning 毎晩〔まいばん〕every night 毎日新聞〔まいにちしんぶん〕Mainichi Newspaper
367	末	IV-2	247	すえ	まつ	end	週末〔しゅうまつ〕weekend 月末〔げつまつ〕end-of-month 年末〔ねんまつ〕end-of-year 末っ子〔すえっこ〕youngest child (in a family)
368	万	II-9	72	X	まん	ten thousand	一万円〔いちまんえん〕10,000 yen 百万〔ひゃくまん〕1,000,000
369	味	III-8	202	あじ	み	taste	いい味〔あじ〕good taste 味見〔あじみ〕sampling 味の素〔あじのもと〕MSG 意味〔いみ〕meaning 中味〔なかみ〕contents 趣味〔しゅみ〕hobby 興味〔きょうみ〕interest 味噌汁〔みそしる〕miso soup
370	未	V-7	455	X	み	not yet	未来〔みらい〕future (distant) 未知〔みち〕unknown
371	無	IV-9	337	X	む	nothing	無料〔むりょう〕free of charge 無理〔むり〕impossible 無力〔むりょく〕powerless 無口〔むくち〕reticence 無記名〔むきめい〕unsigned 無責任〔むせきにん〕irresponsible
372	名	II-13	99	な	めい	name	名前〔なまえ〕name 名古屋〔なごや〕Nagoya 氏名〔しめい〕full name 有名〔ゆうめい〕famous 名人〔めいじん〕expert 名物〔めいぶつ〕famous product 名門校〔めいもんこう〕famous school

漢字

AP#	漢字	AIJ-L.	AIJ#	訓読み	音読み	意味	熟語
373	明	III-1	130	あか（るい）	めい	bright	明るい〔あかるい〕bright 明日〔あした〕tomorrow 明治時代〔めいじじだい〕Meiji Period (1868-1912) 説明〔せつめい〕explanation 明暗〔めいあん〕light and darkness
374	面	V-3	380	おも/ おもて	めん	face	面白い〔おもしろい〕interesting 真面目〔まじめ〕serious 正面〔しょうめん〕front 表面〔ひょうめん〕surface 一面〔いちめん〕one side 地面〔じめん〕ground 面接〔めんせつ〕interview
375	木	I-15	15	き	もく	tree	大きい木〔おおきいき〕big tree 木々〔きぎ〕trees 木本〔きもと〕さん Kimoto-san 木曜日〔もくようび〕Thursday
376	目	II-2	19	め	もく	eye	右目〔みぎめ〕right eye 左目〔ひだりめ〕left eye 目薬〔めぐすり〕eye drops 目的〔もくてき〕purpose 目次〔もくじ〕table of contents
377	問	III-1	333	と（う）	もん	to ask	問題〔もんだい〕problem 質問〔しつもん〕question 訪問〔ほうもん〕visit
378	門	II-6	54	X	もん	gate	門〔もん〕gate 校門〔こうもん〕school gate 正門〔せいもん〕front gate 専門〔せんもん〕speciality
379	夜	III-6	174	よる	や	night	夜中〔よなか〕midnight 今夜〔こんや〕tonight 夜食〔やしょく〕night snack
380	野	IV-9	331	の	や	field	野原〔のはら〕field 野中〔のなか〕さん Nonaka-san 野菜〔やさい〕vegetables 野球選手〔やきゅうせんしゅ〕baseball player 野球場〔やきゅうじょう〕baseball field 野生〔やせい〕wild

漢字

AP#	漢字	AIJ-L.	AIJ#	訓読み	音読み	意味	熟語
381	薬	IV-4	278	くすり	やく	medicine	薬を飲む〔くすりをのむ〕 to take medicine 風邪薬〔かぜぐすり〕 cold medicine 薬指〔くすりゆび〕 ring finger 薬局〔やっきょく〕 pharmacy 薬剤師〔やくざいし〕 pharmacist
382	友	II-10	80	とも	ゆう	friend	友達〔ともだち〕 friend 友人〔ゆうじん〕 friend 友情〔ゆうじょう〕 friendship 親友〔しんゆう〕 best friend 友子〔ともこ〕さん Tomoko-san
383	有	IV-1	233	あ(る)	ゆう	to have	有田〔ありた〕さん Arita-san 有名〔ゆうめい〕 famous 有料〔ゆうりょう〕 a charge
384	由	III-8	205	X	ゆう	reason	自由〔じゆう〕 freedom
385	遊	V-3	392	あそ(ぶ)	ゆう	to play	遊び場〔あそびば〕 playground 水遊び〔みずあそび〕 water play 遊園地〔ゆうえんち〕 amusement park
386	夕	II-3	30	X	ゆう	evening	夕方〔ゆうがた〕 early evening 夕食〔ゆうしょく〕 dinner, supper 夕日〔ゆうひ〕 sunset 七夕〔たなばた〕 Star Festival (July 7)
387	予	V-5	428	X	よ	pre	予習〔よしゅう〕 preview 予定〔よてい〕 plans 予選〔よせん〕 preliminary 予約〔よやく〕 reservation
388	曜	II-2	25	X	よう	day of week	何曜日〔なんようび〕 what day of the week? 日曜日〔にちようび〕 Sunday
389	様	V-7	454	さま	よう	polite equiv. of さん, manner	御客様〔おきゃくさま〕 customers 様々〔さまざま〕 various 様子〔ようす〕 circumstances; condition
390	洋	III-7	185	X	よう	ocean	太平洋〔たいへいよう〕 Pacific Ocean インド洋〔よう〕 Indian Ocean 大西洋〔たいせいよう〕 Atlantic Ocean 西洋〔せいよう〕 the west 東洋〔とうよう〕 the east 洋服〔ようふく〕 Western-style clothes 洋子〔ようこ〕さん Yoko-san

AP#	漢字	AIJ-L.	AIJ#	訓読み	音読み	意味	熟語
391	用	V-6	444	X	よう	task, use	用〔よう〕がある have things to do 用事〔ようじ〕がある have errands to do 台所用品〔だいどころようひん〕kitchenware 婦人用化粧室〔ふじんようけしょうしつ〕restroom for women 用紙〔ようし〕form
392	要	V-3	383	い (る)	よう	need	必要〔ひつよう〕necessary 重要〔じゅうよう〕important
393	来	II-4	35	き/ く/ こ	らい	to come	来て〔きて〕Come. 来る〔くる〕to come 来ないで〔こないで〕Don't come. 来週〔らいしゅう〕next week 来月〔らいげつ〕next month 来年〔らいねん〕next year 未来〔みらい〕future (distant) 将来〔しょうらい〕future (near)
394	絡	V-6	445	X	らく	linkage	連絡〔れんらく〕contact
395	落	V-1	X	お (ちる)/ お (とす)	らく	to fall, to drop	落ちる〔おちる〕to fall 落とす〔おとす〕to drop 落葉〔おちば〕fallen leaves 落選〔らくせん〕election loss 落語〔らくご〕telling of a comic story (*rakugo*)
396	利	V-5	425	X	り	advantage	便利〔べんり〕convenient 利点〔りてん〕advantage 不利〔ふり〕disadvantage 利用〔りよう〕する to use
397	理	III-8	204	X	り	reason	理科〔りか〕science 理想〔りそう〕ideal 理由〔りゆう〕reason 理解〔りかい〕する to understand 料理〔りょうり〕cooking
398	立	II-14	104	た (つ)	りつ	to stand	立つ〔たつ〕to stand 起立〔きりつ〕Stand. 公立〔こうりつ〕publicly established (institution) 私立〔しりつ/わたくしりつ〕private (institution) 市立〔しりつ/いちりつ〕municipal 州立〔しゅうりつ〕state (establishment) 国立公園〔こくりつこうえん〕national park

漢字

AP#	漢字	AIJ-L.	AIJ#	訓読み	音読み	意味	熟語
399	留	V-3	388	とど (める)/ とど (まる)	りゅう/ る	to stop	留学〔りゅうがく〕する to study abroad 留学生〔りゅうがくせい〕foreign exchange student 留守〔るす〕not at home 留守番電話〔るすばんでんわ〕answering machine
400	旅	III-2	139	たび	りょ	trave	日本の旅〔たび〕Japan trip 旅人〔たびびと〕traveller 旅行〔りょこう〕travel 旅行者〔りょこうしゃ〕traveller 海外旅行〔かいがいりょこう〕travel abroad
401	両	IV-1	231	X	りょう	both	両方〔りょうほう〕both 両親〔りょうしん〕parents 両手〔りょうて〕both hands
402	料	III-8	203	X	りょう	material, fee	料理〔りょうり〕cooking 調味料〔ちょうみりょう〕seasoning 材料〔ざいりょう〕ingredients 料金〔りょうきん〕fare; fee 無料〔むりょう〕free of charge 授業料〔じゅぎょうりょう〕tuition 入場料〔にゅうじょうりょう〕admission fee
403	力	V-1	347	ちから	りょく	power	力持ち〔ちからもち〕strong person 協力〔きょうりょく〕する to cooperate 努力〔どりょく〕する to make efforts
404	林	III-4	160	はやし	りん	forest	林〔はやし〕さん Hayashi-san 林田〔はやしだ〕さん Hayashida-san 小林〔こばやし〕さん Kobayashi-san 大林〔おおばやし〕さん Oobayashi-san 森林〔しんりん〕forest 林業〔りんぎょう〕forestry
405	冷	IV-9	329	つめ (たい)	れい	cold	冷たい〔つめたい〕cold (to the touch) 冷蔵庫〔れいぞうこ〕refrigerator 冷凍庫〔れいとうこ〕freezer 冷凍食品〔れいとうしょくひん〕frozen food 冷房〔れいぼう〕air-conditioning
406	礼	V-4	408	X	れい	gratitude, paper bills	失礼〔しつれい〕rude お礼状〔おれいじょう〕thank you letter

AP#	漢字	AIJ-L.	AIJ#	訓読み	音読み	意味	熟語
407	練	V-6	438	ね(る)	れん	to train	練る〔ねる〕to knead; to work over 練習〔れんしゅう〕practice 訓練〔くんれん〕training
408	六	I-14	6	む	ろく	six	六つ〔むっつ〕six (general counter) 六日〔むいか〕the 6th of the month; 6 days 六月〔ろくがつ〕June 六人〔ろくにん〕six people 六個〔ろっこ〕six (general counter)
409	和	III-7	186	X	わ	harmony, Japanese	和〔わ〕harmony 平和〔へいわ〕peace 和風〔わふう〕Japanese style 和食〔わしょく〕Japanese-style meal 和紙〔わし〕Japanese paper 和室〔わしつ〕Japanese-style room 和菓子〔わがし〕Japanese sweets 和楽器〔わがっき〕traditional Japanese musical instrument 和英辞典〔わえいじてん〕Japanese-English dictionary 英和辞典〔えいわじてん〕English-Japanese dictionary 和敬清寂〔わけいせいじゃく〕harmony, respect, purity and tranquility (tea ceremony)
410	話	II-11	92	はな(す)	わ	to talk	話す〔はなす〕to talk 電話〔でんわ〕telephone 会話〔かいわ〕conversation 英会話〔えいかいわ〕English conversation

漢字

AIJにあって、APにない漢字５１字

AIJ#	漢字	AIJ-L	AIJ#	訓読み	音読み	意味	熟語
1	良	II-4	41	よ（い）	りょう	good	良い〔よい〕good 良く出来ました〔よくできました〕Well done. 良心〔りょうしん〕conscience
2	耳	II-6	53	みみ	じ	ear	右耳〔みぎみみ〕right ear 左耳〔ひだりみみ〕left ear 耳鼻科〔じびか〕otolaryngology
3	々	II-7	68	X	X	(repeat)	人々〔ひとびと〕people 山々〔やまやま〕mountains 時々〔ときどき〕sometimes 国々〔くにぐに〕countries
4	玉	II-9	74	たま	ぎょく	ball, jewel	百円玉〔ひゃくえんだま〕100 yen coin お年玉〔おとしだま〕New Year's monetary gift 玉子〔たまご〕egg 目玉焼き〔めだまやき〕sunny-side-up egg
5	米	II-10	84	こめ	まい	rice	米〔こめ〕rice (uncooked) もち米〔もちごめ〕mochi (glutinous) rice 玄米〔げんまい〕brown rice 新米〔しんまい〕new rice
6	戸	II-13	101	と	こ	door	戸を開ける〔とをあける〕open the door 戸田〔とだ〕さん Toda-san 一戸建て〔いっこだて〕(separate) house
7	才	II-15	112	X	さい	ability	一才〔いっさい〕one year old 天才〔てんさい〕genius 才能〔さいのう〕talent, ability 文才〔ぶんさい〕literary talent
8	銀	III-1	132	X	ぎん	silver	銀色〔ぎんいろ〕silver color 銀行〔ぎんこう〕bank 銀座〔ぎんざ〕Ginza
9	糸	III-3	156	いと	し	thread	糸〔いと〕thread, yarn, string 糸〔いと〕こんにゃく shredded konnyaku
10	草	III-4	159	くさ	そう	grass	緑の草〔みどりのくさ〕green grass 雑草〔ざっそう〕weed ほうれん草〔そう〕spinach 草原〔そうげん〕prairie

漢字

AIJ#	漢字	AIJ-L	AIJ#	訓読み	音読み	意味	熟語
11	閉	III-7	194	と (じる)/ し (める)/ し (まる)	へい	to close	本を閉じる〔ほんをとじる〕close a book 窓を閉める〔まどをしめる〕shut the window ドアが閉まる〔しまる〕door closes 閉店時間〔へいてんじかん〕shop closing time
12	竹	III-8	195	たけ	ちく	bamboo	竹の子〔たけのこ〕bamboo shoots 竹中〔たけなか〕さん Takenaka-san 竹林〔ちくりん〕bamboo thicket 松竹梅〔しょうちくばい〕pine, bamboo, plum
13	黄	III-8	200	き	おう	yellow	黄色〔きいろ〕yellow 黄色人種〔おうしょくじんしゅ〕yellow race 黄金時代〔おうごんじだい〕the golden age
14	鉄	III-9	213	X	てつ	iron	地下鉄〔ちかてつ〕subway 鉄道〔てつどう〕railroad 私鉄〔してつ〕private railway
15	客	IV-1	223	X	きゃく	guest, customer	御客様〔おきゃくさま〕customers 客間〔きゃくま〕room where guests are received 乗客〔じょうきゃく〕passenger
16	座	IV-1	225	す (わる)	ざ	to sit	お座り下さい〔おすわりください〕Please sit. 正座〔せいざ〕sit properly 銀座〔ぎんざ〕Ginza 座布団〔ざぶとん〕floor cushion 座席〔ざせき〕seat
17	当	IV-1	234	あ (たる)/ あ (てる)	とう	to hit	ボールが当たる〔あたる〕The ball hits (something). ボールを当てる〔あてる〕to hit a ball 本当〔ほんとう〕true 当選〔とうせん〕to be elected 当用漢字〔とうようかんじ〕kanji for daily use 当番〔とうばん〕being on duty 弁当〔べんとう〕box lunch
18	死	IV-2	241	し (ぬ)	し	to die	死ぬ〔しぬ〕to die 死亡者〔しぼうしゃ〕deaths 戦死〔せんし〕death in war 事故死〔じこし〕accidental death 死者数〔ししゃすう〕number of deaths
19	亡	IV-2	242	な (くなる)	ぼう	to pass away	亡くなる〔なくなる〕to pass away 死亡者〔しぼうしゃ〕deaths 未亡人〔未亡人〕widow

漢字

AIJ#	漢字	AIJ-L	AIJ#	訓読み	音読み	意味	熟語
20	船	IV-3	252	ふね	せん	ship, boat	船の旅〔ふねのたび〕boat trip 船長〔せんちょう〕ship's captain 客船〔きゃくせん〕passenger boat
21	戦	IV-3	257	たたか(う)	せん	to fight	戦う〔たたかう〕to fight; to battle 戦争〔せんそう〕war 第二次世界大戦〔だいにじせかいたいせん〕World War II 戦車〔せんしゃ〕tank (military vehicle) 開戦〔かいせん〕start of a war
22	争	IV-3	258	あらそ(う)	そう	dispute	競争〔きょうそう〕する to compete
23	軍	IV-4	269	X	ぐん	military	軍人〔ぐんじん〕military personnel 海軍〔かいぐん〕navy 空軍〔くうぐん〕air force 陸軍〔りくぐん〕army 米軍〔べいぐん〕U.S. military
24	連	IV-4	270	つ(れる)	れん	compa-nion	連れて行く〔つれていく〕to take (someone) 連れて来る〔つれてくる〕to bring (someone) 連れて帰る〔つれてかえる〕to take (someone) home 連絡〔れんらく〕する to contact 連続〔れんぞく〕ドラマ serial drama 関連〔かんれん〕relation; connection
25	葉	IV-6	283	は/ ば	よう	leaf	葉っぱ〔はっぱ〕leaf 千葉〔ちば〕Chiba 言葉〔ことば〕word; language 紅葉〔こうよう〕autumn leaves 絵葉書〔えはがき〕picture postcard
26	代	IV-6	285	か(わる)	だい	to take place	時代〔じだい〕period, era 本代〔ほんだい〕money for books 代表〔だいひょう〕representative
27	苦	IV-6	292	くる(しい)/ にが(い)	く	painful	苦しい〔くるしい〕painful, have difficulty 苦い〔にがい〕bitter 苦手〔にがて〕to be weak (at) 苦労〔くろう〕する to suffer, struggle
28	仏	IV-7	297	ほとけ	ぶつ	Buddha	仏様〔ほとけさま〕Buddha 仏教〔ぶっきょう〕Buddhism 大仏〔だいぶつ〕a big image of Buddha 仏像〔ぶつぞう〕Buddhist statue

漢字

AIJ#	漢字	AIJ-L	AIJ#	訓読み	音読み	意味	熟語
29	幸	IV-7	300	しあわ (せ)/ さち	こう	happiness	幸せ〔しあわせ〕happy 幸福〔こうふく〕happiness; good fortune 不幸〔ふこう〕unhappiness 幸子〔さちこ〕さん Sachiko-san 幸いに〔さいわいに〕luckily; fortunately
30	福	IV-7	301	X	ふく	fortune	福は内、鬼は外〔ふくはうち、おにはそと〕 In with good fortune, out with the demon. 福田〔ふくだ〕さん Fukuda-san 福島〔ふくしま〕Fukushima 福岡〔ふくおか〕Fukuoka
31	建	IV-7	302	た (てる)	ちく	to build	家を建てる〔いえをたてる〕to build a house 建物〔たてもの〕building 建築〔けんちく〕architecture 建築家〔けんちくか〕architect
32	助	IV-7	304	たす (ける)	じょ	to assist	助けて！〔たすけて〕Help! 助け合う〔たすけあう〕to help each other 助手〔じょしゅ〕assistant 助詞〔じょし〕particle
33	喜	IV-7	306	よろ (こぶ)	き	to be pleased	喜ぶ〔よろこぶ〕to be pleased 喜劇〔きげき〕comedy
34	嬉	IV-7	307	うれ (しい)	き	happy (emotion)	嬉しい〔うれしい〕happy, glad
35	悲	IV-7	308	かな (しい)	ひ	sad	悲しい〔かなしい〕sad 悲劇〔ひげき〕tragedy
36	愛	IV-7	309	X	あい	love, affection	愛〔あい〕している to love 恋愛〔れんあい〕love 愛情〔あいじょう〕affection
37	恋	IV-7	310	こい	れん	love (lomantic)	恋〔こい〕をする to fall in love with 恋愛結婚〔れんあいけっこん〕love marriage 失恋〔しつれん〕broken heart 恋人〔こいびと〕lover, sweetheart
38	宗	IV-8	311	X	しゅう	religion	宗教〔しゅうきょう〕religion 禅宗〔ぜんしゅう〕Zen sect 天台宗〔てんだいしゅう〕Tendai sect

漢字

AIJ#	漢字	AIJ-L	AIJ#	訓読み	音読み	意味	熟語
39	原	IV-8	312	はら	げん	field	野原〔のはら〕field 原田〔はらだ〕さん Harada-san 原宿〔はらじゅく〕Harajuku 秋葉原〔あきはばら〕Akihabara 原因〔げんいん〕reason 原爆〔げんばく〕atomic bomb
40	窓	IV-8	313	まど	そう	window	みどりの窓口〔まどぐち〕JR ticket window 窓側〔まどがわ〕window-side 窓口〔まどぐち〕ticket window 車窓〔しゃそう〕car window
41	雲	IV-8	317	くも	うん	cloud	白い雲〔しろいくも〕white cloud 夏雲〔なつくも〕summer cloud 雨雲〔あまぐも〕rain cloud
42	曇	IV-8	318	くも(る)	どん	to get cloudy	曇りのち晴れ〔くもりのちはれ〕cloudy later clear 曇〔くも〕っている is cloudy 曇り空〔くもりぞら〕cloudy sky
43	交	IV-8	319	まじ(わる)	こう	to cross, intersect	交通〔こうつう〕transportation, traffic 交信〔こうしん〕communication 国際交流〔こくさいこうりゅう〕international exchange 交換〔こうかん〕する to exchange
44	泊	IV-8	321	と(まる)	はく	to sleep over	泊まる〔とまる〕to stay overnight 三泊四日〔さんぱくよっか〕three nights, four days 宿泊〔しゅくはく〕lodging
45	感	IV-8	323	かん	かん	to feel	感じる〔かんじる〕to feel 感謝〔かんしゃ〕する to appreciate 感動〔かんどう〕する to be moved 感心〔かんしん〕する to admire 感想文〔かんそうぶん〕reflection
46	箱	IV-9	328	はこ	X	box	ゴミ箱〔ごみばこ〕trash can 空き箱〔あきばこ〕empty box 箱根〔はこね〕Hakone 弁当箱〔べんとうばこ〕lunch box
47	球	IV-9	332	たま	きゅう	ball	テニスの球〔たま〕tennis ball 野球〔やきゅう〕baseball 球場〔きゅうじょう〕baseball field 地球〔ちきゅう〕earth

AIJ#	漢字	AIJ-L	AIJ#	訓読み	音読み	意味	熟語
48	寄	IV-9	336	よ (る)	き	to stop by	寄る〔よる〕to stop by お年寄り〔おとしより〕elderly person(s) 寄付〔きふ〕する to donate
49	暖	V-2	362	あたた (かい)	だん	warm	暖かい春〔あたたかいはる〕warm spring 地球温暖化〔ちきゅうおんだんか〕global warming 暖房〔だんぼう〕heater
50	服	V-3	376	X	ふく	clothes	制服〔せいふく〕school uniform 私服〔しふく〕plain clothes 洋服〔ようふく〕Western clothes 和服〔わふく〕Japanese clothes [*kimono*]
51	季	V-4	404	X	き	season	季節〔きせつ〕season 四季〔しき〕four seasons 季語〔きご〕seasonal word in *haiku*

漢字

一課	人と生活と趣味 People, Daily Life & Hobbies

 At the end of this lesson, you are expected to be able to handle the following tasks.

【AP-1課 タスク1：私と家族と友達】

A Japanese magazine reporter interviews you for an article. You are a well known personality. The reporter wants to find out some personal information about you.
1. Personal information: age, birthdate, childhood, personal characteristics, hobbies, etc.
2. Family information: family members, relationships, their influence on you, things you appreciate about them.
3. Information about your best friend(s): how you became friends, things you appreciate about your friend(s).

【AP-1課 タスク2：日常生活】

Discuss the following topics with your partner.
1. Most valued time of your day.
2. Things you have learned from the simulation of being a handicapped person.

【AP-1課 タスク3：リクリエーションと趣味とスポーツ】

Discuss your interest. What are you passionate about now? When and how did you start it? Who recommended you to start it? Did you accomplish anything and/or receive any award for it? What have you gained? What challenges have you experienced in relation to this interest? What is your goals do you still want to accomplish?

調べよう！

A. 本音と建前

B. 日本の武道

柔道　剣道　弓道　合気道

「道」とは何か。

C. ウォッシュレット

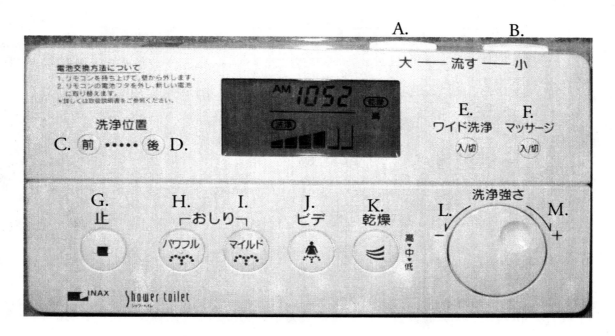

ウォッシュレットの使い方：

Find the most appropriate buttons. Write the matching letters.

1. "Front Cleansing" button　　　　　　（　　　）
2. "Rear Cleansing" button　　　　　　（　　　）
3. "Dryer" button　　　　　　　　　　（　　　）
4. "Rear Cleansing : Gentle" button　　（　　　）
5. "Rear Cleansing : High" button　　　（　　　）
6. "Stop" button　　　　　　　　　　　（　　　）
7. Water pressure adjustment: high　　（　　　）
8. Water pressure adjustment: low　　（　　　）
9. "Wide cleaning" button　　　　　　（　　　）
10. "Massage" button　　　　　　　　（　　　）
11. "Big flush" button　　　　　　　　（　　　）
12. "Little flush" button　　　　　　　（　　　）

13. A man defecated. At minimum, which buttons should he push in which order?
　　（　　　）→（　　　）→（　　　）→（　　　）→（　　　）

14. A woman urinated. At minimum, which buttons should she push in which order?
　　（　　　）→（　　　）→（　　　）→（　　　）→（　　　）

一課

☆ Special reading   [*Kanji* in text font]

1. 初 first   はじ(め)   初めまして。Nice to meet you.

初めて the first time

はつ   初詣〔はつもうで〕the first visit of

the year to the shrine

ショ   最初〔さいしょ〕the first time

初日〔しょにち〕first or opening day

2. 単 single   タン   単語〔たんご〕vocabulary

簡単〔かんたん〕simple

単位〔たんい〕credit(s)

3. 試 to try   シ   試合〔しあい〕sports game

試食〔ししょく〕taste and try

samples

試着室〔しちゃくしつ〕

fitting room

試験〔しけん〕exam

4. 験 testing   ケン   試験〔しけん〕exam

体験〔たいけん〕personal

experience

経験〔けいけん〕experience

実験〔じっけん〕experiment

5. 昨　last　　　サク　　昨年〔さくねん〕last year

昨夜〔さくや〕last night

☆　　昨日〔きのう/さくじつ〕yesterday

6. 皆　everyone　　みな　　皆さん everyone

みんな　皆 everyone

7. 力　power　　　ちから　力持ち〔ちからもち〕a strong man

リョク　努力〔どりょく〕する to make efforts

協力〔きょうりょく〕する to cooperate

能力〔のうりょく〕ability

無力〔むりょく〕powerless, incompetent

集中力〔しゅうちゅうりょく〕ability to concentrate

8. 歳　age,　　　　とし　　歳月〔としつき／さいげつ〕years

- years old　サイ　　何歳〔なんさい〕how old?

百歳〔ひゃくさい〕hundred years old

セイ　　御歳暮〔おせいぼ〕year-end gift

9. 局　station　　キョク　郵便局〔ゆうびんきょく〕

post office

放送局〔ほうそうきょく〕

broadcast station

薬局〔やっきょく〕drug store

65

一課

10. 記 to mark　　キ　　　　日記〔にっき〕diary

伝記〔でんき〕biography

記号〔きごう〕symbol

記事〔きじ〕article; news story

新記録〔しんきろく〕new record

11. 転 to roll　　テン　　　運転〔うんてん〕する to drive

運転手〔うんてんしゅ〕driver

自転車〔じてんしゃ〕bicycle

回転寿司〔かいてんずし〕

conveyor belt *sushi* shop

転校〔てんこう〕school transfer

12. 枚 - sheet(s)　マイ　　　一枚の紙〔いちまいのかみ〕

one sheet of paper

13. 遅 late　　おそ(い)　　　遅くなりました。

I am (sorry to be) late.

おく(れる)　　遅れた。 I am late.

チ　　　　遅刻〔ちこく〕tardy

14. 難 difficult　むずか(しい)　難しい問題〔もんだい〕

difficult problem

-がた(い)　　有難い〔ありがたい〕thankful

ナン　　　難問〔なんもん〕

difficult question

15. 泳 to swim　　　およ(ぐ)　　海〔うみ〕で泳ぐ

　　　　　　　　　　　　　　　　swim in the ocean

　　　　　　　　　エイ　　　水泳〔すいえい〕swimming

16. 落 to fall,　　　お(ちる)　　葉〔は〕が落ちている。

　　　　　　　　　　　　　　　　The leaves are falling.

　　　　　　　　　　　　　　　落ち込んでいる

　　　　　　　　　　　　　　　to be depressed

　　　　to drop　　お(とす)　　お金〔かね〕を落とした。

　　　　　　　　　　　　　　　　I dropped the money.

　　　　　　　　　ラク　　　落語〔らくご〕a comic story

　　　　　　　　　　　　　　presented by a man (*rakugo*)

　　　　　　　　　　　　　　落書き〔らくがき〕graffiti

17. 治 to cure,　　　なお(す)　　病気〔びょうき〕を治す

　　　　　　　　　　　　　　　　to cure illness

　　　to be cured　なお(る)　　病気〔びょうき〕が治る

　　　　　　　　　　　　　　　　illness is curred

　　　　　　　　　ジ　　　　政治〔せいじ〕politics

　　　　　　　　　　　　　　明治〔めいじ〕Meiji

　　　　　　　　　チ　　　　治療〔ちりょう〕treatment

【読みかえの漢字】　　　* Previously introduced.

1. 集 to collect,　　あつ(める)*　　お金を集める to collect money

　　　to gather　　あつ(まる)*　　集まる時間〔じかん〕time to gather

　　　　　　　　　シュウ　　　集中〔しゅうちゅう〕する to concentrate

一課

2. 音　sound　　おと＊　　　雨〔あめ〕の音 sound of rain

オン＊　　　音楽〔おんがく〕music

ネ　　　　本音〔ほんね〕real feeling

音色〔ねいろ〕tone color

3. 待　to wait　ま(つ)＊　　待って下さい。 Please wait.

まち＊　　　待合室〔まちあいしつ〕waiting room

タイ　　　招待状 invitation (card)

4. 当　to hit　トウ＊　　　本当〔ほんとう〕true

あ(たる)　　クイズが当たった。I won the game show.

あ(てる)　　答〔こたえ〕を当てる to guess the answer correctly

3. 止　〜stop(s),　と(まる)＊　止まれ！Stop!

to stop 〜　と(める)＊　車を止めて！Stop the car!

シ　　　　中止〔ちゅうし〕する to cancel

【読めればいい漢字】

1. 趣味	しゅみ	N	hobby
2. 一緒	いっしょ	Adv.	together
3. 成績	せいせき	N	grade(s)
4. 風邪	かぜ	N	a cold
5. 将来	しょうらい	N	future
6. 自己紹介	じこしょうかい	N	self-introduction
7. 誰	だれ	N	who
8. 感謝	かんしゃ	N	gratitude; appreciation
9. 目標	もくひょう	N	goal
10. 賞	しょう	N	prize
11. 夢	ゆめ	N	dream

《Activity A》

1. しんゆう＜親友＞　N　best friend

何でも話せる親友がほしい。　I want a best friend to whom I can talk about anything.

2. ゆうじょう＜友情＞　N　friendship

友情の大切さを感じる。　I feel the importance of friendship.

3. なかま＜仲間＞　N　group of friends

週末仲間といる時が、最高に楽しい。　When I am with a group of my friends, it is the most

enjoyable.

4. ふどうさん＜不動産＞　N　real estate

父は不動産関係の仕事をしている。　My father is working at a real estate related job.

5. ぶどう＜武道＞　N　martial arts

柔道や剣道は伝統的な日本の武道だ。Judo and kendo, etc. are traditional Japanese martial

arts.

6. れいぎただしい＜礼儀正しい＞　A　polite; well mannered; courteous

武道をしている人はとても礼儀正しい。The people who are doing martial arts are very polite.

7. (〜と/に)にて＜似て＞いる／います　V2　to resemble (〜); look like (〜)

私は母によく似ていると言われる。　I have been told that I look like my mother a lot.

8. ぐちをいう＜愚痴を言う＞／言います　V1　to grumble

友達は私が愚痴を言っても、いつも聞いてくれる。　Even though I grumble, my friend

always listens to me.

9. めいわく＜迷惑＞　Na　trouble; bother; imposition

(〜に)めいわく＜迷惑＞を かける／かけます　V2　to trouble 〜; to impose

(on) 〜

(〜の)めいわく＜迷惑＞に なる／なります　V1　to be an imposition (on) 〜

人に迷惑をかけてはいけない。We should not trouble other people.

10. たいがく＜退学＞する／します　V3　to drop out of school

　　たいがく＜退学＞させられる　V3　to be made to drop out of school [passive causative form] → 文法E

　　友達が麻薬を持っていて退学させられた。　My friend was made to drop out of school because he possessed drugs.

11. にゅういん＜入院＞(を)する／します　V3　to be hospitalized

　　一郎君はけがをして今入院している。　Ichiro got injured and is in the hospital now.

《Activity B》

12. しっかりしている／しっかりしています　V2　to be reliable

　　姉はしっかりしていて、妹の世話をよくしてくれる。　An older sister is reliable and she takes care of her younger sister well.

13. (～に)しゅうちゅう＜集中＞(を)する／します　V3　to concentrate (on ～); to focus (on ～)

　　「ボールに集中しろ。」　"Concentrate on the ball."

　　しゅうちゅうりょく＜集中力＞　N　ability to concentrate

　　このゴルファーは集中力がすごい。　This golfer has a tremendous ability to concentrate.

14. きょうそう＜競争＞(を)する／します　V3　to compete

　　私は人と競争することが嫌いだ。　I don't like to compete with others.

　　きょうそうがはげしい＜競争が激しい＞　A　competitive (event)

　　有名大学に入るのは競争がとても激しい。　It's very competitive to get into a famous university.

《Activity C》No new vocabulary

《Activity D》

15. きぼう＜希望＞　N　hope; wish

　　両親にどんな希望がある？　Do you have any hopes for your parents?

16. はげます＜励ます＞／励まします　V1　to encourage

　　両親はいつもよくがんばるように私を励ましてくれる。　My parents always encourage me to do my best.

《Activity E》

17. ほんね＜本音＞　N　true feelings

親友には本音で話せる。　I can tell my true feelings to my good friend.

18. きっかけ　N　initial opportunity; start; trigger

私達が友達になったきっかけは学校のダンスだった。　Our friendship first began at a school dance.

19. なぐさめる＜慰める＞／慰めます　V2　to comfort

悲しかった時、友達が慰めてくれた。　When I was sad, my friend comforted me.

20. あまやかされる＜甘やかされる＞／甘やかされます　V1　to be spoiled; to be pampered [passive form of 甘やかす／甘やかします "to spoil"] → 文法B

私は祖母に甘やかされて育った。　I was spoiled by my grandmother as I grew up.

21. おちこむ＜落ち込む＞／落ち込みます　V1　to feel "down"; to become depressed

成績が悪くて、落ち込んでしまった。　My grades were bad and I became depressed.

22. すごす＜過ごす＞／過ごします　V1　to spend (time)

「仲間と過ごす時間が私には一番幸せな時だ。」 "The time I spend with a group of my friends is the happiest time for me."

23. さそわれた＜誘われた＞　V1　was invited [passive form of さそう／さそいます "to invite"] →文法C

「彼に映画に誘われたの。」 "I was invited to a movie by him."

《Activity F》

24. (〜に)じょうねつ＜情熱＞をかける／かけます V2 to be passionate (about 〜)

今テニスに情熱をかけている。　I am passionate about tennis now.

《Activity G》　No new vocabulary

《Activity H》

25. しょうがいしゃ＜障害者＞　N　(physically) handicapped person

障害者には親切にしてあげよう。　Let's be kind to handicapped people.

一課

26. くるまいす＜車椅子＞　N　wheelchair

祖父は足が弱いので、車いすを使っている。　My grandfather's legs are weak, so he uses a wheelchair.

27. ふじゆう＜不自由＞　Na　disabled

祖母は耳が不自由だ。　My grandmother cannot hear.

28. しゅわ＜手話＞　N　sign language

祖母は耳が聞こえないので、私は手話で話す。　Since my grandmother cannot hear, I talk to her in sign language.

《Activity I》　No new vocabulary

《Activity J》

29. もくひょう＜目標＞　N　goal

今年の目標は希望の大学に入学することだ。　My goal this year is to get into the college of my choice.

30. すすめる＜勧める＞／勧めます　V2　to recommend

先生は私達に日記を書くことを勧めた。　Our teacher recommended that we write a diary.

《1課 - 1・聞く》

31. がん＜癌＞　N　cancer

おばあさんは癌で亡くなった。　My grandmother passed away from cancer.

32. みまい(にいく)＜見舞い(に行く)＞／行きます

　　N+P+V1　(to visit someone) to express concern

病院に友人を見舞いに行った。　I visited my friend at the hospital.

33. たちなおる＜立ち直る＞／立ち直ります　V1　to recover; to regain one's footing

家族のおかげで、私は立ち直ることが出来た。Thanks to my family, I could recover.

《1課 - 2・読む》

34. (illness が)なおる＜治る＞／治ります　V1　(illness) is cured [intransitive]

　☞ (illness を)なおす＜治す＞／治します　V1　to cure (an illness) [transitive]

やっと風邪が治った。　My cold has finally gotten better.

35. にちじょうせいかつ＜日常生活＞　N　daily life

忙しい日常生活の中にほっとする時間がほしい。　I want time to relax in my busy daily life.

36. せいじょう＜正常＞　Na　normal

祖父は目が不自由でも、頭は正常です。　My grandfather is blind, but his mind is sharp.

37. むね＜胸＞　N　breast; chest

「胸がドキドキしている。」　"My heart is beating fast (I am excited)."

38. しんぞう＜心臓＞　N　heart; cardio-

「心臓がドキドキしている。」　"My heart is beating fast."

《1課 - 3a・書く》　No new vocabulary

《1課 - 3b・書く》

39. れい＜例＞　N　example [☞ 例えば "for example"]

武道の一つの例として、柔道について話します。　As an example of martial arts, I will talk about judo.

40. けつろんとして＜結論として＞　Exp　in conclusion

結論として、柔道はすばらしいスポーツだと思います。　in conclusion, I think judo is a wonderful sport.

《1課 - 3c・書く》

41. のべ＜述べる＞／述べます　V2　to describe

武道の例として、柔道について述べたいと思います。I want to describe judo as an example of martial arts, .

42. あいて＜相手＞　N　opponent; partner

昨日の試合の相手は強かった。　My oponent in yesterday's game was strong.

ジョンさんが今日の私の会話の相手だった。　John was my partner for today's conversation.

《1課 - 4a・話す》

43. アンケート　N　survey

「すみません、アンケートに答えて下さい。」　"Excuse me, please answer the survey."

44. はっぴょう＜発表＞しなきゃ(いけない)　Dv　have to present; have to announce [informal conversational form of 発表しなければいけない]

「明日クラスでプロジェクトを発表しなきゃいけないんだ。」"Tomorrow I have to present my project in class."

《1課‐4b・話す》

45. しょうたいけん＜招待券＞　N　complimentary ticket
　　しょうたいじょう＜招待状＞　N　invitation (card)
　　しょうたい＜招待＞(を)する／します　V3　to invite

「映画の招待券を二枚もらったんだけど、一緒に行かない？」"I received two complimentary movie tickets. Won't you go together with me?"

46. クイズにあたる＜クイズに当たる＞／当たります　V1　to win a contest

「クイズに当たって、日本旅行の航空券を二枚もらったんだ。」"I won a contest and received two airline tickets for a trip to Japan."

47. しきゅう＜至急＞　Adv　immediately

「至急、電話して。」"Please call me immediately."

48. ほうそうきょく＜放送局＞　N　broadcast station
　　ラジオきょく＜ラジオ局＞　N　radio station

この放送局では日本語番組をやっている。This Japanese broadcast station is showing Japanese programs.

49. いつものところ＜いつもの所＞　N　the usual place

「いつもの所で一時に会おう。」"Let's meet at one o'clock at the place we always meet at."

《1課‐4c・話す》

50. ようこそ。　Exp　Welcome.

「日本にようこそ。」"Welcome to Japan."

51. ふくそう＜服装＞　N　attire

服装は楽な物を着て下さい。Please wear something comfortable (for your attire).

52. しょうひん＜賞品＞　N　prize [☞ しょうきん＜賞金＞ prize money]

スピーチコンテストに優勝して、賞品としてデジカメをもらった。I won the speech contest and received a digital camera as a prize.

53. ひやけ(を)する＜日焼け(を)する＞／します　V3　to get sun burnt

ひやけどめクリーム＜日焼け止めクリーム＞　N　sunscreen (lotion)

海や山へ行く時には、いつも日焼け止めクリームを持って行く。When I go to the beach and the mountains, I always take sunscreen with me.

54. えんきされる＜延期される＞／延期されます　V3　will be postponed

[passive form of 延期する／します "to postpone"]

コンサートは来月に延期された。　The concert was postponed to the next month.

55. (～を)ちゅうし＜中止＞する／します　V3　to cancel ～ [transitive]

(～が)ちゅうし＜中止＞になる／なります　V1　～ is canceled [intransitive]

今日のサッカーの試合は雨のため中止になった。　Today's soccer game was canceled because of rain.

56. しゅっせき＜出席＞(を)する／します　V3　to attend

けっせき＜欠席＞(を)する／します　V3　to be absent

「出席か欠席かを知らせて下さい。」"RSVP, please."

《1課 - 4 d・話す》

57. しつれん＜失恋＞(を)する／します　V3　to have a broken heart

姉は彼に失恋して、ずっと泣いている。My older sister has a broken heart and has been crying all the time.

58. (～を)やぶる＜破る＞／破ります　V1　to tear (～) [transitive]

(～が)やぶれる＜破れる＞／破れます　V2　(～) tears [intransitive]

思い出の写真を全部破ってしまった。I tore up all the photos of our memories.

59. てをたたく＜手を叩く＞／叩きます　V1　to clap one's hands

祖母は手を叩いて、喜んでくれた。My grandmother clapped her hands with joy (for me).

60. いじょうです。＜以上です。＞　Exp.　This is all. [Used at the end of a
　　　presentation.]

【分かればいい単語】

1. ゆうじん＜友人＞　　　　　　　　　　N　　friend [formal equiv. of 友達]
2. そのた＜その他＞　　　　　　　　　　N　　etc. [written]; otherwise
3. て＜手＞をつなぐ／つなぎます　　　　V1　to hold hands
4. -リットル　　　　　　　　　　　　　Na　liter (ℓ) [1 gallon = 3.6 liters]
5. こどく＜孤独＞　　　　　　　　　　　Na　lonely; isolated
6. ありがたい＜有難い＞　　　　　　　　A　　thankful
7. リハビリ　　　　　　　　　　　　　　N　　rehabilitation
8. ぐうぜん＜偶然＞　　　　　　　　　　Adv　(by) chance; unexpectedly
9. ごかつやくください。＜御活躍下さい。＞／活躍します

　　　　　　　　　　　　　　　　Exp　　I wish you success in your work.
10. できごとがおこる＜出来事が起こる＞　N+P+V1　something happens
11. あたりまえ＜当たり前＞　　　　　　　N　　ordinary; common; expected
12. どうじょう＜道場＞　　　　　　　　　N　　training room for martial arts
13. のぞく＜覗く＞／覗きます　　　　　　V1　to peek in
14. めがさめる＜目が覚める＞／覚めます　V2　to awaken
15. めざましどけい＜目覚まし時計＞　　　N　　alarm clock
16. ひげをそる＜髭を剃る＞／剃ります　　V1　to shave one's
　　　　　　　　　　　　　　　　　　　　　 beard/moustache

17. びよういん＜美容院＞　　　　　　　　N　　beauty shop
　　　　　　　　　　　　　　　　　　　　　 [≠病院〔びょういん〕hospital]

18. とこや＜床屋＞　　　　　　　　　　　N　　barber shop

* Previously learned.

A. "do ～ (as a favor)"　　　　　　　　　　　　　→ AIJ 2 L.15 *

　　Giver は　Receiver (equal) に　　　Verb (TE form)　あげます。
　　Giver は　Receiver (inferior) に　　Verb (TE form)　やります。
　　Giver は　Receiver (me) に/を　　　Verb (TE form)　くれます。
　　Receiver は　Giver に　　　　　　　Verb (TE form)　もらいます。

1. 私は友達にシャツを買ってあげました。　　I bought a shirt for my friend (as a favor).

2. 私は妹に本を読んでやりました。　　　　　I read a book to my younger sister (as a favor).

3. 父は私を迎えに来てくれました。　　　　　My father came to pick me up (as a favor).

4. 私は姉に宿題を手伝ってもらいました。　　I had my older sister help me with my homework (as a favor).

Complete the following sentences using TE + giving/receiving verb.

1. 両親は私の授業料を　　_____。

2. 両親は私がほしい物を　_____。

3. 友達は私の問題を　　　_____。

4. 祖母が夕食を　　　　　_____。

5. 私は両親に何も　　　　_____。

6. 私は友達の宿題を　　　_____。

7. 私は弟におもちゃを　　_____。

8. 私は兄に車を　　　　　_____。

B.　Verb 1 (TE form) 、～　　　　　　　"do V1, and do ～"　　　　→ AIJ 1 L.14 *

　　Verb 1 (stem form) ＋ ながら、～　　"While doing V1, does ～."　→ AIJ 3 L.6 *
　　　　Used when one subject performs two actions concurrently.

　　Verb 1 (informal form) ＋ 間に、～　"While doing V1, does ～."　→ AIJ 3 L.6 *
　　　　Used when one or two subject(s) exist and/or perform(s) two actions.

　　Verb 1 (dictionary form) ＋ 前に、～ "Before doing V1, does ～"　→ AIJ 3 L.6 *

　　Verb 1 (TA form) ＋ 後で、～　　　"After doing V1, does ～"　　→ AIJ 3 L.6 *

　　Verb (TE form) ＋ から、～　　　　"After doing V, does ～"　　　→ AIJ 3 L.4 *

1. うちへ帰って、服を着替えた。　　　　　　　I returned home and changed my clothes.
2. 運転をしながら、ラジオを聞く。　　　　　　I listen to a radio while driving.
3. 日本にいる間に、いろいろな所へ旅行したい。
　　　　I want to travel to various places while I am in Japan.
4. 母が朝食を作っている間に、父は本を読んでいた。
　　　　While my mother was cooking breakfast, my father was reading a newspaper.
5. ゆうべ寝る前に、お風呂に入った。
　　　　I took a bath before I went to bed last night.
6. 明日友達と映画を見た後で、友達のうちへ行くつもりだ。
　　　　After seeing a movie with my friend tomorrow, I plan to go to my friend's house.
7. 昼食を食べてから、映画を見に行こう。　　　Let's go to watch a movie after eating lunch.

These are some activities you and/or your family members do in daily life. Write sentences using all of the choices in the ( ).

1. (- て、シャワーをあびる、朝食を食べる)

　　_____。

2. (- ながら、おどる、歌う)

　　_____。

3. (- 後で、宿題をする、アイスクリームを食べる)

　　_____。

4. (- 前に、寝る、歯をみがく)

　　_____。

5. (- 間に、父、母、掃除する、車を洗う)

　　_____。

C. Verb passive form　　　　　　　　　　　　→ AIJ 4 L.2＊

Group 1 verbs:　のむ　→のまれる　　　　is drunk
Group 2 verbs:　たべる→たべられる　　　is eaten
Irregular verbs:　くる　→こられる　　　　come
　　　　　　　　　する　→される　　　　　is done

1. 教科書がぬすまれた。　　　　　　　　　　My textbook was stolen.
2. お弁当は犬に食べられた。　　　　　　　　My box lunch was eaten by my dog.
3. 兄はどろぼうに自動車をぬすまれた。　　　My older brother had his car stolen by a thief.
4. 母は父に死なれて、生活は大変だったそうだ。
　　I understand that after my father died, my mother was left alone and life was difficult (for her).

Fill in the ( ) with correct particles and the blanks with correct passive forms.

1. 彼は私をさそった。＝ 私 （　） 彼に （　） ＿＿＿＿＿＿＿＿＿＿＿＿＿＿＿＿＿＿＿＿＿。

2. 彼は私をふった。＝ 私 （　） 彼に （　） ＿＿＿＿＿＿＿＿＿＿＿＿＿＿＿＿＿＿＿＿。

3. 祖母は私を育てた。＝ 私 （　） 祖母に （　） ＿＿＿＿＿＿＿＿＿＿＿＿＿＿＿＿＿＿＿。

4. 祖母は私を甘やかした。＝ 私 （　） 祖母に （　） ＿＿＿＿＿＿＿＿＿＿＿＿＿＿＿＿＿＿。

5. 母は私に勉強しなさいと言った。

　　＝ 私 （　） 母に （　） 勉強しなさいと＿＿＿＿＿＿＿＿＿＿＿＿＿＿＿＿＿＿。

6. 両親はいつも私と姉を比べた。

　　＝ 私 （　） 姉 （　） いつも両親 （　） ＿＿＿＿＿＿＿＿＿＿＿＿＿＿＿＿＿。

7. 友達は私をなぐさめた。＝ 私 （　） 友達に （　） ＿＿＿＿＿＿＿＿＿＿＿＿＿＿＿＿＿。

D. Verb causative form　　　　　　　　　　　　　　　→ AIJ 4 L.4＊

Group 1 verbs:	いう →いわせる	make/let someone say
Group 2 verbs:	たべる→たべさせる	make/let someone eat
Irregular verbs:	くる →こさせる	make/let someone come
	する →させる	make/let someone do

1. 先生は生徒に漢字を書かせる。　　　The teacher makes his/her students write *kanji*.

2. 両親は私を日本旅行に行かせてくれた。　My parents let me go on a trip to Japan.

3. 母は私にピアノを練習させる。　　　My mother makes me practice the piano.

4. 「お待たせしました。」　　　　　　"I'm sorry for making you wait."

Complete the sentences using the causative form of the verb in the (　).

1. 先生は私達に日本語を＿＿＿＿＿＿＿＿＿＿＿＿＿＿＿。　（話す）

2. 両親は毎晩私に皿を＿＿＿＿＿＿＿＿＿＿＿＿＿＿。　（洗う）

3. 体育の先生は生徒をよく＿＿＿＿＿＿＿＿＿＿＿＿＿＿。　（泳ぐ）

4. コーチは週末も私達を＿＿＿＿＿＿＿＿＿＿＿＿＿＿。　（練習する）

5. 疲れているので、もっと＿＿＿＿＿＿＿＿＿＿＿＿下さい。　（寝る）

6. 両親は授業料が高くても、大学に＿＿＿＿＿＿＿＿＿＿＿くれる。　（行く）

E. Verb causative passive form [Recognition only]

Group 1 verbs:	いう	→いわせられる	be forced to say
Group 2 verbs:	たべる	→たべさせられる	be forced to eat
Irregular verbs:	くる	→こさせられる	be forced to come
	する	→させられる	be forced to do

1. 友達は学校を退学させられた。　　　　My friend was forced to drop out of school.

2. これは考えさせられる問題です。　　　This is a problem that I am made to think about.

Translate to English.

1. 私達は毎日一時間もコーチに走らされた。　_____

2. 授業の後、先生に教室を掃除させられた。　_____

3. 友達に長い間駅の前で待たされた。　_____

F. ～んです，　～のです　　　　　　　　　　　→ AIJ 3 L.3＊

The ～んです and ～のです endings are frequently used in speaking. When it appears in a statement form, it suggests that the speaker feels obligated to explain him/herself or his/her actions. When it appears in a question form, it serves the purpose of inviting an explanation from the listener. ～のです is used in formal situations and ～んです is used in less formal situations. The copula だ changes to な before ～んです and ～のです.

1. 友達が麻薬を使っているんですよ。　　My friend is using drugs.

2. この本は本当に高かったんですよ。　　This book was really expensive, you know.

3. 明日が試験なんですよ。　　　　　　　Tomorrow is the exam day.

4. あの子が好きなんだ。　　　　　　　　I like that person.

5. 僕はあの子が好きだったんだ。　　　　I liked that girl.

6. 本当にいいんですか。　　　　　　　　Is it really o.k.?

7. なぜ分からないんですか。　　　　　　Why don't you understand it?

Rewrite the underlined endings using ～んです.

1. 母は教師でした。　　　　　　　→_____。

2. 兄はスキーが上手です。　　　　→_____。

3. 祖父が亡くなりました。　　　　→_____。

4. 祖母が私を世話をしてくれました。　→_____。

5. 友達は麻薬も使い出しました。　　　　→＿＿＿＿＿＿＿＿＿＿＿＿＿＿＿＿＿＿＿＿＿＿。

6. 僕は友達のおかげで立ち直る事が出来ました。→＿＿＿＿＿＿＿＿＿＿＿＿＿＿＿＿＿＿。

7. 友達になったきっかけは何でしたか。　→＿＿＿＿＿＿＿＿＿＿＿＿＿＿＿＿＿＿＿＿＿。

8. 仲間がたくさんいます。　　　　　　　→＿＿＿＿＿＿＿＿＿＿＿＿＿＿＿＿＿＿＿＿＿。

9. 賞をもらいました。　　　　　　　　　→＿＿＿＿＿＿＿＿＿＿＿＿＿＿＿＿＿＿＿＿＿。

G. Verb potential form　　　　　　　　　　　→ AIJ 2 L.10＊

Group 1 verbs:　　はな<u>す</u>→はな<u>せる</u>　　　can speak

Group 2 verbs:　　たべ<u>る</u>→たべ<u>られる</u>　　can eat

Irregular verbs:　　くる　→こられる　　　can come

　　　　　　　　　する　→出来る　　　　can do

1. 父は中国語が<u>話せ</u>ますが、私は<u>話せ</u>ません。　My father can speak Chinese, but I cannot.

2. 母はさしみが<u>食べられ</u>ません。　My mother cannot eat raw fish.

3. 「この土曜日に家へ<u>来られ</u>ますか。」　"Can you come to my house this Saturday?"

　「はい、もちろん<u>行け</u>ますよ。」　"Yes, of course I can."

4. 七時に予約<u>出来ました</u>。　I was able to make a reservation for 7 o'clock.

Complete the sentences using the potential form of a verb in the (　).

1. 私は何も上手に＿＿＿＿＿＿＿＿＿＿＿＿＿＿＿＿＿。（しない）

2. 熱があって今日学校へ＿＿＿＿＿＿＿＿＿＿＿＿＿＿。（行かない）

3. 誰にもほかの人の＿＿＿＿＿＿＿＿＿＿＿＿＿ことがある。（役に立つ）

4. 祖母は足が悪くて＿＿＿＿＿＿＿＿＿＿＿＿＿＿＿。（歩かない）

5. 妹は病気でもっと生きたくても＿＿＿＿＿＿＿＿＿＿＿＿＿。（生きない）

6. 明日のパーティーにケーキを＿＿＿＿＿＿＿＿＿＿＿＿＿。（持って来ない）

H. 「起きなさい。」　　"Wake up!"　　　　　　→ AIJ 4 L.3＊

　This informal command forms are used by superiors to persons of lesser status (parent to child; boss to subordinate, etc.).

　Superior males use the command forms and the negative command form ("Don't do ～."). These forms are also used in public signs, i.e., とまれ (for "Stop.") or およぐな ("Don't swim.").

一課

The -なさい (command) and negative form, -ないで are polite commands which are used by superiors such as parents or teachers to their inferiors (= people of younger age and of lower rank). It may also be used in written instructions, i.e., instructions on a test.

	Dic. Form	Command	Neg. Command	Polite Command	Polite Neg. Command
Group 1 Verbs	話す	話せ Speak! - e	話すな Don't talk! Dic. form + な	話しなさい Speak. Stem form + なさい	話さないで Don't talk. NAI form + で
Group 2 Verbs	食べる	食べろ Eat! Stem form + ろ	食べるな Don't eat! Dic. form + な	食べなさい Eat. Stem form + なさい	食べないで Don't eat! NAI form + で
Irregular Verb	する	しろ Do it!	するな Don't do it! Dic. form + な	しなさい Do it. Stem form + なさい	しないで Don't do it. NAI form + で
Irregular Verb	来〔く〕る	来〔こ〕い Come!	来〔く〕るな Don't come! Dic. form + な	来〔き〕なさい Come. Stem form + なさい	来〔こ〕ないで Don't come. NAI form + で

1. 父はいつももっと<u>勉強しろ</u>と言う。

My father always tells me to study harder.

2. 私が運転する時、両親はいつもスピードを<u>出すな</u>と言う。

When I drive the car, my parents always tell me not to speed.

3. 私が外へ出かける時、母はいつも「<u>気をつけなさい</u>」と言う。

When I go out, my mother always tells me, "be careful."

Fill in the blanks with an appropriate verb in the command form.

1. 母は私が遅くまで寝ていると、「＿＿＿＿＿＿＿＿＿＿＿＿＿」と言う。

2. 父は私が遅く家に帰ると、「＿＿＿＿＿＿＿＿＿＿＿＿＿」と言う。

3. 母は私が遅くまで起きていると、「＿＿＿＿＿＿＿＿＿＿＿＿＿」と言う。

4. 父は私の成績が悪いと、「＿＿＿＿＿＿＿＿＿＿＿＿＿」と言う。

5. 母は私が夕食を食べないで、ケータイで友達と話していると、

「＿＿＿＿＿＿＿＿＿＿＿＿＿」と言う。

6. 父は私が宿題をしないでテレビを見ていると、「＿＿＿＿＿＿＿＿＿＿＿＿」と言う。

A. ビンゴゲーム ：クラスワーク

This is a variation of Bingo. In order to win, students must circulate throughout the classroom and find persons who fit the descriptions in as many boxes as possible. Have the student who fits the description sign your card. No name must appear twice anywhere on the card. Complete the card as quickly as possible. Your teacher will give you a time limit. The winner is the student who has the most completed Bingo lines (horizontal, vertical or diagonal.)

性格〔せいかく〕が明るいと思う？	絵を描〔か〕くのが得意〔とくい〕？	スポーツが上手？	人の役〔やく〕に立つ部活をしている？	趣味はアニメ？
＿＿＿＿	＿＿＿＿	＿＿＿＿	＿＿＿＿	＿＿＿＿
将来の夢は俳優〔はいゆう〕になること？	一人っ子？	韓国系〔かんこくけい〕？	親が不動産〔ふどうさん〕の仕事をしている？	おばあさんと一緒に住んでいる？
＿＿＿＿	＿＿＿＿	＿＿＿＿	＿＿＿＿	＿＿＿＿
礼儀〔れいぎ〕正しい？	今、親に迷惑〔めいわく〕をかけている？	おまけ（ボーナス）	お姉さんがいる？	親と顔が似〔に〕ている？
＿＿＿＿	＿＿＿＿		＿＿＿＿	＿＿＿＿
入院したことがある？	今つき合っている人がいる？	自然の中で遊ぶのが好き？	親友がいる？	退学〔たいがく〕させられた人を知っている？
＿＿＿＿	＿＿＿＿	＿＿＿＿	＿＿＿＿	＿＿＿＿
けっして愚痴〔ぐち〕を言わない？	音楽の才能〔さいのう〕がある？	賞をもらったことがある？	武道〔ぶどう〕を習っている？	仲間〔なかま〕がたくさんいる？
＿＿＿＿	＿＿＿＿	＿＿＿＿	＿＿＿＿	＿＿＿＿

83

一課

B. 自分の事：ペアーワーク

Check all the words that accurately describe you. Work with your partner.

1. どんな性格をしている？

__おとなしい　__にぎやか　__明るい　__暗い　__まじめ　__しっかりしている

__よくばり __うそつき　__なまけ者　__わがまま　__ぜいたく　__幸福 __不幸

__道徳的　__才能が多い　__自信がある __正直　__誠実　__謙虚　__努力家

__協力的　__完全主義者　__寛大　__集中力がある　__競争することが好き

その他：＿＿＿＿＿＿＿＿＿＿＿＿＿

2. 何が得意？

__野球　__水泳　__ダンス　__歌　__ピアノ　__数学　__科学　__料理　__車の運転

その他：＿＿＿＿＿＿＿＿＿＿＿＿＿

3. 趣味は何？

__走ること　__食べること　__寝ること　__テレビを見ること　__音楽を聞くこと

__おしゃべりすること __読書　__泳ぐこと　__コンピューターゲームをすること

その他：＿＿＿＿＿＿＿＿＿＿＿＿＿

4. 将来の夢は何？

__医者になること　__日本で仕事すること　__有名になること　__賞をもらうこと

その他：＿＿＿＿＿＿＿＿＿＿＿＿＿

C. 自己紹介：一人ワーク→クラスワーク

Write your self-introduction. Discuss your personality, hobbies, skills, passion, and your dreams. Do not write your grade and age. Then your teacher will collect the papers and he/she will read them. Guess who the teacher is describing.

私の名前：＿＿＿＿＿＿＿＿＿＿＿＿＿＿＿＿

自己紹介：

D. 家族のこと：ペアーワーク

Check all the responses that accurately answer the questions. Work with your partner.

1. 家族にいる人は？

＿父　＿母　＿兄　＿姉　＿弟　＿妹　＿祖父　＿祖母　＿犬　＿猫

その他（た）：＿＿＿＿＿＿＿＿＿＿＿＿＿＿

2. 親に感謝していることは何？

＿食べさせてくれる　＿授業料（じゅ）を払ってくれる　＿信じてくれる

＿はげましてくれる　＿しかってくれる　＿問題を聞いてくれる

＿ほしい物を買ってくれる　＿お小遣い（づか）をくれる　その他（た）：＿＿＿＿＿＿＿＿＿＿＿＿

3. 親に希望（きぼう）がある？

＿うるさく言わないでほしい　その他（た）：＿＿＿＿＿＿＿＿＿＿＿＿＿＿

E. 友人のこと：ペアーワーク

Check all the words that describe your friend. Work with your partner.

1. 好きな友達（or 親友）はどんな人？

＿成績がいい　＿音楽の才能（のう）がある　＿運動の才能（のう）がある　＿本音が言える

＿親に甘（あま）やかされている　＿性格（かく）が似（に）ている　＿謙虚（けんきょ）　＿にぎやか　＿おとなしい

その他（た）：＿＿＿＿＿＿＿＿＿＿＿＿＿＿

2. 親友（or 友人）になったきっかけは何だった？　＿＿＿＿＿＿＿＿＿＿＿＿＿＿＿＿＿＿＿

3. 仲間（なか）がたくさんいる？仲間（なか）でどんなことをする？

＿＿＿＿＿＿＿＿＿＿＿＿　＿＿＿＿＿＿＿＿＿＿＿＿＿＿＿＿＿＿＿

4. 友人や仲間（なか）の良さは何？

＿私を心配（ぱい）してくれる　＿落ち込（こ）んでいる時なぐさめてくれる　＿一緒にいてくれる

＿一緒に楽しい時間を過（す）ごせる　＿悩（なや）みを聞いてくれる

＿映画やパーティーに誘（さそ）ってくれる　その他（た）：＿＿＿＿＿＿＿＿＿＿＿＿＿＿

F. 「自分と家族と友人」会話：3、4人ワーク

Discuss the following 3 topics with your group. Express your opinions and feelings.

1. Something you are passionate about　（情熱（じょうねつ）をかけてやっていること）

2. What you appreciate about your family　（家族に感謝（しゃ）していること）

3. Virtue of friendship　（友情（じょう）の大切さ）

一課

G. お話：ペアワーク

Narrate Ken's day with your partner. Use a variety of patterns 〜て(から), 〜間に, Stem + ながら, TA + 後で, Dic. + 前に. Include as many details as you can.

H. 会話「障害者〔しょうがいしゃ〕になったら、どんな感じかな？」：ペアワーク

1. 目をつぶって見よう。目が不自由な人の気持ちを分かろう。
Put on a blindfold (目かくし). Your partner will give you directions in Japanese. Walk around the classroom. Find your seat and sit down. Remove the blindfold. Share your experiences and your feelings to the class in Japanese.
(目をつぶって。= "Close your eyes." どいて。= "Move.")

2. 耳をふさいでみよう。手話で話してみよう。耳が不自由な人の気持ちを分かろう。
Wear earplugs. Discuss each of the following topics with your partner. Try to read your partner's lips, use sign language and communicate by writing or any means of communication other than listening. (ふさぐ "to plug up")

Topic 1: 放課後にすることを決める。

Topic 2: 週末に行く所を決める。

Topic 3: 今、一番興味を持っていることについて話し合う。
Remove the earplugs. Share your experiences and your feelings to the class in Japanese.

3. 車いすを体験してみよう。足が不自由な人の気持ちを分かろう。
Sit in a wheelchair and try to maneuver around the classroom. Share your experience and feelings with your class in Japanese.

I. 会話「週末はどうだった？」：グループワーク→クラスワーク
Discuss your weekend with your classmates. Share at least one interesting true thing that happened to you. Listen to your classmates. Vote for the funniest story, the most surprising story, and the most unbelievable story. Tell the class your choices and the reasons.

J. 会話「趣味について」：グループワーク→クラスワーク
Discuss the following questions with your partner. Share the interesting findings with your class.

1. 今一番情熱をかけてしていることは何？

2. いつ始めた？

3. 始めたきっかけは？誰かすすめてくれた人がいる？

4. 何か賞をもらったことがある？

5. 一番の思い出は何？

6. 一番大変だったことは何？

一課

7. 一番影響を与えた人は誰？<ruby>影響<rt>えいきょう</rt></ruby> <ruby>与<rt>あた</rt></ruby>

8. これからの目標は何？

K. 「俳優〔はいゆう〕インタビュー」Pre-listening activity：グループワーク

Discuss a famous or infamous person's childhood and his or her occupation as an adult. (e.g., President Lincoln, Hitler). Discuss how his/her childhood influenced him/her in his/her later life. Discuss your opinions and feelings.

L. 会話「一リットルの涙〔なみだ〕」

Pre-reading activity：グループワーク→クラスワーク

Discuss the following topics with your group.
1. The title of a television drama is "一リットルの涙〔なみだ〕." Guess from the title what the content of the drama might be.
2. Share about a time when you became ill or injured. Share what happened and how you felt.

M. 会話「一リットルの涙〔なみだ〕」

Post-reading activity：グループワーク→クラスワーク

1. List three things you learned about Aya. State your opinions and feelings.
2. Discuss your observations with your group.
3. Share your group's observations for two minutes with your class.
4. Write your group's observations in 20 minutes using 300 - 400 words.

＜1課 - 1・聞く＞

聞く：Movie Star Interview

(Narrator)   Now you will listen once to an interview.

聞く：Movie Star Interview

(Narrator)   Now answer the questions for this selection.

1.   What kind of family did he have?
   (A)   His mother was a movie star.
   (B)   His father worked at the post office.
   (C)   He had no siblings.
   (D)   He didn't have his grandparents.

2.   What happened to his family?
   (A)   His mother died in a car accident.
   (B)   His parents separated.
   (C)   His parents divorced.
   (D)   His father remarried.

3.   Who helped him the most when he was going through his drug rehabilitation?
   (A)   his mother
   (B)   his grandmother
   (C)   his father
   (D)   his friends

4.   What was the major reason for his recovery from drug abuse?
   (A)   religion
   (B)   friendship
   (C)   drug rehabilitation program
   (D)   career

5.   Who recommended him for an acting job?
   (A)   himself
   (B)   his father
   (C)   his friend's father
   (D)   his teacher

読む：Movie Review

　最近見た「一リットルの涙」というテレビドラマについて紹介します。このドラマは本当にあったお話で、普通の明るくにぎやかな家族に突然ひとつの出来事が起こりました。長女の亜也さんは１５歳の時、難病にかかって、医者から治らないと宣言されました。体がだんだん不自由になって、２５歳で亡くなりました。彼女は日常生活でごく当たり前と思うことがだんだん出来なくなり、苦しみました。少しずつ歩けなくなって、車いすを使うようになりました。そして、話せなくなっていきました。書くことも難しくなりました。でも、頭は正常です。亜也さんが歩けなくなっていった時に、自分がまだ歩けることを嬉しく思いました。亜也さんが学校へ行けなくなった時に、私はまだ学校へ行けるんだと喜びました。亜也さんが友達に「親切にしてくれてありがとう」と言ったり、いつも彼女の気持ちや悩みを聞いてくれる男友達に「いつもそばで話を聞いてくれてありがとう」と言ったりするたびに、私自身は誰にも感謝していないなあって反省させられました。そして、亜也さんのために何でもしてあげる家族の愛から、家族の有り難さを感じました。亜也さんが「自分は人のために役に立つことをしたいと思っていたけど、何にも出来ないよ。」とお母さんにぐちを言った時、お母さんは亜也さんに日記を書くことを勧めました。亜也さんの書いた日記は多くの人を励ましました。だれでも人の役に立てるんですね。「生きる」ということがどういうことか考えさせられ、今を大事に生きようと思いました。

　このドラマは２００５年に親が子供に見せたいテレビ番組」の一位に選ばれました。亜也さんの言葉に、多くの人達が励まされたからだと思います。彼女の言葉の一つです。「胸に手をあててみる。ドキドキ、ドキドキ、音がする。心臓が動いている。嬉しい。私は生きている。」

　皆さんもぜひこのドラマを見て下さい。

一課

読む: Movie Review

(Narrator)　Now answer the questions for this selection.

1.　How old was Aya when she became ill?
　　(A)　5
　　(B)　10
　　(C)　15
　　(D)　25

2.　Even though Aya gradually could not do what she normally did, what thing could she still do?
　　(A)　walk
　　(B)　talk
　　(C)　think
　　(D)　write

3.　What made Aya write her journal?
　　(A)　She enjoyed writing.
　　(B)　Her mother advised her to.
　　(C)　Her friend encouraged her.
　　(D)　Her teacher advised her to.

4.　How did Aya's life change the writer's life?
　　(A)　The writer decided to make more friends.
　　(B)　The writer decided to write a journal.
　　(C)　The writer decided to write thank-you cards to her family and friends.
　　(D)　The writer decided to live every moment fully.

5.　Who in particular wanted to show this drama to children?
　　(A)　parents
　　(B)　teachers
　　(C)　students
　　(D)　Department of Education

書く　Text Chat : Daily Life

30点
90秒Ｘ6

You will participate in a simulated exchange of text-chat messages. Each time it is your turn to write, you will have 90 seconds. You should respond as fully and as appropriately as possible.

You will have a conversation with Mrs. Kondo, who was your host mother in Japan last summer.

1.　Respond. (90 seconds)

　　おひさしぶりですね。そちらの生活はどうですか。

2.　Respond. (90 seconds)

　　ちゃんと食事していますか。皿洗いとか食事の片付けを手伝っていますか。

3.　Respond. (90 seconds)

　　ちゃんと部屋を掃除したり、洗濯をしたりしていますか。

4.　Describe a specific occasion. (90 seconds)

　　何か運動していますか。

5.　Justify your opinion. (90 seconds)

　　今、趣味と勉強とどっちの方が大事だと思いますか。

6.　Ask a specific question. (90 seconds)

　　では、元気でね。こちらの皆について何か聞きたいことがありますか。

一課

＜１課 - 3b・書く＞

Compare and Contrast: Japanese Pop Culture & American Pop Culture

You are writing an article for the student newspaper of your sister school in Japan.　Write an article in which you compare and contrast Japanese pop culture such as *anime, manga* and J-pop songs, and American pop culture. Choose one example.　Based on your personal experience, describe at least THREE similarities and differences between Japanese pop culture and American pop culture.　Also state your preference and give reasons for it.

Your article should be 300 to 400 characters or longer.　Use the *desu/masu* or *da* (plain) style, but use one style consistently.　Also, use kanji wherever *kanji* from the AP Japanese *kanji* list is appropriate.　You have 20 minutes to write.

【自分の作文のアウトラインを書こう！】

Introduction:

_____

One example:

_____

Three similarities and/or differences:

1. _____

2. _____

3. _____

Your preference and reasons:

_____

_____

Cultural Topic Posting: Japanese Martial Arts

You are responding to a posting in a Web forum for high school students of Japanese. The posting asks about Japanese martial arts. Select ONE example from among the Japanese martial arts, such as judo, kendo, aikido, karate, sumo, etc. Describe in detail at least THREE characteristics of that Japanese martial art. Also, express your opinion or feelings about the martial art.

Your posting should be 300 to 400 characters or longer. Use the *desu/masu* or *da* (plain) style, but use one style consistently. Also, use kanji wherever *kanji* from the AP Japanese *kanji* list is appropriate. You have 20 minutes to write.

【自分の作文のアウトラインを書こう！】

Introduction:

_____

One example:

_____

Three characteristics:

1. _____

2. _____

3. _____

Your opinion and feelings:

_____

_____

＜１課 - 4a・話す＞

話す　Conversation : Daily Life

You will participate in a simulated conversation. Each time it is your turn to speak, you will have 20 seconds to record. You should respond as fully and as appropriately as possible.

You will have a conversation with Taro, your Japanese friend, about your daily life.

(Taro)

(20 seconds)

(Taro)

(20 seconds)

(Taro)

(20 seconds)

(Taro)

(20 seconds)

話す　Return Telephone Call: Concert

You will participate in a simulated telephone conversation with someone you are calling back after receiving a message. First, you will listen to the voice message. Then the telephone call will begin. Each time it is your turn to speak, you will have 20 seconds to record. You should respond as fully and as appropriately as possible.

(Narrator)   Listen to the voice message.

(Female speaker)

(Narrator)   Now the telephone call will begin. After the phone is answered, begin with a greeting and then explain why you are calling.

(Female speaker) [Telephone] [Rings twice and picks up]

(20 seconds)

(Female speaker)

(20 seconds)

(Female speaker)

(20 seconds)

(Female speaker)

(20 seconds)

10点
1分＋1分

School Announcement: Excursion

Directions: Imagine that you are making an announcement in Japanese to an assembly of Japanese students visitng your school. First, you will see some notes in English about what to include in your announcement. You will have 1 minute to prepare your announcement while you look at the notes. Then you will have 1 minute to record your announcement. Your announcement should have an opening remark, details according to the notes, and a closing remark. Deliver your announcement using complete sentences in *desu/masu* style.

Camping:
Friday April 20, 8:30 a.m. - 3:30 p.m.
Meet at the bus stop by the school gate at 8:30 a.m.
Attire: shorts, shirt, swim suit, towel
Things to bring: snacks, drinks, game prizes, camera, sunscreen
In case of rain, it will be canceled.
RSVP to Mari by Wednesday at 3:00 p.m.

10点
4分＋2分

話す　Story Narration:

Directions: Imagine that you are making an oral presentation to your Japanese class. In your presentation, you will narrate a story. First, you will see pictures depicting the story. You will have 4 minutes to prepare your narration while you look at the pictures. Then you will have 2 minutes to record your narration. Narrate your story using complete sentences in *desu/masu* style.

一課

＜１課 - 4e・話す＞

Cultural Perspective Presentation: Japanese Toilets and Bath

Directions: Imagine you are making an oral presentation to your Japanese class. First, you will read and hear the topic for your presentation. You will have 4 minutes to prepare your presentation. Then you will have 2 minutes to record your presentation. Your presentation should be as full as possible.

Present your own view or perspective on Japanese toilets and baths. Discuss at least FIVE aspects or examples of Japanese toilets and baths.

Begin with an appropriate introduction, give details about your example, explain your own view or perspective, and end with a concluding remark.

【Let's take notes!】

1. Begin with an appropriate introduction.

_____

2. Discuss five aspects/examples of the topic.

    1.) _____

    2.) _____

    3.) _____

    4.) _____

    5.) _____

3. Explain your view or perspective.

_____

4. End with a concluding remark.

_____

| 二課 | ●●● | 家と都市と自然環境《かんきょう》
Homes, Cities & The Environment | ●●● |

At the end of this lesson, you are expected to be able to handle the following tasks.

【AP-2課 タスク1：家でコミュニティーで】

Why do you think community service is important? What are your feelings and opinions about the community service you have participated in so far? What did you learn from performing community service?

【AP-2課 タスク2：都市と町と田舎《いなか》】

Introduce your hometown, which you are proud of, to Japanese visitors. Where do YOU recommend that they visit? Why? What do you recommend that they taste? What do you recommend that they buy as souvenirs?

【AP-2課 タスク3：自然と環境《かんきょう》】

Discuss the environmental problems we face in the world. What do you think we should do in order to protect nature and the environment? What are you actually doing now in this area?

調べよう！

A. 日本はなぜ地震が多い？

B. 日本はなぜ台風が多い？

C. 京都議定書って何？

☆ Special reading　　　　　　　　　　　　　[*Kanji* in text font]

1. 向　to face　　む(ける)　　靴<ruby>くつ</ruby>を外に向ける
　　　　　　　　　　　　　　　　to face shoes outward

　　　　　　　　　む(く)　　　私の方〔ほう〕を向いて。
　　　　　　　　　　　　　　　　Face me.

　　　　　　　　　むか　　　　向井〔むかい〕さん Mukai-san

　　　　　　　　　コウ　　　　どちらの方向〔ほうこう〕？ Which direction?

向

2. 置　to put　　お(く)　　　自転車置き場〔じてんしゃおきば〕
　　　　　　　　　　　　　　　　bicycle parking area

置

3. 祭　festival　　まつ(り)　　桜<ruby>さくら</ruby>祭り Cherry Blossom Festival
　　　　　　　　　　　　　　　　秋祭り〔あきまつり〕
　　　　　　　　　　　　　　　　autumn festival

祭

4. 温　warm　　あたた(かい)　温かいお茶〔ちゃ〕warm tea
　　　　　　　　オン　　　　温度〔おんど〕temperature
　　　　　　　　　　　　　　温室〔おんしつ〕green house
　　　　　　　　　　　　　　体温〔たいおん〕body temperature

温

5. 暖　warm　　あたた(かい)　　暖かい春〔はる〕 warm spring

　　　　　　　　ダン　　　　　地球温暖化〔ちきゅうおんだんか〕
　　　　　　　　　　　　　　　global warming

6. 熱　hot　　　あつ(い)　　熱いコーヒー hot coffee
　　　　　　　　　　　　　　[⇔暑い夏〔あついなつ〕
　　　　　　　　　　　　　　hot summer]

　　　　fever　　ねつ　　　　高〔たか〕い熱 high fever

7. 速　fast　　　はや(い)　　速く走〔はし〕る ro run fast
　　　　　　　　　　　　　　[⇔早〔はや〕く起〔お〕きる
　　　　　　　　　　　　　　to get up early]

　　　　　　　　ソク　　　　速度〔そくど〕 speed
　　　　　　　　　　　　　　快速〔かいそく〕 rapid train
　　　　　　　　　　　　　　風速〔ふうそく〕 wind speed

8. 氷　ice　　　こおり　　　氷水〔こおりみず〕 ice water
　　　　　　　　　　　　　　かき氷〔ごおり〕 shaved ice;
　　　　　　　　　　　　　　snow cone

　　　　　　　　ヒョウ　　　氷山〔ひょうざん〕 iceberg

9. 工　industry　　コウ　　　工業〔こうぎょう〕 industry
　　　engineering　　　　　　工場〔こうば/こうじょう〕 factory
　　　　　　　　　　　　　　工学部〔こうがくぶ〕 department
　　　　　　　　　　　　　　of engineering
　　　　　　　　　　　　　　マサチューセッツ工科大学〔こうかだいがく〕M.I.T.

10. 伝 to convey　つた(える)　手伝う〔てつだう〕to help

伝えたいメッセージ
a message I want to convey

デン　伝統的〔でんとうてき〕traditional

伝記〔でんき〕biography

伝言〔でんごん〕message

11. 昔 a long time むかし　昔話〔むかしばなし〕folk tale
ago

昔々〔むかしむかし〕a long long
time ago

12. 身 body　シン　身長〔しんちょう〕height (of a person)

長身な男性〔ちょうしんなだんせい〕
tall man

心身〔しんしん〕mind and body

13. 宿 inn　やど　宿屋〔やどや〕Japanese inn

シュク/　宿題〔しゅくだい〕homework

ジュク　新宿〔しんじゅく〕Shinjuku

原宿〔はらじゅく〕Harajuku

宿泊〔しゅくはく〕lodging

14. 答 answer　こた(え)　正〔ただ〕しい答え
correct answer

トウ　解答用紙〔かいとうようし〕
answer sheet

105

15. 期 term　　　キ　　　　学期〔がっき〕semester
　　　　　　　　　　　　　春学期〔はるがっき〕
　　　　　　　　　　　　　spring semester
　　　　　　　　　　　　　学期末試験〔がっきまつしけん〕
　　　　　　　　　　　　　semester exam

16. 点 point(s)　　　テン　　　　百点〔ひゃくてん〕hundred points
　　　　　　　　　　　　　満点〔まんてん〕perfect score
　　　　　　　　　　　　　問題点〔もんだいてん〕
　　　　　　　　　　　　　problem point(s)
　　　　　　　　　　　　　良い点〔よい (or いい) てん〕good point

17. 数 number　　　かず　　　　車〔くるま〕の数 number of cars
　　　to count　　　かぞ(える)　　お金を数える to count money
　　　　　　　　　　スウ　　　　数学〔すうがく〕math
　　　　　　　　　　　　　数字〔すうじ〕number
　　　　　　　　　　　　　学生数〔がくせいすう〕
　　　　　　　　　　　　　number of students

【読みかえの漢字】　　　* Previously introduced.

1. 南 south　　　みなみ*　　　日本の南 the south of Japan
　　　　　　　　ナン　　　　南部〔なんぶ〕the southern part
　　　　　　　　　　　　　南極〔なんきょく〕the South Pole
2. 地 land　　　チ*　　　　　地下鉄〔ちかてつ〕subway
　　　　　　　　ジ　　　　　地震〔じしん〕earthquake

3. 元　original　　ゲン＊　　　元気〔げんき〕healthy

　　　　　　　　ガン　　　　元旦〔がんたん〕New Year's Day

　　　　　　　　もと　　　　地元〔じもと〕local

　　　　　　　　　　　　　元大統領〔もとだいとうりょう〕former President

　　　　　　　　　　　　　(of a country)

4. 間　between　　あいだ＊　　病院〔びょういん〕と学校〔がっこう〕の間

　　　　　　　　　　　　　between the hospital and the school

　　　interval　　カン＊　　　時間〔じかん〕time

　　　　　　　　ゲン　　　　人間〔にんげん〕human beings

5. 色　color　　　いろ＊　　　黄色〔きいろ〕yellow

　　　　　　　　シキ　　　　景色〔けしき〕scenery

　　　　　　　　　　　　　色紙〔しきし〕square drawing paper

6. 好　like　　　す(き)＊　　大好き〔だいすき〕like very much

　　　　　　　　こう　　　　好奇心〔こうきしん〕curiosity

7. 重　heavy　　　おも(い)＊　重い本〔ほん〕heavy book

　　　　　　　　ジュウ　　　体重〔たいじゅう〕(body) weight

　　　　　　　　　　　　　重力〔じゅうりょく〕gravity

8. 中　middle　　なか＊　　　家〔いえ〕の中 inside the house

　　　　　　　　チュウ＊　　中学〔ちゅうがく〕intermediate school

　　　　　　　　ジュウ　　　一年中〔いちねんじゅう〕throughout the year

【読めればいい漢字】

1. 嫌い　　　　きらい　　　　dislike
2. 観光地　　　かんこうち　　sightseeing spot(s)
3. 御土産　　　おみやげ　　　souvenirs

《Activity A》

1. とくちょう＜特徴＞　N　special characteristics

山田さんの顔の特徴は目がとても大きいことです。The special characteristic of Yamada's face is her big eyes.

2. かぎをかける＜鍵をかける＞／かけます　V2　to lock [transitive]

教室は授業がない時、たいてい鍵がかけてある。When there is no class, the classrooms are usually locked.

3. かぎがかかる＜鍵がかかる＞／かかります　V1　to be locked [intransitive]

今この部屋は鍵がかかっている。This room is locked now.

4. (〜を)むける＜向ける＞／向けます　V2　to face 〜 [transitive]

「靴は玄関のドアの方に向けて置くはずです。」"You are supposed to face your shoes toward the front door."

5. (〜が)むく＜向く＞／向きます　V1　〜 faces [intransitive]

「私の方に向いて座って下さい。」"Please sit facing me."

《Activity B》

6. ていあん＜提案＞　N　suggestion; proposal

「この町のリサイクルについて何か提案がありませんか。」"Don't you have any suggestions about the recycling for this town?"

《Activity C》No new vocabulary

《Activity D》

7. こうがい＜郊外＞　N　suburb

家は郊外にあって、朝夕の交通ラッシュが大変だ。My home is in the suburbs and the traffic is terrible in the morning and the evening.

8. じもと＜地元＞　N　local

地元の果物や野菜は本当においしい。The local fruits and vegetables are really tasty.

9. さんぎょう＜産業＞　N　industry; business

地元に産業があまりないので、若い人達がこの町に帰って来ない。Since there are not enough businesses here, young people do not come back to this town.

10. こうぎょう＜工業＞　N　industry; technology

田中さんは東京工業大学でコンピューター工学を専攻している。Tanaka is majoring in computer technology at Tokyo University of Technology.

11. きこう＜気候＞　N　climate

日本の気候は、夏とても蒸し暑く過ごしにくい。As for the Japanese climate, the summer is very hot and humid, and it is hard to live (there).

12. おすすめ＜お勧め＞　N　recommendation; recommended

すすめる＜勧める＞／勧めます　V2　to recommend

「この町のお勧めのレストランはどこですか。」"Where is the restaurant you recommend in this town?"

13. （お）まつり＜（お）祭り＞　N　festival

お祭りがある度に、わくわくする。Every time when we have a festival, I get excited.

《Activity E》No new vocabulary

《Activity F》

14. しぜんさいがい＜自然災害＞　N　natural disaster

日本は自然災害が多い。There are lots of natural disasters in Japan.

15. じしん＜地震＞　N　earthquake

東京に大きい地震があったら、どうなるんだろうか。If a big earthquake occurs in Tokyo, I wonder what will happen.

16. たいふう＜台風＞　N　typhoon

最近、台風がだんだん大きくなっているようだ。The typhoon recently seems to gradually be getting bigger.

17. かざんふんか＜火山噴火＞　N　volcanic eruption

火山が噴火し出したというニュースを聞いた。I heard the news about the volcano starting to erupt.

《Activity G》

18. ちきゅうおんだんか＜地球温暖化＞　N　global warming

地球温暖化によっていろいろな問題が起きている。Various problems are occuring as a result of global warming.

19. きおん＜気温＞　N　temperature

地球の気温がだんだん高くなっているそうだ。I heard that the temperature of the earth is gradually getting higher.

20. こおり＜氷＞　N　ice

氷を入れた冷たいジュースを飲みたい。I want to drink cold juice with some ice in it.

21. (〜が)とける＜溶ける＞　V2　〜 melts [intransitive]

「ああ、アイスクリームが溶けちゃった。」"Oh, the ice cream melted."

22. ほっきょく＜北極＞　N　North Pole

北極の氷がだんだん溶けているそうだ。I heard that the ice of the North Pole is gradually melting.

23. なんきょく＜南極＞　N　South Pole

南極の上のオゾンの穴がだんだん大きくなっているそうだ。I heard that the ozone hole over the South Pole is gradually getting larger.

24. (〜が)ふえる＜増える＞／増えます　V2　〜 increases [intransitive]

事故の数が増えている。The number of the accidents is increasing.

25. (〜を)ふやす＜増やす＞／増やします　V1　to increase 〜 [transitive]

「お金を増やしたいんだ。」"I want to increase the amount of money (I have.)"

26. (〜が)へる＜減る＞／減ります V1　〜 decreases [intransitive]

日本は子供の数が減っているそうだ。I heard that the number of children is decreasing in Japan.

27. (〜を)へらす＜減らす＞／減らします　V1 to decrease 〜 [transitive]

「ごみを減らそう。」"Let's decrease garbage."

28. げんいん＜原因＞　N　cause

試合に負けた原因は練習を十分しなかったからだ。The cause of our loss at the game was that we didn't practice enough.

29. けっか＜結果＞　N　result; consequence

「昨日のテニスの試合の結果はどうだった？」"What was the result of the yesterday's tennis game?"

30. はいきガス＜排気ガス＞　N　exhaust fumes

自動車の排気ガスによる公害はだんだん悪くなっている。The pollution by the car's exhaust fumes are getting worse.

31. こうば or こうじょう＜工場＞　N　factory

この町には工場がたくさんあって、公害もひどい。There are lots of factories in this town and the pollution is also terrible.

32. うえる＜植える＞／植えます　V2　to plant

祖母が植えたトマトが赤くなった。The tomato my grandmother planted became red.

33. しょくぶつ＜植物＞　N　plants

祖父は植物をを育てることが好きだ。My grandfather likes to raise the plants.

《2課‐1・聞く》

34. しんど＜震度＞／マグネチュード　N　magnitude

新潟の地震は震度7だったそうだ。I heard that the earthquake at Niigata was magnitude 7.

35. ひがい＜被害＞　N　damage

地震の被害もひどかったそうだ。I heard that the damage from the earthquake was terrible.

36. どうろ＜道路＞　N　road

ラッシュの時、道路はいつも混んでいる。The roads are always crowded during the rush hour.

37. しぼうしゃすう＜死亡者数＞　N　number of death

交通事故からの死亡者数は今年もう５００人以上だそうだ。I heard that the number of deaths from traffic accidents is already more than 500 this year.

38. やく＜約＞〜　PN　about 〜

この学校の学生数は約三千人だ。The number of students at this school is about 3,000.

39. ひなん＜避難＞(を)する／します　V3　to evacuate

大きい台風が来ているので、たくさんの人が学校の体育館に避難した。Because a big

typoon is coming, lots of people evacuated to the school gym .

40. わかもの＜若者＞　N　young people

日本で結婚をしたくない若者が増えているらしい。Young people who don't want to marry

seem to be increasing in Japan.

41. ぜんこく＜全国＞　N　nation wide

地震の時、全国から寄付が送られた。When the earthquake occured, lots of donations were

sent in from all over the nation.

42. きゅうじょ＜救助＞(を)する／します　V3　to rescue

お年寄りが火事の中から救助された。The elderly person was rescued from the fire.

《2課 - 2・読む》

43. こうきしん＜好奇心＞　N　curiosity

妹は好奇心がいっぱいだ。My younger sister is full of curiosity.

44. こわがる＜怖がる＞／怖がります　V1　to fear; to be afraid of

竹中先生は猫が嫌いで、子猫さえ怖がる。Takenaka Sensei dislikes cats and she is even scared

of kittens.

45. ぼうけん＜冒険＞　N　adventure

始めての日本旅行は冒険でいっぱいだった。My first trip to Japan was full of adventures.

46. ふしぎ＜不思議＞　Na　mysterious

トトロは不思議な動物だ。Totoro is a mysterious animal.

47. つたえる＜伝える＞／伝えます　V2　to convey

メッセージを伝えたい。I want to convey my message.

48. かいせつ＜解説＞　N　explanation; commentary

映画の解説を読んで、この映画を見たいと思った。When I read the movie review, I thought

that I wanted to see this movie.

49. のんびり　Adv　carefree; at leisure; relaxed

しばらくのんびりしたい。I want to relax for a while.

50. くらす＜暮らす＞／暮らします　V1　to live (a daily life)

[住む to live/reside, 生きる to live (a life)]

父は退職したら田舎でのんびり暮らしたいと言っていた。My grandfather was saying that he

wants to live leisurely in the country after his retirement.

51. にんげん＜人間＞　N　human being

人間はなぜいつも戦争をするんだろうか。Why do human beings always have wars?

52. ふえ(をふく)＜笛(を吹く)＞／吹きます　N　(to play) a flute

トトロは木の上でオカリナという笛を吹いていた。Totoro was playing a flute called the

ocarina in the tree.

53. しんちょう＜身長＞　N　(body) height

私の身長は１６５センチだ。My height is 165 cm.

54. たいじゅう＜体重＞　N　(body) weight

体重が減って、嬉しい。I'm happy to have lost weight.

《2課 - 3a, b, c・書く》No new vocabulary

《2課 - 4a・話す》

55. ～ぶり　Nd　after ～ (a long time)

「おひさしぶりです。一年ぶりですねえ。」"I haven't seen you for a long time. It's almost

one year since the last time we met, isn't it?"

56. おせわになります。＜お世話になります。＞

Exp　Thank you for taking care of me. {from now on}

☞おせわになりました。＜お世話になりました。＞

Exp.　Thank you for taking care of me. [in the past]

《2課 - 4b・話す》

57. たすかった。＜助かった。＞　Exp　I'm saved.

たすかりました。＜助かりました。＞　Exp　Thank you for your help.

(たすかる＜助かる＞／助かります　V2　to be helpful [intransitive])

「わあ、助かった！」"Oh, I'm saved!"

☞たすける＜助ける＞　V2　to rescue; to help [transitive]

58. りゆう＜理由＞　　N　　reason

「昨日学校を休んだ理由は、風邪をひいて、熱があったからなんです。」"The reason

I was absent from school yesterday was that I caught a cold and had a fever."

59. うけつけ＜受付＞　　N　　reception (desk); information desk

病院へ行くと、まず受付に行くはずだ。When we go to the hospital, we are supposed to go to

the reception desk first.

60. じかん(どおり)に＜時間(通り)に＞　　Adv　　on time

「時間通りに来て下さい。」"Please come on time."

《2課 - 4d・話す》　No new vocabulary

《2課 - 4e・話す》　No new vocabulary

【分かればいい単語】

1. げたばこ＜下駄箱＞　　　　　　N　　shoe box/shoe stand [originally for *geta* (wooden clogs)]

2. かけじく＜掛け軸＞　　　　　　N　　scroll

3. おしいれ＜押し入れ＞　　　　　N　　closet (for *futon*)

4. ふすま＜襖＞　　　　　　　　　N　　sliding door (opaque)

5. あぐらをかく／かきます　　　　V1　　to sit cross-legged

6. しょうぎょう＜商業＞　　　　　N　　business; commerce

7. ぎょぎょう＜漁業＞　　　　　　N　　fishing industry

8. つなみ＜津波＞　　　　　　　　N　　tidal wave

9. たつまき＜竜巻＞　　　　　　　N　　tornado

10. かんばつ＜干ばつ＞　　　　　　N　　drought

11. こうずい＜洪水＞　　　　　　　N　　flood

＊ Previously learned.

A. Transitive verbs and Intransitive verbs → AIJ 4 L.4＊
   direct object を ＋ Transitive verb
   subject が ＋ Intransitive verb

1. クラスは9時に始まるはずなのに、先生はいつもクラスを遅く始める。
   The class is supposed to begin at 9:00, but the teacher always starts class late.

2. ドアが壊れているけど、誰がドアを壊したの。
   The door is broken, but who broke the door?

3. お金を増やしたいけど、お金はなかなか増えないんだ。
   I want to increase my finances, but money doesn't increase easily.

4. 体重を減らしたいけど、体重はなかなか減らないんだ。
   I want to lose weight, but it doesn't decrease easily.

Fill in the blanks with the correct intransitive verbs after the ～が.

	Transitive verb ～を	(someone) does (something)	Intransitive verb ～が	(something) does
1.	～を 始める	(SO) starts (ST)	～が	(ST) starts
2.	～を こわす	(SO) breaks (ST)	～が	(ST) be broken
3.	～を 見つける	(SO) finds (ST)	～が	(ST) be found
4.	～を 変える	(SO) changes (ST)	～が	(ST) changes
5.	～を 落とす	(SO) drops (ST)	～が	(ST) falls
6.	～を 起こす	(SO) causes (ST)	～が	(ST) happens
7.	～を 開ける	(SO) opens (ST)	～が	(ST) opens
8.	～を 閉める	(SO) closes (ST)	～が	(ST) closes
9.	～を つける	(SO) turns on (ST)	～が	(ST) turns on
10.	～を けす	(SO) turns off (ST)	～が	(ST) turns off
11.	～を 決める	(SO) decides (ST)	～が	(ST) is decided
12.	～を 集める	(SO) collects (ST)	～が	(Some people) gather
13.	～を ふやす	(SO) increases (ST)	～が	(ST) increases
14.	～を へらす	(SO) decreases (ST)	～が	(ST) decreases
15.	かぎを かける	(SO) lockes (ST)	かぎが	(ST) be locked
16.	～を 向ける	(SO) faces (ST)	～が	(ST) faces

B. (Subject が) + Transitive verb (TE form) + ある

has been done; be done → AIJ 3 L.7＊

Used to describe an existing state which is the result of an action previously done by someone.

1. 床<small>とこ</small>の間<small>ま</small>に掛<small>か</small>け軸<small>じく</small>がかけてある。   A scroll has been hung in the alcove.

2. パーティーの食べ物はもう買ってある。   Food for the party has already been bought.

Answer the following questions based on fact. Include the verb in the answers.

1. 日本語の教室に日本語のポスターが貼<small>は</small>ってありますか。   _____

2. 日本語の教室にお花が飾<small>かざ</small>ってありますか。   _____

3. 日本語の教室はよく掃除<small>そうじ</small>してありますか。   _____

4. 日本語の教室にリサイクルの袋<small>ふくろ</small>が置いてありますか。   _____

5. 日本語の教室は先生がいない時、鍵<small>かぎ</small>がかけてありますか。   _____

C. Verb (TE form) ＋おく   do something in advance → AIJ 3 L.8＊

Means "do something in advance and leave as is for future convenience."
-ておく is often contracted or shortened to -とく in informal conversation.
Examples: 話しておく→話しとく　読んでおく→読んどく

1. いつか日本に留学したいので、日本語を勉強しておく。

Since I want to study in Japan someday, I will study Japanese (to prepare for it).

2. 母は今晩出かけるので、晩ご飯を作っておいてくれた。

Since my mother is going out tonight, she made our dinner ahead of time for us.

3. 「トイレに行っとくね。」　 "I will go to the bathroom ahead of time."

4. 「明日マラソンだから、今スパゲティーをたくさん食べとこう。」

"Since the marathon is tomorrow, let's eat lots of spaghetti now (to prepare for it)."

You are planning a birthday party at your house. Write three things you have to prepare for it using the -ておく pattern.

1. _____

2. _____

3. _____

二課   116

D. Intransitive verb (TE form) + いる　　Description of a state　→ AIJ 4 L.4＊

Describe a state. For example, to say, "The window is open," one would use the intransitive form of the verb (TE form) + いる． The subject of intransitive sentences often take the particle が.

1. 窓が 開いている。 The window is open.

2. 電気が ついている。 The electricity is on.

3. 電気が 消えている。 The electricity is off.

a. Describe the state of your classroom by filling the blanks with an appropriate intransitive verb + いる form.

1. 教室の窓は、今＿＿＿＿＿＿＿＿＿＿＿＿＿＿＿＿＿＿＿＿＿。

2. 教室の戸は、今＿＿＿＿＿＿＿＿＿＿＿＿＿＿＿＿＿＿＿＿＿。

3. 教室の電気は、今＿＿＿＿＿＿＿＿＿＿＿＿＿＿＿＿＿＿。

4. 教室のコンピューターは、今＿＿＿＿＿＿＿＿＿＿＿＿＿＿＿。

5. 教室のエアコンは、今＿＿＿＿＿＿＿＿＿＿＿＿＿＿＿＿。

練習： Circle the correct verbs.

1. 窓は今（開いて　開けて）いる。

2. 空き缶を（集めて　集まって）、リサイクルしている。

3. 「お金を（落として　落ちて）しまった。」

4. 「テレビを（つけて　ついて）おいて下さい。」

5. 「電気を（消して　消えて）下さい。」

6. 「レストランはもう（閉めて　閉まって）いるよ。」

7. 私の時計は今（壊して　壊れて）いるから、時間が分からない。

8. 友達がお金を（見つけて　見つかって）くれた。

9. 私は今日、交通事故を（起こした　起きた）。

10. 毎日アイスクリームやケーキを食べていたら、体重が（増やした　増えた）。

11. 次郎君はレスリングの試合の前に、いつも体重を（減らす　減る）。

12. 私の方に（向けて　向いて）座って下さい。

117

二課

A. 日本の家の特徴〔とくちょう〕は？：ペアワーク→クラスワーク

What are the characteristics of a Japanese house and appropriate manners to follow while in a Japanese home? Circle the correct words.

日本の家：

1. （畳　カーペット）の部屋は伝統的である。

2. 風呂とトイレが（同じ　違う）所にある。

3. 玄関に下駄箱という（傘　靴）を入れる所がある。

4. 床の間には（生け花　掛け軸）がかけてある。

5. （ふとん　ざぶとん）は朝起きた時に、押し入れに入れる。

6. 畳の部屋の戸は襖や障子で、鍵は（かけられる　かけられない）。

日本の家の中でのマナー：

1. 日本の家の中で靴を（はいていてもいい　はいていてはいけない）。

2. 靴をぬぐ時、靴は（玄関のドアに　家の中に）向けて置くはずだ。

3. 畳の部屋でスリッパを（はいてもいい　はいてはいけない）。

4. 床の間に（立ってもいい　立ってはいけない）。

5. トイレを使っていない時、トイレの戸は（開けておく　閉めておく）べきだ。

6. 日本のお風呂の中で石鹸を（使ってもいい　使ってはいけない）。

7. 茶道で畳の上に座る時、女性は（あぐらをかいてもいい　あぐらをかいてはいけない）。

8. トイレのスリッパをほかの部屋で（はいてもいい　はいてはいけない）。

9. 襖や障子は足で（開けてもいい　開けてはいけない）。

10. 食事の時、ぼうしを（かぶっていてもいい　かぶっていてはいけない）。

B. 会話「リサイクルについて」：ペアワーク→クラスワーク

Discuss the following topics with your partner. Share your opinions and suggestions with your class.

1. あなたの家では、どんなリサイクルをしているか。

2. 学校では、どんなリサイクルをしているか。

3. リサイクルについてどんな意見を持っているか。提案があるか。

C. 会話「ボランティア活動について」：ペアワーク→クラスワーク

Discuss the following topics with your partner. Share your opinions and suggestions with your class.

1. どんなボランティア活動に参加(さんか)したか。

2. ボランティア活動についてどんな意見を持っているか。提案(ていあん)があるか。

3. ボランティア活動から何を習ったか。

D. 会話「私の住んでいる所」：ペアワーク→クラスワーク

Circle the correct choice or write an appropriate word in the blanks below. Share your highlights with your class.

1. 私の住んでいる所は（アメリカの東海岸(がん)　アメリカの西海岸(がん)　アメリカの中西部

   アメリカの南部　太平洋　アラスカ　日本）にある。

2. 私の住んでいる所は（都会(こう)　郊外(いなか)　田舎(た)　町　その他(た)：＿＿＿＿＿）だ。

3. 地元の一番の産業(さん)は（農業(のう)　工業　商業(しょう)　漁業(ぎょ)　観光業(かんこう)　その他(た)：＿＿＿＿＿）だ。

4. 地元の気候(こう)が一番いい季節(きせつ)は（春　夏　秋　冬）だ。

5. 一番景色(け)のいい所は＿＿＿＿＿＿＿＿＿＿＿＿＿＿＿＿＿＿＿だ。

6. この町のお勧(すす)めのレストランは＿＿＿＿＿＿＿＿＿＿＿＿＿＿＿＿＿＿だ。

7. 地元で有名なお土産(みやげ)は＿＿＿＿＿＿＿＿＿＿＿＿＿＿＿＿＿＿だ。

8. 一番のお祭りは＿＿＿＿＿＿＿＿＿＿＿＿＿＿＿＿＿だ。

9. 地元の一番の問題点は＿＿＿＿＿＿＿＿＿＿＿＿＿＿＿＿＿だ。

E. ディベート「町に住むのと田舎〔いなか〕に住むのとどちらの方がいいか」：

   グループワーク→クラスワーク

List the good points of living in town and in the countryside. Have a debate.

町に住むことの良い点：＿＿＿＿＿＿＿＿＿＿＿＿＿＿＿＿＿＿＿＿＿＿＿。

＿＿＿＿＿＿＿＿＿＿＿＿＿＿＿＿＿＿＿＿＿＿＿。

＿＿＿＿＿＿＿＿＿＿＿＿＿＿＿＿＿＿＿＿＿＿＿。

田舎(いなか)に住むことの良い点：＿＿＿＿＿＿＿＿＿＿＿＿＿＿＿＿＿＿＿＿＿＿＿。

＿＿＿＿＿＿＿＿＿＿＿＿＿＿＿＿＿＿＿＿＿＿＿。

＿＿＿＿＿＿＿＿＿＿＿＿＿＿＿＿＿＿＿＿＿＿＿。

二課

F. 会話「自然災害〔しぜんさいがい〕」：ペアワーク→クラスワーク

What are the natural disasters that occur in Japan and your area? Determine the 3 most common natural disasters. Mark the most common 1, next common 2, and least common of the 3 with a 3.

日本の自然災害：

_____地震　　_____津波　　_____台風/ハリケーン　　_____竜巻

_____干ばつ　　_____山火事　　_____火山噴火　　　　_____洪水

私の住んでいる所の自然災害：

_____地震　　_____津波　　_____台風/ハリケーン　　_____竜巻

_____干ばつ　　_____山火事　　_____火山噴火　　　　_____洪水

G. 会話「地球温暖化〔ちきゅうおんだんか〕」：ペアワーク→クラスワーク

Discuss the following topics with your partner and share it with your class.

1. 地球温暖化によってどんな問題が起きているか。

    a. 気温がもっと高くなっている。　　　　　　　　　（はい　いいえ）

    b. 台風やハリケーンがもっと大きくなっている。　（はい　いいえ）

    c. 北極や南極の氷が溶け始めている。　　　　　　（はい　いいえ）

    d. 地震がもっと増えている。　　　　　　　　　　（はい　いいえ）

    e. その他　_____

2. 地球温暖化を起こしている原因は何か。

    a. 自動車からの排気ガス　　　　　　　　　　　　（はい　いいえ）

    b. 工場から出る CO_2　　　　　　　　　　　　　（はい　いいえ）

    c. コンピューターを使う。　　　　　　　　　　　（はい　いいえ）

    d. その他　_____

3. 私達は地球温暖化を解決するために何をするべきか。

    a. 木を植える。　　　　　　　　　　　　　　　　（はい　いいえ）

    b. 森の木を切る。　　　　　　　　　　　　　　　（はい　いいえ）

    c. 自動車の運転を減らす。　　　　　　　　　　　（はい　いいえ）

    d. ごみをたくさん捨てる。　　　　　　　　　　　（はい　いいえ）

    e. エアコンを使う。　　　　　　　　　　　　　　（はい　いいえ）

    f. その他　_____

H. 会話「地震〔じしん〕」Pre-listening activity：ペアワーク→クラスワーク

下の質問に答えましょう。

1. 日本のどこに大きい地震がありましたか。いつでしたか。
2. 大きな自然災害のために何を準備したらいいと思いますか。

I. 会話「地震〔じしん〕」Post-listening activity：ペアワーク→クラスワーク

下の質問に答えましょう。

1. What did you learn from this listening passage? List three things. Write about them or make a short speech. Include your opinions and feelings.
2. Discuss any natural disaster that has occured in your area and how people have coped with it.

J. 会話「トトロ」Pre-reading activity：ペアワーク→クラスワーク

1. Look at the picture of "*Totoro.*" What kind of creature do you think it is?
2. List any facts you know about "*Totoro.*" Share them with the class.
3. If you have seen the movie "*Tonari no Totoro,*" what do you think is the theme of the movie? What did you think of the movie? Share your opinions and feelings in Japanese.

K. 会話「トトロ」Post-reading activity：ペアワーク→クラスワーク

What did you learn about "Totoro"? List three things. Write about them or make a short speech.

＜2課 - 1・聞く＞

聞く： Earthquake

(Narrator)   Now you will listen once to a report.

＜2課 - 1・聞く (質問)＞

聞く: Earthquake

(Narrator)　Now answer the questions for this selection.

1. When did the Kobe earthquake happen?
   (A)　January 19th, 1995
   (B)　February 17th, 1995
   (C)　January 17th, 1995
   (D)　January 19th, 1985

2. How big was the Kobe earthquake?
   (A)　Magnitude 7.0
   (B)　Magnitude 7.2
   (C)　Magnitude 8.0
   (D)　Magnitude 8.2

3. What damage did NOT occur in the Kobe earthquake?
   (A)　Lots of buildings and roads were destroyed.
   (B)　Lost of houses were burned.
   (C)　Almost 5,300 people died.
   (D)　Lots of houses were destroyed by a tidal wave.

4. What did NOT happen after the Kobe earthquake?
   (A)　Lots of people evacuated to school gyms.
   (B)　Lots of young volunteers went to Kobe to assist with the rescues.
   (C)　Lots of young volunteers were from the Tokyo area.
   (D)　Lots of people donated things and money to people in Kobe.

5. What is the purpose of this announcement?
   (A)　Asking people to evacuate for the coming disaster.
   (B)　Explaining the effects of the disaster and how to prepare for the coming disaster.
   (C)　Explaining the importance of community service and encouraging people to participate in it.
   (D)　Reporting the damage from the earthquakes in Japan in general.

＜2課-2・読む＞

読む: Totoro

　「トトロ」が何か知っていますか。有名なアニメです。そのアニメの本当の名前は「となりのトトロ」と言います。私はこのアニメを何度も何度も見ました。好奇心いっぱいの妹のメイが可愛くて、その何も怖がらない冒険心が楽しくて、また不思議な動物のトトロが現われたりして、最後には心が温かくなり、見るたびに元気が出て来ます。だから、トトロについていろいろ考えたし、本を読んだりもしました。

　そのアニメの制作者そして監督が宮崎駿という人なんですが、宮崎駿さんが「トトロ」というアニメの中で伝えたかったメッセージは何なのでしょうか。

　「トトロ」って何でしょうか。私が読んだトトロの本の解説によるとトトロは、人間より昔から住んでいる生き物。どんぐりなどの木の実を食べ、森でのんびり暮らしている。でも、普通は人間には見えない。昼間はたいてい寝ていて、月夜の晩に、オカリナという笛を吹くのが好き。空を飛ぶことも出来る。トトロというのは、メイ（４歳の女の子）がつけた名前。このアニメの中の大トトロは、1300歳ぐらいで、身長２メートル。中トトロは600歳ぐらい。小トトロは100歳ぐらいだそうです。小学４年生の姉のサツキと４歳の妹のメイは、困っている時に、いつもトトロに助けられました。

　私は宮崎駿さんが「自然を大切にしなさい。森を大切にしなさい。そうすれば、自然も森もあなたを助けてくれますよ。」と言っているような気がします。この変な生き物はまだいろいろな村にまだいるかも知れませんね。たぶん。

読む: Totoro

(Narrator)　Now answer the questions for this selection.

1.　What are the writer's thoughts about "Totoro"?
(A)　This is one of her favorite stories.
(B)　There are many things she did not understand.
(C)　There are some parts that need improvement.
(D)　This must be shown to both children and adults.

2.　Who is the most adventurous in this story?
(A)　Totoro
(B)　Mei
(C)　Satsuki
(D)　father

3.　What is NOT a correct description of Totoro?
(A)　Totoro existed even before human beings.
(B)　Totoro eats leaves.
(C)　Totoro lives in a forest.
(D)　Totoro is usually invisible to people.

4.　What is a correct description of Totoro?
(A)　Totoro sleeps at night.
(B)　Totoro likes to play a violin.
(C)　Totoro can fly.
(D)　Big Totoro is youngest.

5.　What is the author's opinion about the animator's intention in creating "Totoro"?
(A)　To respect nature
(B)　To respect animals
(C)　To take care of children
(D)　To promote family values

＜２課 - 3a・書く＞
Text Chat: Your Town

You will participate in a simulated exchange of text-chat messages. Each time it is your turn to write, you will have 90 seconds. You should respond as fully and as appropriately as possible.

You will have a conversation about your town with Hideki Matsuo, a student in a Japanese school.

1.   Respond. (90 seconds)

それでは、よろしくお願いします。最初の質問です。住んでいらっしゃる所は何州の何市ですか。都会ですか。田舎ですか。

2.   Explain your preference. (90 seconds)

一年の気候はどうですか。どの季節が一番いいですか。

3.   State your opinion. (90 seconds)

町で一番有名な観光地やお祭りやお勧めのお土産などを紹介して下さい。

4.   Give a specific example. (90 seconds)

景色の一番美しい所はどこですか。どんな景色が見えますか。

5.   Justify your opinion. (90 seconds)

高校生が卒業した後、地元にいた方がいいと思いますか。それとも、ほかの場所へ行った方がいいと思いますか。

6.   Ask a specific question. (90 seconds)

そうですか。ありがとうございました。では、何か僕達の町について質問して下さい。

＜２課 - 3b・書く＞

Compare and Contrast: Living in city and living in village

You are writing an article for the student newspaper of your sister school in Japan. Write an article in which you compare and contrast living in the city and living in a village. Based on your personal experience, describe at least THREE similarities and differences between living in the city and living in a village. Also state your preference and give reasons for it.

Your article should be 300 to 400 characters or longer. Use the *desu/masu* or *da* (plain) style, but use one style consistently. Also, use *kanji* wherever *kanji* from the AP Japanese *kanji* list is appropriate. You have 20 minutes to write.

【自分の作文のアウトラインを書こう！】

Introduction:

_____

Three similarities and differences between living in the city and living in a village:

1. _____

2. _____

3. _____

Your preference and reasons:

_____

_____

15点
20分

Cultural Topic Posting: Japanese House

You are responding to a posting in a Web forum for high school students of Japanese. The posting asks about the Japanese house. Select ONE example of Japanese house, such as the building materials used, the structure of the house, the furnitures in the house, etc. Describe in detail at least THREE characteristics of the Japanese house. Also, express your opinion or feelings about the Japanese house.

Your posting should be 300 to 400 characters or longer. Use the *desu/masu* or *da* (plain) style, but use one style consistently. Also, use kanji wherever *kanji* from the AP Japanese *kanji* list is appropriate. You have 20 minutes to write.

【自分の作文のアウトラインを書こう！】

Introduction:

_____

One example:

_____

Three characteristics of the Japanese house:

1. _____

2. _____

3. _____

Your opinion and feelings:

_____

_____

＜２課 - 4a・話す＞

Conversation: Visiting Town

You will participate in a simulated conversation. Each time it is your turn to speak, you will have 20 seconds to record. You should respond as fully and as appropriately as possible.

You will have a conversation about staying at your house next week with Yuko, your Japanese host family's daughter who is an 8th grader,

(Girl)

(20 seconds)

(Girl)

(20 seconds)

(Girl)

(20 seconds)

(Girl)

(20 seconds)

＜2課 - 4b・話す＞

Return Telephone Call: I got lost!

You will participate in a simulated telephone conversation with someone you are calling back after receiving a message from the caller. First, you will listen to the voice message. Then the telephone call will begin. Each time it is your turn to speak, you will have 20 seconds to record. You should respond as fully and as appropriately as possible.

(Narrator)   Listen to the voice message.

(Girl)

(Narrator)   Now the telephone call will begin. After the phone is answered, begin with a greeting and then explain why you are calling.

(Girl)   [Telephone] [Rings twice and picks up]

(20 seconds)

(Girl)

(20 seconds)

(Girl)

(20 seconds)

(Girl)

(20 seconds)

School Announcement: Community service

Directions: Imagine that you are making an announcement in Japanese to an assembly of Japanese students visiting your school. First, you will see some notes in English about what to include in your announcement. You will have 1 minute to prepare your announcement while you look at the notes. Then you will have 1 minute to record your announcement. Your announcement should have an opening remark, details according to the notes, and a closing remark. Deliver your announcement using complete sentences in *desu/masu* style.

Community service: Children's Day Festival sign up
Shifts: Sunday, May 5, 8:00 a.m. - 12:00 or 11:00 a.m. - 3:00 p.m.
Receive a Japanese Cultural Center T-shirt and a free lunch.
Work at a booth of crafts, games, or food.
Report to an adult in case you are leaving the booth for any reason.
Report to the registration booth on time.

＜２課 - 4d・話す＞

Story Narration: Pollution

Directions: Imagine that you are making an oral presentation to your Japanese class. In your presentation, you will narrate a story. First, you will see pictures depicting the story. You will have 4 minutes to prepare your narration while you look at the pictures. Then you will have 2 minutes to record your narration. Narrate your story using complete sentences in *desu/masu* style.

Cultural Perspective Presentation: Manners in the Japanese Home

Directions: Imagine you are making an oral presentation to your Japanese class. First, you will read and hear the topic for your presentation. You will have 4 minutes to prepare your presentation. Then you will have 2 minutes to record your presentation. Your presentation should be as full as possible.

Present your own view or perspective on manners in the Japanese home. Discuss at least FIVE examples of manners in the Japanese home.

Begin with an appropriate introduction, give details, explain your own view or perspective, and end with a concluding remark.

【Let's take notes!】

1. Begin with an appropriate introduction.

_____

2. Discuss five aspects/examples of the topic.

    1.) _____

    2.) _____

    3.) _____

    4.) _____

    5.) _____

3. Explain your view or perspective.

_____

4. End with a concluding remark.

_____

●●● 教育と服装とテクノロジー ●●●
Education, Clothes & Technology

At the end of this lesson, you are expected to be able to handle the following tasks.

【AP-3課 タスク1：学校と教育】

Where are you in your college application process now? What are the most important factors you will consider when selecting a college? What are the real goals of education? What is your immediate goal in academics now? Once you get into a college of your choice, will you stop studying? Do you think you may have a different attitude toward education after graduating from high school and after college? What are your life goals?

【AP-3課 タスク2：服装】

Discuss the pros and the cons of having school uniforms. How did your school decide on the present dress code? What are your feelings and opinions about your school dress code? What fashion is popular now? How do the media influence new fashions, and why? What is your opinion about the present fashion trends?

【AP-3課 タスク3：コミュニケーションとメディアとテクノロジー】

What three functions of your cellular phone do you use the most? What do you use a computer for the most? What ethical issues do you face when you use a computer? Which is better, using the telephone or e-mail? Which is better, printed newspapers or internet newspapers?

調<ruby>べよう<rt>しら</rt></ruby>！

A. 少子高齢化社会

B. 日本の受験システム

C. 生涯教育

D. 多世代コミュニティーマンション

E. 日本の制服、セーラー服、学生服

F. 日本の若者ファッション―裏原宿ファッション

G. 日本のケータイ

H. 日本のロボット―介護用ロボット、災害救助用ロボット、地雷爆弾用ロボット

☆ Special reading [*Kanji* in text font]

1. 制 system   セイ   制度 〔せいど〕 system

2. 服 clothes   フク   制服 〔せいふく〕 school uniform

服装 〔ふくそう〕 clothes

私服 〔しふく〕 plain clothes

洋服 〔ようふく〕 Western clothes

和服 〔わふく〕 Japanese clothes [kimono]

3. 進 to advance   すす(む)   前へ進め！〔まえへすすめ〕

Go forward!

進 〔すすむ〕 さん

Susumu [male name]

シン   進学 〔しんがく〕 go on to university

進歩 〔しんぽ〕 progress

4. 相 together   あい   相手 〔あいて〕 partner

ソウ   相談 〔そうだん〕 する

to consult

5. 願　wish　　　　　ねが(う)　　お願いします
Please. [I will ask a favor
of you.]

ガン　　　願書〔がんしょ〕
written application

6. 面　face　　　　　メン　　　帳面〔ちょうめん〕notebook
[old word for ノート]
正面〔しょうめん〕front
☆イケメン good-looking man
[slang]

7. 接　to connect　　セツ　　　面接〔めんせつ〕する
to have an interview
接待〔せったい〕する
to welcome; serve food
接続時間〔せつぞく〕する
to connect

8. 必　certainly　　　かなら(ず)　必ず行く I will go without fail.
ヒツ　　　必勝〔ひっしょう〕certain victory
必読書〔ひつどくしょ〕
required reading

9. 要　need　　　　　い(る)　　　お金が要る (I) need money.

ヨウ　　　　必要〔ひつよう〕necessary

重要人物〔じゅうようじんぶつ〕

important person

主要な道路〔しゅようなどうろ〕

main road

10. 術 skill　　　　ジュツ　　　美術〔びじゅつ〕fine arts

芸術〔げいじゅつ〕the arts

手術〔しゅじゅつ〕surgery

技術〔ぎじゅつ〕technique; technology

忍術〔にんじゅつ〕

fighting art of the *ninja*

11. 組 group　　　　くみ　　　　赤組〔あかぐみ〕red team

テレビ番組〔ばんぐみ〕

TV program

一年一組〔いちねんいちくみ〕

1st year class #1

12. 個 individual　　コ　　　　　個人〔こじん〕individual; private

個人的〔こじんてき〕な問題

〔もんだい〕personal problem

個性〔こせい〕individual personality

一個〔いっこ〕の飴 one piece of candy

13. 実 truth　　ジツ　　実は as a matter of fact

理科〔りか〕の実験〔じっけん〕

science experiment

現実〔げんじつ〕reality

事実〔じじつ〕fact; truth

実力〔じつりょく〕real ability

14. 留 to remain　　リュウ　　留学〔りゅうがく〕する

to study abroad

留学生〔りゅうがくせい〕

overseas student

ル　　留守〔るす〕not at home

15. 遠 far　　とお(い)　　遠い国〔くに〕faraway country

エン　　遠足〔えんそく〕hike

(from school)

遠泳〔えんえい〕long-distance

swimming

遠慮〔えんりょ〕する to hesitate

16. 反 to oppose　　ハン　　反省〔はんせい〕する to reflect

交通違反〔こうつういはん〕

traffic violation

反則〔はんそく〕foul (play)

17. 対 versus, the opposite   タイ

2対3〔にたいさん〕2 to 3 [score]

A高校対B高校〔Aこうこうたい Bこうこう〕A High School vs. B High School

反対〔はんたい〕する to oppose

18. 遊 to play   あそ(ぶ)

公園〔こうえん〕で遊ぶ
play at the park

遊び場〔あそびば〕playground

水遊び〔みずあそび〕water play

ユウ   遊園地〔ゆうえんち〕
amusement park

【読みかえの漢字】

* Previously introduced.

1. 足 foot   あし*   足が痛い (My foot) is sore.

    enough   たり(る)   お金が足りない There is not enough money.

2. 行 to go   い(く)*   行こう Let's go.

    コウ*   旅行〔りょこう〕travel

    to conduct   ギョウ*   年中行事〔ねんちゅうぎょうじ〕annual event

    おこな(う)   式〔しき〕を行う to conduct a ceremony

3. 青 blue   あお*   青い空〔そら〕blue sky

    セイ   青春〔せいしゅん〕youth

4. 春 spring   はる*   春休み〔はるやすみ〕spring vacation

    シュン   青春〔せいしゅん〕youth

    春分の日〔しゅんぶんのひ〕Vernal Equinox Holiday (March 20 or 21)

三課

【読めればいい漢字】

1. 合格　　　　ごうかく　　　　　to pass (an exam)
2. 相談　　　　そうだん　　　　　consultation
3. その他　　　そのた　　　　　　etc.
4. 掃除　　　　そうじ　　　　　　cleaning
5. 洗濯　　　　せんたく　　　　　laundry
6. 返す　　　　かえす　　　　　　to return (something)
7. 郵便局　　　ゆうびんきょく　　post office

《Activity A》

1. しんがく＜進学＞(を)する／します　V3　to go on to college/university

　　大学に進学するつもりだ。I plan to go on to college.

2. そうだん＜相談＞(を)する／します　V3　to consult

　　カウンセラーの先生に問題を相談した。I consulted with a counselor about the problem.

3. がんしょ＜願書＞　N　application form (for admission)

　　六つの大学に願書を送った。I sent application forms to six universities.

4. しめきり＜締め切り＞　N　deadline

　　この大学の願書の締め切りがいつか知らない。I don't know when the deadline for this university's application form is.

5. だい＜題＞　N　title

　　作文の題は「親友」だ。The title of my composition is "My Best Friend."

6. めんせつ＜面接＞(を)する/します　V3　to have an interview

　　昨日、大学の面接を受けた。I had a college interview yesterday.

7. つうち＜通知＞(を)する/します　V3　to inform; notice

　　三月の末ごろに大学からの通知が来るはずだ。My college entrance results are supposed to come around the end of March.

8. もうしこむ＜申し込む＞／申し込みます　V1　to apply
　　もうしこみしょ＜申込書＞　N　application form

　　奨学金を申し込むつもりだ。I am planning to apply for a scholarship.

9. かのうせい＜可能性＞　N　possibility

　　希望の大学に入学出来る可能性は５０％くらいかな。I wonder if the possibility for me to be able to enter the college of my choice might be about 50%.

10. じゅけん＜受験＞(を)する／します　V3　to take an entrance exam

　　大輔は東大に受験したけど、失敗したと言っていた。Daisuke said that he took the entrance exam for Tokyo University, but he failed.

11. せいど＜制度＞　N　system

日本とアメリカの受験制度はとても違う。The systems for taking entrance exams in Japan and America are very different.

《Activity B》

12. もくてき＜目的＞　N　purpose　[☞もくひょう＜目標＞ goal]

大学へ行く目的は何ですか。What is the purpose of going to college?

13. せいしんりょく＜精神力＞　N　mental strength

スポーツに勝つのに体力だけでなく精神力も大事だ。In order to win in sports, not only is physical strength important, but also mental strength.

14. ちしき＜知識＞　N　knowledge

正しく考えるために十分な知識が必要だ。In order to think correctly, we (also) need sufficient knowledge.

15. げいじゅつ＜芸術＞　N　the arts

芸術を愛する心を持つ方がいい。It's better to have a love of the arts.

16. えんげき＜演劇＞　N　play (theatrical)

夏川さんは演劇が大好きで、将来女優になりたいそうだ。I heard that Ms. Natsukawa loves acting and wants to become an actress in the future.

17. りかい＜理解＞(を)する／します　V3 to understand [formal equiv. of 分かる]; to comprehend

ほかの国の文化を理解することは、とても大事だ。It's very important to understand other countries' cultures.

18. ちょうせん＜挑戦＞(を)する／します　V3　to challenge (one's ability)

今この「すどく」というゲームに挑戦している。I am taking on the challenge of *sudoku* game now.

19. たいど＜態度＞　N　attitude

山田君は態度がとても良い。Yamada has a good attitude.

20. げんざい＜現在＞　N　present time

現在の希望の大学はどこですか。What college do you wish to get into at present?

《Activity D》

21. しふく＜私服＞　N　plain/private (own) clothes

この高校は制服がなくて、皆私服を着ている。There is no school uniform at this high school and everyone wears their own clothes.

22. だらしない　A　loose; slovenly; sloppy

私服はだらしなく見えると思う。I think the plain clothes look inappropriate.

23. まよう＜迷う＞／迷います　V1　to lose (one's way); to be perplexed; to be puzzled

制服があれば、朝何を着るか迷わなくてもいい。If we had a school uniform, we wouldn't have to be undecided about what to wear in the morning.

24. せいしゅん＜青春＞　N　youth

友達と過ごした時間が青春の思い出だ。The time I spent with my friends is my memory of my youth.

25. ほこり＜誇り＞　N　pride

この制服に誇りを感じる。I feel pride in this school uniform.

26. かっこう＜格好＞　N　shape; appearance

「変な格好をしないで下さい。」"Please don't wear something inappropriate."

27. こせい＜個性＞　N　individuality; personality

リサさんは個性が強くて、人とよくけんかをする。Lisa has a strong personality and often fights with people.

28. おしゃれ＜お洒落/オシャレ＞　Na　fashion-conscious

おしゃれ＜お洒落/オシャレ＞(を)する／します　V3　to dress up

姉はとってもオシャレです。My older sister is very fashionable.

姉は今日もおシャレをして、出かけた。My older sister dressed up today, too, and went out.

29. あきる＜飽きる＞／飽きます　V2　to get tired of

もうインスタントラーメンに飽きてしまった。I already got tired of instant noodles.

30. あせをかく＜汗をかく＞／かきます　V1　to perspire

汗をかいたので、シャツがちょっと臭い。Because I perspired, my shirt is a little smelly.

31. ふけつ＜不潔＞　Na　unclean; unsanitary

田中君はいつも同じシャツを着ていて、汗臭くて、不潔な感じがする。Tanaka is always wearing the same shirt and is smelly, so I feel that he is unclean.

《Activity E》

32. はやる＜流行る＞／流行ります　V1　to be popular; to come into fashion

今、変なファッションが流行っている。Now a strange fashion is in style.

33. メディア　N　media

メディアがファッションに大きな影響を与えている。The media has a big influence on fashion.

《Activity F》

34. きのう＜機能＞　N　(mechanical) function

「ケータイのどの機能を一番よく使っている？」"What function of the cellular phone do you use the most?

35. (お)さいふ＜(お)財布＞　N　purse; wallet

財布を落としてしまったらしい。It seems that I dropped my wallet.

36. じょうほう＜情報＞　N　information

個人の情報を盗まれてしまった。Personal information was stolen.

《Activity G》

37. とうろんかい＜討論会＞　N　discussion; debate

とうろん＜討論＞(を)する／します　V3　to discuss

「今日は制服について討論しよう。」"Let's discuss school uniforms today."

《3課 - 1・聞く》No new vocabulary

38. ロボット　N　robot

ロボットは平和のために使ってほしい。I want people use the robots for peace.

39. しょうしか＜少子化＞　N　decrease in the number of children

少子化で日本の学校の数が少なくなるそうだ。I heard that the number of schools in Japan

will lessen because of the decrease in the number of children.

40. こうれいか＜高齢化＞　N　aging

日本は高齢化社会でお年寄りが多い社会になる。Because of its aging society, Japan will

become a society with lots of elderly people.

41. かいご＜介護＞(を)する／します　V3　to care

母はおばあちゃんをうちで介護しているが、大変そうだ。My mother is taking care of my

grandmother at home, but it seems to be hard.

42. かならず＜必ず＞　Adv　without fail; certainly

将来必ず故郷に帰って来る。I will definitely come back to my hometown in the future.

43. たりる＜足りる＞／足ります　V2　to be sufficient; to be enough

今お金が足りないから、ほしい物が買えない。Since I don't have enough money, I cannot

buy the things I want.

44. とうなんアジア＜東南アジア＞　N　Southeast Asia

東南アジアからの多くの移民が日本に住んでいる。There are lots of immigrants from

Southeast Asia living in Japan.

45. うけいれる＜受け入れる＞／受け入れます　V2　to accept

早稲田大学はたくさんの留学生を受け入れているそうだ。I heard that Waseda University

is accepting lots of overseas students.

46. たよる＜頼る＞／頼ります　V1　to depend on; to rely on

一生両親に頼って生きるべきではない。We should not depend on our parents all our lives.

47. おてつだいさん＜お手伝いさん＞　N　a maid

母はうちを掃除して、料理をしてくれるお手伝いさんをほしがっている。My mother

wants a maid who does house cleaning and cooking.

48. ぎじゅつ＜技術＞　N　technology; technique

日本人は伝統的にいい物を作り出す技術を持っているようだ。Japanese people traditionally seem to have the technology to create good products.

49. はったつ＜発達＞(を)する／します　V3　(something) develops; advance(s)

日本はロボット技術が発達しているらしい。The Japanese robotic technology seems to be advanced.

50. しつ＜質＞　N　quality

少し高くても質のいい物を買いたい。I want to buy things of good quality even though they are a little more expensive.

51. りょう＜量＞　N　quantity

お年寄りには「量より質」が大事らしい。Quality seems to be more important than quantity for elderly people.

52. きたい＜期待＞(を)する／します　V3　to look forward to 〜; to anticipate

両親は私の将来に期待をしている。My parents are looking forward to my future.

《3課 - 3 a, b, c・書く》 No new vocabulary

《3課 - 4 a・話す》

53. おこなう＜行う＞／行います　V1　to practice; to conduct

日本語の卒業式は、学校のチャペルで行われる。The Japanese graduation ceremony is held at the school chapel.

54. ごきょうりょくおねがいします。＜御協力お願いします。＞

Exp　I request your cooperation.

55. しちょうりつ＜視聴率＞　N　ratings (of a television program)

NHKの「紅白歌合戦」は、毎年視聴率が高いそうだ。I heard that the ratings of the NHK Red and White Song Festival are high every year.

56. ぐたいてき＜具体的＞　Na　concrete

ぐたいてきに＜具体的に＞　Adv　concretely

「どんな人が好きですか。具体的に話して下さい。」"What kind of person do you like? Please answer in concrete terms."

《3課 - 4b・話す》

57. ゲームき＜ゲーム機＞　N　video game machine

「ごめん、君のゲーム機を壊しちゃった。」 "Sorry, I broke your video game machine."

58. じつは＜実は＞　Exp　by the way; as a matter of fact; to tell you the truth

「ごめん。実は、今日のデート、行けなくなっちゃった。」 "Sorry. As a matter of fact, I cannot go on our date today."

《3課 - 4c・話す》 No new vocabulary

《3課 - 4d・話す》

59. かがみ＜鏡＞　N　mirror

姉は鏡の前で、いろいろなドレスを着てみている。 My older sister is trying on various dresses in front of the mirror.

60. にあう＜似合う＞／似合います　V1　to suit; to match

「そのドレス、よく似合ってるね。」 "That dress looks good on you."

《3課 - 4e・話す》 No new vocabulary

【分かればいい単語】

1. めざまし(どけい)＜目覚まし(時計)＞　N　alarm (clock)
2. しっぱいはせいこうのもと＜失敗は成功のもと＞

   Prov. Failure teaches success.

3. ちえ＜知恵＞　　　　　　　　　　N　wisdom
4. がくりょく＜学力＞　　　　　　　N　academic ability
5. セーラーふく＜セーラー服＞　　　N　sailor suit
6. がくせいふく＜学生服＞　　　　　N　school uniform for boys [black color]

* Previously learned.

A. 〜か（どうか）　　　whether or not; if (〜 or not)　　　→ AIJ 3 L.9 *

This construction is used when one expresses uncertainty about a certain condition, event or fact. When the optional どうか is used, the embedded question has to be a yes-no question. If it is not used, then the question can be either a yes-no question or a WH-question. Typical final verbs include, among others, verbs of knowing, examining, understanding, asking, remembering and deciding. Use the plain form before か. だ is omitted after な adjectives and nouns.

1. この大学が<u>いいか</u>(どうか)知らない。　　I do not know if this university is good or not.

2. 次の試験が<u>いつか</u>忘れた。　　　　　　I forgot when the next exam is.

3. <u>どこ</u>の大学に<u>行くべきか</u>考えている。　I am thinking about what university I should go to.

4. 一郎が<u>誰</u>を<u>好きか</u>知っている？　　　　Do you know who Ichiro likes.

Combine the two sentences into one and translate the sentence to English.

1. トトロは何ですか。知っていますか。

_____　　_____

2. お土産（みやげ）は何がいいですか。困っています。

_____　　_____

3. 田中君はどこの大学へ行きますか。教えて下さい。

_____　　_____

4. 京都大学は合格しにくいですか。知りません。

_____　　_____

5. 毎朝何を着ますか。迷（まよ）わなくてもいいです。

_____　　_____

B.　～と、　　　　　　　　　　　　　　　　　→ AIJ 3 L.9＊
　　　～たら、
　　　～ば、

All of the above can be expressed as "If . . ." Although they may be interchangeable in usage, there are certain restrictions on each.

a. Verb (Dictionary/ NAI form - Nonpast Plain form) ＋ と、Sentence 2.
Normally used when stating fact, mathematical or scientific principles. Is not generally used when expressing opinion or information of a personal nature.

　　1. 右にまがると、大きいデパートがある。
　　　　If you turn right, there is a large department store.
　　2. 冬になると、雪が降る。
　　　　When it becomes winter, it will snow.

b. Verb (TA/ NAKATTA form) ＋ら、Sentence 2.
Used to make general statements, often of a more personal nature. Sentence 2 (the main clause) may express volition, suggestion, invitation, request, permission, prohibition or opinion. Though it is considered a conditional, -たら is also often expressed as "When."

　　3. お酒を飲んだら、ぜったい車を運転してはいけない。
　　　　When you drink alcohol, you definitely should not drive a car.
　　4. このハワイ旅行クイズが当たったら、一緒にハワイへ行こう。
　　　　If I win this game for a trip to Hawaii, let's go to Hawaii together.

c. Verb (-ば)、Sentence 2.
Used in hypothetical statements, i.e., "if and only if . . ."
　　いAdjective (-ば)、Sentence 2.
　　なAdjective (なら)、Sentence 2.
　　Noun　　　　(なら)、Sentence 2.

　　5. (もし)試験が明日なら、今日勉強しなくちゃいけない。
　　　　If the exam is tomorrow, I have to study today.
　　6. 日本の大学へ行けば、日本語が上手になるでしょう。
　　　　If I go to college in Japan, my Japanese will probably become good.

a. Choose the most appropriate answer of the three.

1. 宿題が早く（終わると　終わったら　終われば）、アイスクリームを食べよう。

2. ひまが（あると　あったら　あれば）、ぜひうちに遊びに来て下さい。

3. 高校を（卒業すると　卒業したら　卒業すれば）、日本へ行きませんか。

4. 秋葉原へ（行くと　行ったら　行けば）、電気製品やゲームの店がたくさんあります。

5. モールへ（行くと　行ったら　行けば）、先生に会った。

三課

b. Change the word in the (　) to the correct conditional form.

1. 今百ドル_____、何を買いたい？（もらう）

2. この道をまっすぐ_____、郵便局は右にありますよ。（行く）

3. 漢字を二千_____、新聞が読める。（知っている）

4. 希望の大学に合格_____、ぜったい行く。（出来る）

5. 成績が_____、悲しい。（悪い）

6. 天気が_____、テニスをしよう。（いい）

7. 彼女が_____、わかれた方がいいよ。（好きじゃない）

C. 〜と(いうの)は、　Noun＋の/Sentence＋という　＋ことだ。

This structure is used in interpreting, explaining, or defining a word, a phrase, or a sentence.

1. デジカメと(いうの)は、デジタルカメラのことです。

　Dejikame means digital camera.

2. 少子化と(いうの)は、子供がだんだん減るということです。

　Shooshika means that the number of children decreases gradually.

3. 「猿も木から落ちる」と(いうの)は、上手な人でも時々間違えるということです。

　Saru mo ki kara ochiru (lit. even monkeys fall from trees) means that even a skillful person sometimes makes mistakes.

Fill in the blanks with the correct description.

1. 高齢化と(いうの)は、_____ことです。

2. ウォッシュレットと(いうの)は、_____ことです。

3. トトロと(いうの)は、_____ことです。

4. 本音と(いうの)は、_____ことです。

5. 「笑う門には福来る」と(いうの)は、_____

　ことです。

D. 〜かも　知れない／知れません　　　might 〜; may 〜　　　　　　→ AIJ 3 L.7＊

　　〜だろう／でしょう　　　　　　　probably 〜　　　　　　　　→ AIJ 2 L.7＊

　　〜に　違いない／違いありません　there is no doubt that 〜; must be 〜

　　　　　　　　　　　　　　　　　　　　　　　　　　　　　　　→ AIJ 4 L.8＊

These structures express different degrees of doubt.

1. 明日、雨が降る<u>かも知れません</u>。　　It might rain tomorrow.

2. 明日、雨が降る<u>でしょう</u>。　　　　It will probably rain tomorrow.

3. 明日、雨が降る<u>に違いありません</u>。　It will certainly rain tomorrow.

Make a sentence about your future using the following structures.

1. 〜かも知れません　　　_____

2. 〜でしょう　　　　　　_____

3. 〜に違いありません　　_____

E. Indirect quotation (Plain form) ＋と＋　思う/言う/答える/聞く　　→ AIJ 2 L.11＊

　　　　　　　　　　　think/say/answer/hear that 〜

The subject of the sentence, that is, the person who thinks, says, answers, etc. is usually marked by the particle は. The subject of the quote, if different from the subject of the sentence, is followed by が.

1. 私はケンが日本へ<u>行く</u>と聞いた。　　I heard that Ken will go to Japan.

2. 私はケンが<u>やさしい</u>と思う。　　　　I think that Ken is nice.

3. ケンは日本が<u>好きだ</u>と言った。　　　Ken said that he likes Japan.

4. 私はケンがいい<u>人だ</u>と思う。　　　　I think Ken is a good person.

5. ケンは私が<u>好きだった</u>と思う。　　　I think that Ken liked me.

Complete the sentences using the word in the (　) in a correct form.

1. 母は今_____と思う。（４６歳）

2. 母は日本語がとても_____と思う。（難しい）

3. 母はゴルフがまだ_____と思う。（下手）

4. 母は以前_____と思う。（小学校の先生）

5. 母の夢は私がいい大学へ_____と思う。（行く）

153

三課

A. 大学進学について：ペアワーク→クラスワーク

Discuss the following with your partner and share the findings with your class.

1. 大学進学について先生と何度相談した？　＿＿＿＿＿＿＿＿＿＿＿＿＿＿
2. 大学についてコンピューターでよく調べた？　＿＿＿＿＿＿＿＿＿＿＿＿＿＿
3. 何校の大学に願書を送るつもり？　＿＿＿＿＿＿＿＿＿＿＿＿＿＿
4. 最後の大学の願書の締め切りはいつ？　＿＿＿＿＿＿＿＿＿＿＿＿＿＿
5. 大学の推薦状をもう先生にお願いした？　＿＿＿＿＿＿＿＿＿＿＿＿＿＿
6. 大学のエッセイをもう書いた？題は何？　＿＿＿＿＿＿＿＿＿＿＿＿＿＿
7. もう大学の面接をした？　＿＿＿＿＿＿＿＿＿＿＿＿＿＿
8. 大学からいつごろ結果の通知をもらう？　＿＿＿＿＿＿＿＿＿＿＿＿＿＿
9. 奨学金を申し込むつもり？　＿＿＿＿＿＿＿＿＿＿＿＿＿＿
10. 大学進学について何か親と問題がある？　＿＿＿＿＿＿＿＿＿＿＿＿＿＿
11. 希望の大学に合格出来る可能性は何パーセント？　＿＿＿＿＿＿＿＿＿＿＿
12. 最後に大学を決める時、一番大事な事は何？　＿＿＿＿＿＿＿＿＿＿＿＿
13. 日本の受験について何か知っている？　＿＿＿＿＿＿＿＿＿＿＿＿＿＿
14. 日本とアメリカの受験制度はどちらの方がいいと思う？なぜ？

＿＿＿＿＿＿＿＿＿＿＿＿＿＿

B. 教育の目的について：ペアワーク→クラスワーク

The following are some educational goals of schools. How well do you think you have achieved these goals? Discuss with your partner and share the findings with your class.

1. 道徳的な人間か。　＿＿＿＿＿＿＿＿＿＿＿＿＿＿
2. 健康な体を作っているか。　＿＿＿＿＿＿＿＿＿＿＿＿＿＿
3. 強い精神力を持っているか。　＿＿＿＿＿＿＿＿＿＿＿＿＿＿
4. 正しく考えるための知識を十分持っているか。　＿＿＿＿＿＿＿＿＿＿
5. 芸術（音楽、美術、演劇など）を愛する心を持っているか。　＿＿＿＿＿＿
6. 文化の違いに理解を持っているか。　＿＿＿＿＿＿＿＿＿＿＿＿＿＿
7. 社会の役に立てる人間か。　＿＿＿＿＿＿＿＿＿＿＿＿＿＿
8. 自分に挑戦し続ける態度を持っているか。　＿＿＿＿＿＿＿＿＿＿＿＿
9. 大学に入学出来る学力があるか。　＿＿＿＿＿＿＿＿＿＿＿＿＿＿

C. 現在と将来の目標について：ペアワーク→クラスワーク

Discuss the following topics with your partner and share the findings with your class.

1. 今の目標は何？　　　　　　　　　　　_____

2. 大学に合格した後の目標は何？　　　_____

3. 大学で何を専攻したい？　　　　　　　_____

4. 大学にいる間に、してみたいことは何？　_____

5. 大学を卒業した後、どんな仕事をしてみたい？_____

6. どんな人生を生きたい？　　　　　　　_____

D. 制服について Pre-listening activity：ペアワーク→クラスワーク

Do you support having a school uniform or not? Determine your three most important reasons for supporting or opposing school uniforms. Mark your choices #1 - 3, with #1 being your most important reason. Finally, add your own reason.

制服に賛成する理由：

____ 1. 制服を着ていると、どこの学校か分かりやすい。

____ 2. 制服は見た目がきれいだが、私服はだらしなく見える。

____ 3. 制服があれば、毎日何を着るか迷わなくていい。

____ 4. 制服は学生の時にだけ着られるので、青春の思い出になる。

____ 5. 制服は学校のシンボルだから、学校に誇りを持つようになる。

____ 6. 制服は私服より経済的だ。

____ 7. セーラー服は可愛い。

____ 8. 女子学生がセクシーな格好が出来ないので、勉強に集中出来る。

____ 9. その他の理由：_____

制服に反対する理由：

____ 1. 皆が同じ服を着ていると、個性がなくなる。

____ 2. 制服ではオシャレが出来ない。

____ 3. 毎日同じ制服を着ると、飽きてしまう。

____ 4. 毎朝服装について考えなくていいので、ファッションセンスがなくなる。

____ 5. 制服は汗をかいてもあまり洗濯をしないから、不潔だ。

____ 6. その他の理由：_____

三課

E. ファッションについて：ペアワーク→クラスワーク

Draw the most popular fashion now and describe it in Japanese. What is your opinion about this fashion? How do the media influence fashion? Share your opinion with your class.

1. 今はやっているファッションを描きなさい。2. ファッションを説明しなさい。

それか、写真を貼りなさい。

_____

_____

_____

_____

3. このファッションについての意見を

書きなさい。

_____

_____

4. メディアがファッションにどのような影響を与えていると思いますか。

_____

F. テクノロジーについて：ペアワーク→クラスワーク

Discuss the following questions with your partner and share the findings with your class.

1. ケータイの機能で何をよく使っていますか。よく使うベスト３に１〜３の番号を書きなさい。

____電話　____テキストメール　____目覚まし　____インターネット　____時計

____カメラ　____音楽　____ゲーム　____おさいふケータイ

____ナビゲーター　____テレビ　____電車の改札

2. コンピューターで一番よく使っている機能は何ですか。

____情報　____ゲーム　____ワープロ　____ビデオ　____買物　その他：_____

3. コンピューターを使って、道徳的にどんな問題がありますか。

_____

G. 討論会〔とうろんかい〕 「テクノロジーについて」：ペアワーク→クラスワーク
Debate the following topics with your group and share the findings with your class.

1. 「電話」と「Eメール」とどちらの方がいいですか。

電話の良い点： _____

電話の悪い点： _____

Eメールの良い点： _____

Eメールの悪い点： _____

どちらが好き？： _____

好きな理由： _____

2. 紙の「新聞」と「インターネットの新聞」とどちらの方がいいですか。

紙の新聞の良い点： _____

紙の新聞の悪い点： _____

ネット新聞の良い点： _____

ネット新聞の悪い点： _____

どちらが好き？： _____

好きな理由： _____

H. 会話 「制服について」Post-listening activity：ペアワーク→クラスワーク
Discuss your school dress code. List at least three facts and include your feelings and opinions.

I. 会話 「ロボットについて」Pre-reading activity：ペアワーク→クラスワーク
Pre-reading activity: Answer the following questions in Japanese.

1. どんなロボットを知っていますか。

2. 少子高齢化社会には、どんな問題があると思いますか。

3. ロボットがお年寄りの介護にどう役に立つと思いますか。

J. 作文 「制服について」Post-reading activity：ペアワーク→クラスワーク
What did you learn about robots? List at least three facts and include your feelings and opinions. (300-400 letters)

三課

＜３課 - 1・聞く＞

聞く： School Uniform Debate

(Narrator)　Now you will listen once to a school debate by Ken and Mari.

＜3課-1・聞く(質問)＞

聞く： School Uniform Debate

(Narrator)   Now answer the questions for this selection.

1. What kind of students are Ken and Mari?
(A)   Both Ken and Mari graduated from this school.
(B)   Both Ken and Mari are students at this school now.
(C)   Ken is a study abroad student and Mari graduated from this school.
(D)   Both Ken and Mari are study abroad students.

2. What is Mari's opinion about school uniforms?
(A)   Mari is for uniforms.
(B)   Mari thinks that students can have individuality with uniforms.
(C)   Mari thinks that students can dress up with uniforms.
(D)   Mari thinks that students will get tired of uniforms.

3. What is Ken's opinion about school uniforms?
(A)   Ken does not like uniforms.
(B)   Ken thinks people cannot tell student's schools by their uniforms.
(C)   Ken thinks uniforms look good.
(D)   Ken thinks that students who wear their own clothes look good.

4. Which statement by Ken and Mari is NOT correct?
(A)   Ken thinks that students don't have to worry about what to wear in the morning with uniforms.
(B)   Ken thinks wearing uniforms will become a memory of their youth.
(C)   Mari thinks uniforms become unsanitary from perspiration.
(D)   Ken thinks that students do not like uniforms.

5. What is Ken's and Mari's opinions about school uniforms?
(A)   Both Ken and Mari generally like uniforms.
(B)   Neither Ken nor Mari like uniforms.
(C)   Only Ken likes uniforms.
(D)   Only Mari likes uniforms.

三課

＜３課‐２・読む＞

読む：Robot

　日本はこれから少子高齢化社会を迎える。少子化というのは、子供がだんだん減るということで、高齢化とは、お年寄りがだんだん増えるということだ。もうすぐ日本の人口の２５％が６０歳以上のお年寄りになるそうだ。少子化によって、子供の数が少なくなるので、お年寄りを介護する人が必ず足りなくなるに違いない。東南アジアから若い移民を受け入れて、その移民達にお年寄りの介護を頼らなければならないかも知れない。

　そんな時に、お年寄りの介護をするためのロボットが役に立つかも知れない。うちの中で掃除や洗濯や料理をしてくれるロボット、話し相手になってくれるロボット、介護もしてくれるロボット、そんなロボットがいれば、きっとお年寄りのいいお手伝いさんになるだろう。ロボットは掃除機や冷蔵庫やテレビのような電気製品の一つとして、電気屋さんで売られているかも知れない。

　ロボットの技術がどんどん発達して、質のいいロボットが作られることを期待している。そんな日が来るのは、遠い将来ではないような気がする。

読む: Robot

(Narrator)   Now answer the questions for this selection.

1.   What is the problem Japan has faced in recent years?
   (A)   Decreased number of children
   (B)   Increased number of elderly people
   (C)   Both (A) and (B)
   (D)   None of the above

2.   What role will the immigrants from Southeast Asia play in Japan?
   (A)   They will help to care for children.
   (B)   They will help to build robots.
   (C)   They will help to care for elderly people.
   (D)   They will help Japanese with domestic work.

3.   The author is describing the possible capabilities of robots. Which one was NOT mentioned in this passage?
   (A)   Speaking and listening to a person
   (B)   Laundry
   (C)   Repairing
   (D)   Cooking

4.   Where does the author think robots will be sold in the future?
   (A)   Electric goods shop
   (B)   Computer shop
   (C)   Robot shop
   (D)   Department store

5.   What opinion does the author have about robots?
   (A)   Robots will help with the problems that Japan will face in the future.
   (B)   Robots will expand the problems that Japan will face in the future.
   (C)   Robots will not replace people.
   (D)   Robots will help only rich people who can afford them.

＜3課‑3a・書く＞

Text Chat: School

Note: In this part of the exam, the student may not move back and forth among questions.

You will participate in a simulated exchange of text-chat-messages. Each time it is your turn to write, you will have 90 seconds. You should respond as fully and as appropriately as possible.

You will have a conversation with Mari, a student in a Japanese school, about your school.

1. Start the conversation.   (90 seconds)

    それでは、よろしくお願いします。最初の質問です。そちらの高校は、どんな高校ですか。教えて下さい。

2. Respond. (90 seconds)

    そうですか。次の質問です。授業料はいくらですか。入学は難しいですか。

3. Describe a specific example. (90 seconds)

    分かりました。次の質問です。学校の歴史について何か知っていますか。

4. Explain your preference. (90 seconds)

    分かりました。次の質問に行きましょう。学校の行事で何が一番好きですか。

5. State your opinion. (90 seconds)

    そうですか。では、最後の質問です。学校のいい点と悪い点を一つずつ教えて下さい。

6. Ask a specific question. (90 seconds)

    ありがとうございました。ところで、日本の学校について何か質問がありますか。

三課

162

15点
20分

Compare and Contrast: Public School & Private School

You are writing an article for the student newspaper of your sister school in Japan. Write an article in which you compare and contrast public schools and private schools. Based on your personal experience, describe at least THREE similarities and differences between public schools and private schools. Also state your preference and give reasons for it.

Your article should be 300 to 400 characters or longer. Use the *desu/masu* or *da* (plain) style, but use one style consistently. Also, use *kanji* wherever *kanji* from the AP Japanese *kanji* list are appropriate. You have 20 minutes to write.

【自分の作文のアウトラインを書こう！】

Introduction:

_____

Three similarities and differences of public schools and private schools:

1. _____

2. _____

3. _____

Your preference and give reasons:

_____

_____

三課

Cultural Topic Posting: Japanese Clothing

You are responding to a posting in a web forum for high school students of Japanese. The posting asks about Japanese clothes. Select ONE example of Japanese clothing, such as traditional *kimono*, present Japanese fashion, etc. Describe in detail at least THREE characteristics of Japanese clothes. Also, express your opinion or feelings about Japanese clothes.

Your posting should be 300 to 400 characters or longer. Use the *desu/masu* or *da* (plain) style, but use one style consistently. Also, use *kanji* wherever *kanji* from the AP Japanese *kanji* list are appropriate. You have 20 minutes to write.

【自分の作文のアウトラインを書こう！】

Introduction:

_____

One example:

_____

Three characteristics of Japanese clothes:

1. _____

2. _____

3. _____

Your opinion and feelings:

_____

_____

Conversation: Media

You will participate in a simulated conversation. Each time it is your turn to speak, you will have 20 seconds to record. You should respond as fully and as appropriately as possible.

You will have a conversation with a person who conducts a survey for a TV station about media.

(Interviewer)

(20 seconds)

(Interviewer)

(20 seconds)

(Interviewer)

(20 seconds)

(Interviewer)

(20 seconds)

三課

＜３課 - 4b・話す＞

Return Telephone Call: Game Machine

You will participate in a simulated telephone conversation with someone you are calling back after receiving a message. First, you will listen to the voice message. Then the telephone call will begin. Each time it is your turn to speak, you will have 20 seconds to record. You should respond as fully and as appropriately as possible.

(Narrator)   Listen to the voice message.

(Boy)

(Narrator)   Now the telephone call will begin. After the phone is answered, begin with a greeting and then explain why you are calling.

(Boy)   [Telephone] [Rings twice and you pick it up]

(20 seconds)

(Boy)

(20 seconds)

(Boy)

(20 seconds)

(Boy)

(20 seconds)

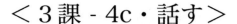
School Announcement: Basketball game

Directions: Imagine that you are making an announcement in Japanese to an assembly of Japanese students visiting your school. First, you will see some notes in English about what to include in your announcement. You will have 1 minute to prepare your announcement while you look at the notes. Then you will have 1 minute to record your announcement. Your announcement should have an opening remark, details based on the notes, and a closing remark. Deliver your announcement using complete sentences in *desu/masu* style.

Saturday, November 26, 4:30 p.m. - 7:00 p.m.
Basketball, vs. Lincoln High School at the Lincoln High School gym
School bus departure: 3:00 p.m. in front of the science building.
Free of charge, but ticket required.
RSVP to the school office by Friday, November 20

＜３課‐4d・話す＞

Story Narration: Clothes Shopping

Directions: Imagine that you are making an oral presentation to your Japanese class. In your presentation, you will narrate a story. First, you will see pictures depicting the story. You will have 4 minutes to prepare your narration while you look at the pictures. Then you will have 2 minutes to record your narration. Narrate your story using complete sentences in *desu/masu* style.

Cultural Perspective Presentation: Japanese School

Directions: Imagine you are making an oral presentation to your Japanese class. First, you will read and hear the topic for your presentation. You will have 4 minutes to prepare your presentation. Then you will have 2 minutes to record your presentation. Your presentation should be as complete as possible.

Present your own view or perspective on Japanese school. Discuss at least FIVE aspects or examples of Japanese school.

Begin with an appropriate introduction, give details, explain your own view or perspective, and end with a concluding remark.

【Let's take notes!】

1. Begin with an appropriate introduction.

_____

2. Discuss five aspects/examples of the topic.

    1.) _____

    2.) _____

    3.) _____

    4.) _____

    5.) _____

3. Explain your view or perspective.

_____

4. End with a concluding remark.

_____

三課

四課	●●● 仕事と冠婚葬祭と年中行事 ●●●
	Work, Rites of Life, & Annual Events

At the end of this lesson, you are expected to be able to handle the following tasks.

【AP-4課 タスク1：仕事と職業】

Discuss your college major preference(s). Discuss your possibilities for higher degrees, such as master's degree, Ph. D., MBA, etc. Discuss your preferences for your future career. What is important as you decide on your occupation - high salary, contribution to the community, your passion, location, etc.?

【AP-4課 タスク2：冠婚葬祭】

What would be an ideal life for you? Discuss what would be your ideal college life, ideal career, ideal marriage, ideal partner, ideal place of residence, ideal family, ideal retirement life and ideal way of dying. Who do you respect as a person the most and why? What is most important in your life? What are your favorite proverbs or sayings?

【AP-4課 タスク3：祭りと年中行事】

Select one annual event from the Japanese calendar and discuss three characteristics of the event. Discuss your thoughts and opinions about it. Compare and contrast them with characteristics of the same or a similar annual event on an American calendar.

四課

A. 日本の県名

県 prefecture

日本の県と県庁(capital)がある市： 空いているところに読みがなを書きなさい。

都道府県	読みがな	県庁所在地	読みがな	都道府県	読みがな	県庁所在地	読みがな
1. 北海道		札幌市		25. 滋賀県	しがけん	大津市	おおつし
2. 青森県		青森市		26. 京都府		京都市	
3. 岩手県		盛岡市	もりおかし	27. 大阪府		大阪市	
4. 宮城県	みやぎけん	仙台市		28. 兵庫県	ひょうごけん	神戸市	
5. 秋田県		秋田市		29. 奈良県		奈良市	
6. 山形県	やまがたけん	山形市		30. 和歌山県		和歌山市	
7. 福島県		福島市		31. 鳥取県	とっとりけん	鳥取市	
8. 茨城県	いばらぎけん	水戸市	みとし	32. 島根県		松江市	まつえし
9. 栃木県	とちぎけん	宇都宮市	うつのみやし	33. 岡山県		岡山市	
10. 群馬県	ぐんまけん	前橋市		34. 広島県		広島市	
11. 埼玉県	さいたまけん	さいたま市		35. 山口県		山口市	
12. 千葉県		千葉市		36. 徳島県		徳島市	
13. 東京都		新宿区		37. 香川県	かがわけん	高松市	
14. 神奈川県	かながわけん	横浜市		38. 愛媛県	えひめけん	松山市	
15. 新潟県	にいがたけん	新潟市		39. 高知県	こうちけん	高知市	
16. 富山県	とやまけん	富山市		40. 福岡県		福岡市	
17. 石川県		金沢市	かなざわし	41. 佐賀県	さがけん	佐賀市	
18. 福井県		福井市		42. 長崎県		長崎市	
19. 山梨県	やまなしけん	甲府市	こうふし	43. 熊本県	くまもとけん	熊本市	
20. 長野県		長野市		44. 大分県	おおいたけん	大分市	
21. 岐阜県	ぎふけん	岐阜市		45. 宮崎県	みやざきけん	宮崎市	
22. 静岡県		静岡市		46. 鹿児島県	かごしまけん	鹿児島市	
23. 愛知県	あいちけん	名古屋市		47. 沖縄県		那覇市	
24. 三重県	みえけん	津市	つし				

四課

B. 日本の氏名トップ１０

1位	佐藤（さとう）	6位	伊藤（いとう）
2位	鈴木（すずき）	7位	中村（なかむら）
3位	高橋（たかはし）	8位	小林（こばやし）
4位	田中（たなか）	9位	山本（やまもと）
5位	渡部（わたなべ）	10位	加藤（かとう）

C. 生年月日と干支

西暦	和暦	干支〔えと〕	干支〔英〕	西暦	和暦	干支〔えと〕	干支〔英〕
1868	明治元年	辰〔たつ〕	Dragon	1995	平成7年	亥〔いのしし〕	Boar
1912	大正元年/明治45年	子〔ね〕	Rat	1996	平成8年	子〔ね〕	Rat
1926	昭和元年/大正15年	寅〔とら〕	Tiger	1997	平成9年	丑〔うし〕	Ox
1945	昭和20年	酉〔とり〕	Cock	1998	平成10年	寅〔とら〕	Tiger
:	:	:	:	1999	平成11年	卯〔うさぎ〕	Rabbit
1987	昭和62年	子〔ね〕	Rat	2000	平成12年	辰〔たつ〕	Dragon
1987	昭和62年	丑〔うし〕	Ox	2001	平成13年	巳〔み〕	Snake
1987	昭和62年	寅〔とら〕	Tiger	2002	平成14年	午〔うま〕	Horse
1987	昭和62年	卯〔うさぎ〕	Rabbit	2003	平成15年	未〔ひつじ〕	Ram
1988	昭和63年	辰〔たつ〕	Dragon	2004	平成16年	申〔さる〕	Monkey
1989	平成元年/昭和64年	巳〔み〕	Snake	2005	平成17年	酉〔とり〕	Cock
1990	平成2年	午〔うま〕	Horse	2006	平成18年	戌〔いぬ〕	Dog
1991	平成3年	未〔ひつじ〕	Ram	2007	平成19年	亥〔いのしし〕	Boar
1992	平成4年	申〔さる〕	Monkey	2008	平成20年	子〔ね〕	Rat
1993	平成5年	酉〔とり〕	Cock	2009	平成21年	丑〔うし〕	Ox
1994	平成6年	戌〔いぬ〕	Dog	2010	平成22年	寅〔とら〕	Tiger

D. 干支と性格

	子	Rat ねずみ	1924, 1936, 1948, 1960, 1972, 1984, 1996, 2008	節約〔せつやく〕(saving) が上手、 よく気をつける
	丑 (牛)	Ox うし	1925, 1937, 1949, 1961, 1973, 1985, 1997, 2009	静か、 がまん強い、 がんこ
	寅 (虎)	Tiger とら	1926, 1938, 1950, 1962, 1974, 1986, 1998, 2010	よく考える、 気が短い
	卯 (兎)	Rabbit うさぎ	1927, 1939, 1951, 1963, 1975, 1987, 1999, 2011	話が上手、 才能〔さいのう〕がある、 おとなしい
	辰 (竜/龍)	Dragon たつ	1928, 1940, 1952, 1964, 1976, 1988, 2000, 2012	元気、 正直〔しょうじき〕、 勇気〔ゆうき〕がある
	巳 (蛇)	Snake へび	1929, 1941, 1953, 1965, 1977, 1989, 2001, 2013	頭がいい、 お金持ち、 静か
	午 (馬)	Horse うま	1930, 1942, 1954, 1966, 1978, 1990, 2002, 2014	人気がある、 明るい性格〔せいかく〕、 おしゃべり
	未 (羊)	Sheep ひつじ	1931, 1943, 1955, 1967, 1979, 1991, 2003, 2015	明るい、 芸術〔げいじゅつ〕的、情熱〔じょうねつ〕的、 おとなしい
	申 (猿)	Monkey さる	1932, 1944, 1956, 1968, 1980, 1992, 2004, 2016	頭がいい、 何でも上手
	酉 (鶏)	Rooster にわとり	1933, 1945, 1957, 1969, 1981, 1993, 2005, 2017	よく考える、 よく働く、 人が好き
	戌 (犬)	Dog いぬ	1934, 1946, 1958, 1970, 1982, 1994, 2006, 2018	責任感〔せきにんかん〕がある、 正直〔しょうじき〕、 いい友達、がんこ
	亥 (猪)	Boar いのしし	1935, 1947, 1959, 1971, 1983, 1995, 2007, 2019	強い心、 やさしい心、 気が短い

四課

E. 星占い（ほしうらな）

Capricorn	やぎ座	12/22 - 1/19	努力する、真面目（まじめ）、人に厳（きび）しい積極的（せっきょく）
Aquarius	みずがめ座	1/20 - 2/18	自由、リーダー、孤独（こどく）がまん強い、
Pisces	うお座	2/19 - 3/20	優しい、芸術的（げいじゅつ）、頼（たよ）りない
Aries	おひつじ座	3/21 - 4/19	積極的（せっきょく）、行動力（こうどうりょく）がある、短気（たん）
Taurus	おうし座	4/20 - 5/20	がまん強い、責任感（せきにん）がある、嫉妬（しっと）する
Gemini	ふたご座	5/21 - 6/21	好奇心（こうき）が強い、器用（きよう）（何でも上手に作れる）、すぐ飽（あ）きる
Cancer	かに座	6/22 - 7/22	優（やさ）しい、マイペース、感情（かんじょう）をコントロール出来ない
Leo	しし座	7/23 - 8/22	リーダー、プライドが高い
Virgo	おとめ座	8/23 - 9/22	完全主義者（かんぎ）、努力（ど）する、頑固（がんこ）
Libra	てんびん座	9/23 - 10/23	バランスがいい、協力的（きょうりょく）、なかなか決められない
Scorpio	さそり座	10/24 - 11/21	がまん強い、本音（ね）を出さない
Sagittarius	いて座	11/22 - 12/21	自由、前向き、人の言う事を聞かない

F. 血液型（けつえきがた）

A 型（がた）　　まじめ
B 型（がた）　　情熱的（じょうねつ）
O 型（がた）　　リーダー的
AB型（がた）　　まじめで情熱的（じょうねつ）

G. 浪人（ろうにん）と予備校（よび）

H. リクルートスーツ

四課　　　　　176

[*Kanji* in text font]

1. 法　law　　　　ホウ

法律〔ほうりつ〕law
法学部〔ほうがくぶ〕law school
文法〔ぶんぽう〕grammar

2. 経　to pass　　ケイ

経済〔けいざい〕economics
日経〔にっけい〕Nikkei
(newspaper, stock index)
経歴〔けいれき〕personal history

3. 商　business　ショウ

商業〔しょうぎょう〕commerce;
business
商品券〔しょうひんけん〕
gift certificate
商売〔しょうばい〕(small) business

4. 計　to calculate　ケイ

計算〔けいさん〕する to calculate
時計〔とけい〕clock; watch
会計〔かいけい〕account
会計士〔かいけいし〕accountant
計画〔けいかく〕a plan

177

四課

5. 授　to grant　　ジュ　　　授業〔じゅぎょう〕class

授業料〔じゅぎょうりょう〕tuition

教授〔きょうじゅ〕professor

6. 科　section,　　カ　　　科目〔かもく〕(school) subject

department　　　　　自然科学〔しぜんかがく〕

natural science

理科〔りか〕science

7. 究　to investigate　キュウ　研究〔けんきゅう〕research

8. 専　to face　　セン　　専攻〔せんこう〕major

専門〔せんもん〕specialty

専門店〔せんもんてん〕

specialty shops

専門家〔せんもんか〕specialist

専門学校〔せんもんがっこう〕

vocational school

9. 結　to tie　　むす(ぶ)　ひもを結ぶ to tie strings

ケツ　　　結果〔けっか〕result

10. 婚 marriage　コン　結婚〔けっこん〕marriage

新婚旅行〔しんこんりょこう〕

honeymoon

初婚〔しょこん〕first marriage

離婚〔りこん〕divorce

再婚〔さいこん〕second marriage

11. 式 ceremony　シキ　卒業式〔そつぎょうしき〕

graduation ceremony

入学式〔にゅうがくしき〕

school entrance ceremony

結婚式〔けっこんしき〕

wedding ceremony

お葬式〔そうしき〕funeral

12. 季 season　キ　四季〔しき〕four seasons

季語〔きご〕seasonal word

in haiku

13. 節 to face　セツ　季節〔きせつ〕season

節分〔せつぶん〕The day before

the beginning of spring (Bean

Throwing Night)

　　　　melody　ブシ　ソーラン節 Sooran Song

四課

14. 贈 to send　おく(る)　贈り物〔おくりもの〕present; gift

ゾウ　贈答品〔ぞうとうひん〕gift

15. 失 to lose　うしな(う)　信用〔しんよう〕を失う to lose trust

シツ　失業〔しつぎょう〕unemployment

失業者〔しつぎょうしゃ〕

unemployed person

失敗〔しっぱい〕する to fail

失明〔しつめい〕する to lose one's eyesight

16. 礼 courtesy　レイ　礼を言う to say thank you

失礼〔しつれい〕rude

お礼状〔れいじょう〕thank-you

note

17. 非 non-　ヒ　非常口〔ひじょうぐち〕emergency exit

非常〔ひじょう〕に very, extremely

18. 表 front,　おもて　表玄関〔おもてげんかん〕front door

chart　ヒョウ　時刻表〔じこくひょう〕timetable

発表〔はっぴょう〕する to announce

代表〔だいひょう〕する to represent

代表者〔だいひょうしゃ〕representative

表現〔ひょうげん〕する to express

【読みかえの漢字】　　　*Previously introduced.

1. 飲　to drink　　の(む)*　　　水を飲む to drink water

　　　　　　　　　イン　　　　飲料水〔いんりょうすい〕drinking water

2. 学　to learn　　まな(ぶ)　　日本語を学ぶ to study Japanese

　　　　　　　　　ガク*　　　　学校〔がっこう〕school

3. 重　heavy　　　おも(い)*　　重い本 a heavy book

　　　　　　　　　ジュウ*　　　体重〔たいじゅう〕(body) weight

　　　　　　　　　チョウ　　　　貴重品〔きちょうひん〕valuables

【読めればいい漢字】

1. 専攻　　　せんこう　　　　major subject
2. 希望　　　きぼう　　　　　hope
3. 職業　　　しょくぎょう　　occupation
4. 給料　　　きゅうりょう　　salary
5. 教師　　　きょうし　　　　(classroom) teacher
6. 氏名　　　しめい　　　　　full name
7. 得意　　　とくい　　　　　one's strong point
8. 習慣　　　しゅうかん　　　habit; custom
9. 祝う　　　いわう　　　　　to congratulate; to celebrate
10. 研究　　　けんきゅう　　　research
11. 非常口　　ひじょうぐち　　emergency exit

《Activity A》

1. しょくぎょう＜職業＞　N　occupation

将来どんな職業をしたい？ What kind of occupation do you want to have in the future?

《Activity B》

2. しゅうしごう＜修士号＞　N　Master's degree

姉は今大学院で教育学の修士号を取っている。My older sister is now getting a master's degree in education at graduate school.

3. はくしごう or はかせごう＜博士号 or 博士号＞　N　doctoral degree; Ph.D.

　　〜はかせ＜博士＞　Nd　Dr. 〜

兄は去年コンピューター工学の博士号を取った。My older brother got his doctorate degree in computer science last year.

《Activity C》

4. せいざ＜星座＞　N　constellation; astronomy

吉島さんの星座は乙女座です。Mr. Yoshijima's zodiac sign is Virgo.

5. けつえきがた＜血液型＞　N　blood type

吉島さんの血液型はA型だ。Mr. Yoshijima's blood type is A.

6. とくぎ＜特技＞　N　special skill

吉島さんの特技は料理とデッサンだそうだ。I heard that Mr. Yoshijima's special skills are cooking and sketching.

《Activity D》

7. しゅうしょく＜就職＞(を)する／します　V3　to find employment

吉島さんは大松組に就職することになりました。It was decided that Mr. Yoshijima be employed at the Omatsu Group.

8. せいけつ＜清潔＞　Na　clean; sanitary [⇔ふけつ＜不潔＞ unclean; dirty]

手を清潔にしておこう。Let's keep your hand clean.

9. はで＜派手＞　Na　showy; flashy

あの歌手はいつも派手な服を着ている。That singer is always wearing showy cloths.

10. じみ＜地味＞　Na　plain; simple; conservative

日本のおばあさんはたいてい地味な服を着ている。Japanese older ladies usually wear

conservative clothes.

11. こん(いろ)＜紺(色)＞　N　navy blue (color)

先生はいつも紺色のスカートを履いている。My teacher is always wearing a navy blue skirt.

《Activity E》

12. けんこうほけん＜健康保険＞　N　health insurance

大学へ行く前に健康保険に入っておくべきだ。We should have health insurance before we go

to college.

《Activity F》

13. かつやく＜活躍＞(を)する／します　V3　to be active

彼は学生時代サッカー部で活躍していた。He was active in the soccer club during his college

days.

14. すすむ＜進む＞／進みます　V1　to go forward; to advance

「赤は止まれ、黄色は注意、青は進め。」"Red is stop, yellow is caution and green is to go

(move forward)."

15. もどる＜戻る＞／戻ります　V1　to turn back; to return

忘れ物を取りにうちへ戻った。I returned home to get the things I forgot.

16. よびこう＜予備校＞　N　prep school (for students during their *ronin* year)

受験に失敗して浪人している間に予備校へ通っていた。While I was not in college after

failing to get in, I was going to a prep school.

17. はつこい＜初恋＞　N　first love

僕の初恋は四年生の時だった。My first love was when I was in the fourth grade.

18. こいびと＜恋人＞　N　sweetheart; lover

「恋人がほしいなあ。」"I wish I had a sweetheart."

四課

19. つゆ/ばいう＜梅雨＞　N　rainy monsoon season in Japan (June and July)

梅雨の間は毎日雨が降っている。During the monsoon season, it rains every day.

20. おくりもの＜贈り物＞　N　present; gift

贈り物をもらうと嬉しい。When I receive a present, I am happy.

21. しゅうかん＜習慣＞　N　habit; custom

日本にはいろいろな贈り物の習慣がある。In Japan, there are various gift customs.

22. としのくれ＜年の暮れ＞　N　year end

　　ねんまつ＜年末＞　N　year end

日本人は年の暮れには御歳暮をお世話になった人にあげる。Japanese people give *oseibo* gifts to people who took care of them.

23. ちょくせつ(に)＜直接(に)＞　Adv　directly

日本人はたいてい御歳暮をデパートから直接うちに送ってもらう。Japanese people usually ask the department store to send the *oseibo* gift directly to their houses.

24. かんせつてき(に)＜間接的(に)＞　Adv　indirectly

この話をほかの人から間接的に聞いた。I heard this story indirectly from other person.

25. いっぱんてき＜一般的＞　Na　general; typical

　　いっぱんてきに＜一般的に＞　Adv　in general

日本人が人のうちを訪問する時、手土産を持って行くのが一般的だ。When Japanese people visit people at home, they generally take a small gift.

26. げんきん＜現金＞　N　cash

日本人は結婚式やお葬式の時に、現金をのし袋に入れてあげる。Japanese people give cash in the *noshibukuro* envelope at weddings and funerals.

27. しょうひんけん＜商品券＞　N　gift certificates

日本人はお中元や御歳暮によく商品券をあげる。Japanese often give gift certificates for mid summer gifts and year end gifts.

28. きちょう＜貴重＞　　Na　precious; valuable

　　きちょうひん＜貴重品＞　　N　valuables

　　貴重品は車の中に置いておかないで下さい。Please don't leave (your) valuables in the car.

《4課‐1・聞く》

29. けいれき＜経歴＞　　N　personal history; career

　　仕事の経歴について話して下さい。Please talk about your personal work history.

30. きぎょう＜企業＞　　N　commercial enterprise

　　日本の企業で働きたいです。I want to work at a Japanese firm.

31. けんしゅう＜研修＞　　N　training

　　けんしゅうかい＜研修会＞　　N　workshop

　　留学中、日本の企業で研修を受けました。While I was studying abroad, I received training at a Japanese firm.

32. きかい＜機会＞　　N　opportunity; chance

　　日本に留学する機会があれば、ぜひ行きたいです。If I have an opportunity to study abroad in Japan, I definitely want to go.

33. いんりょうすい＜飲料水＞　　N　drinking water

　　海の水をどうやって飲料水に変えられるんですか。How can you change sea water to drinking water?

34. つき＜月＞　　N　moon

　　月から地球を見てみたい。I want to try and see the earth from the moon.

35. たいよう＜太陽＞　　N　sun

　　夏の太陽は暑い。In the summer, the sun is hot.

36. ほし＜星＞　　N　star

　　今夜は星が美しい。The stars are beautiful tonight.

37. ひじょうに＜非常に＞　　Adv　extremely

　　ひじょうぐち＜非常口＞　　N　emergency exit

　　東大に合格するのは非常に難しい。It's extremely difficult to enter Tokyo University.

38. きょうみぶかい＜興味深い＞　A　very interesting

地球の写真を見るのは非常に興味深い。It's extremely interesting to see the photos of the earth.

39. けんきゅう＜研究＞(を)する／します　V3　to research

兄は大学院でDNAの研究をしている。My older brother is doing research on DNA at graduate

school.

40. まなぶ＜学ぶ＞／学びます　V1　to learn [formal equiv. of 習う]

日本語をもっと学びたい。I want to learn more Japanese.

41. やりがい　N　worthwhile

やりがいのある仕事をしたい。I want to have a job that is worthwhile.

《4課 - 2・読む》

42. そうぎょうしゃ＜創業者＞　N　founder (of a company)

そうりつしゃ＜創立者＞　N　founder (of an organization)

HONDAの創業者は本田宗一郎という人だ。The founder of Honda is a person named

Soichiro Honda.

43. どんぞこ＜どん底＞　N　very bottom; depths

そこ＜底＞　N　bottom

日本は第二次世界大戦後、貧乏のどん底にあった。Japan was at the very depths of poverty

after World Wat II.

44. だいひょう＜代表＞(を)する／します　V3　to represent

だいひょうしゃ＜代表者＞　N　representative; delegate

ホンダは現代の日本を代表する企業だ。Honda is an enterprise that represents modern Japan.

45. せいひん＜製品＞　N　manufactured product

自動車は日本を代表する製品だ。Automobiles are representative of products manufactured in

Japan.

46. (country)せい＜(country)製＞　Nd　made in (a country)

日本製のカメラは質がとてもいい。The cameras made in Japan are good quality.

47. つける＜付ける＞／付けます　V2　to attach

日本人はケータイにたくさんアクセサリーを付けている。Japanese people attach lots of accessories to their cellular phones.

48. こういん＜工員＞　N　factory worker

山本さんは自動車工場の工員として働いている。Mr. Yamamoto is working at the car factory as a factory worker.

49. どなる＜怒鳴る＞／怒鳴ります　V1　to shout; to yell

父は怒ったら、よく怒鳴る。When my father is upset, he often yells.

50. したう＜慕う＞／慕います　V1　to adore

松田先生は多くの生徒に慕われていた。Matsuda Sensei was adored by many students.

51. せいぜん＜生前＞　N　while alive

生前祖母は私をよく世話してくれた。My grandmother took good care of me while she was alive.

52. がくれき＜学歴＞　N　educational background

祖父は学歴が小学校だけだった。My grandfather's educational background only went through elementary school.

53. はずかしい＜恥ずかしい＞　A　ashamed; shy

分からない時人に聞くことは、恥ずかしい事ではない。It's not shameful to ask a person questions when you don't understand.

54. しっぱい＜失敗＞(を)する／します　V3　to fail

失敗しなければ成功しない。If you don't fail, you won't succeed.

55. おそれる＜怖れる＞／怖れます　V2　to fear; to be afraid [same as 怖がる]

失敗を怖れてはいけない。You should be afraid of failure.

56. じつりょく＜実力＞　N　real ability; merit

運も実力のうちだ。Luck is also part of your real ability.

57. のうりょく＜能力＞　N　ability; capability

自分の能力に挑戦し続けたい。I want to keep challenging my own abilities.

58. しんらい＜信頼＞(を)する／します　V3　to trust; to rely

しんらいできる＜信頼出来る＞／出来ます　V3　can rely on; can trust

本当に信頼出来る人が一人でもいればいい。It's good to have at least one person whom you can really trust.

《4課 - 3a・書く》

59. よてい＜予定＞　N　plans; schedule

この週末、何か予定がある？ Do you have any plans this weekend?

《4課 - 4b・話す》

60. ろうそく＜蝋燭＞　N　candle

バースデーケーキのろうそくにマッチで火をつけた。 I lit the candles for the birthday cake with a match.

《4課 - 4c・話す》 No new vocabulary

《4課 - 4d・話す》 No new vocabulary

《4課 - 4e・話す》 No new vocabulary

【分かればいい単語】

1. がくぶ＜学部＞	N	(university) academic department
2. くうはく＜空白＞	N	blank
3. けん＜県＞	N	prefecture
4. がくい＜学位＞	N	(university) degree
5. がくしごう＜学士号＞	N	bachelor's degree
6. しめい＜氏名＞	N	full name
7. せいねんがっぴ＜生年月日＞	N	full birthdate
8. ぼうずあたま＜坊主頭＞	N	shaven head (like a monk)
9. いれずみ＜入れ墨＞	N	tattoo
10. のべる＜述べる＞／述べます	V2	to describe; to mention
11. きゅうか＜休暇＞	N	vacation
12. てんきん＜転勤＞	N	(job) transfer

13. きすう＜奇数＞	N	odd number
14. ぐうすう＜偶数＞	N	even number
15. じょうし＜上司＞	N	boss
16. のしぶくろ＜のし袋＞	N	envelope for special occasions
17. かたみ＜形見＞	N	memento
18. ばかやろう＜馬鹿野郎＞	N	Idiot! [slang]
19. おやじさん＜親父さん＞	N	one's father; old man; one's boss [colloquial]

Noshi-bukuro for wedding (red & white)

Noshi-bukuro for funeral (black & white)

* Previously learned.

A. おいし＋そうだ。	It looks delicious.	→ AIJ 2 L.5＊
おいしい＋そうだ。	I heard that it is delicious.	→ AIJ 3 L.6＊
1a. 太郎君は頭が<u>良〔よ〕さ</u>そうだ。	Taro looks smart.	
1b. 太郎君は頭が<u>いい</u>そうだ。	I heard that Taro is smart.	
2a. このレストランは<u>静か</u>そうだ。	This restaurant looks quiet.	
2b. このレストランは<u>静かだ</u>そうだ。	I heard that this restaurant is quiet.	
3a. 今日は雨が<u>降り</u>そうだ。	It looks like it will rain today.	
3b. 今日は雨が<u>降る</u>そうだ。	I heard that it will rain today.	

英語に訳しなさい。

1. 島田さんはアルバイトをしたいそうだ。　_____

2. この大学は入学が難しそうだね。　_____

3. 松本さんは大学に進学しないそうだ。　_____

4. 姉は彼にふられて、泣きそうな顔をしている。　_____

B. 歌える＋ように＋なる	to become able to sing	→ AIJ 4 L.4＊
安く＋なる	to become cheap	→ AIJ 2 L.14＊
静か＋に＋なる	to become quiet	→ AIJ 2 L.14＊
先生＋に＋なる	to become a teacher	→ AIJ 2 L.14＊

「〜なる」の文型（けい）を使って文を終わらせなさい。

1. 毎日漢字を勉強しているから、日本語の新聞が少し_____。

2. 日本語を勉強して、日本人と日本語で_____。

3. 地球温暖化で地球が少しずつ_____。

4. 私は将来_____。

5. 弟はだんだん背（せ）が_____。

6. このクリームを使ったら顔がだんだん_____と書いてある。

C. 行く＋ことに＋した／決めた　　　decided to go　　　　　　→ AIJ 4 L.2＊

行く＋ことに＋なった／決まった　It has been decided that (I) go. → AIJ 4 L.2＊
The ことにする construction indicates the action of one's own decision. The ことに
なる construction is a common expression which allows the speaker to indicate
that he/she is obligated or is somehow doing the action not entirely at his/her own
will.

a. 英訳しなさい。

1. 「先生、私はプリンストン大学へ行くことになりました。」

_____

2. 「先生、私は日本に留学することになりました。楽しみにしています。」

_____

3. 「先生、日本語のスピーチコンテストに優勝して、日本へ行くことになりました。」

_____

4. 「先生、JETプログラムで日本の中学校で英語を教えることになったんですよ。」

_____

b. なぜ日本人は「〜ことになりました」をよく使うのでしょうか。意見を書きなさい。

_____

c. 次の文型を使って文を作りなさい。そして、その英訳も書きなさい。

1. 〜ことにしました

_____

2. 〜ことになりました

_____

D. 飲まず(に)　　　　　　without/instead of drinking　　　→ AIJ 4 L.7＊

食べず(に)　　　　　　without/instead of eating

勉強せず(に)　　　　　without/instead of studying

来〔こ〕ず(に)　　　　without/instead of coming

This form is the formal negative form of -ないで and is used most commonly in
written form, but it is also occasionally used in more formal speaking situations.

四課

下線に適当な動詞を「-ず(に)」を使って書きなさい。

1. 大学に＿＿＿＿＿＿＿＿＿＿、働くつもりだ。

2. 今日試験があったので、ゆうべ＿＿＿＿＿＿＿＿＿＿、勉強した。

3. 感謝の気持ちを＿＿＿＿＿＿＿＿＿、生きて行きたい。

4. 花子はプロムに彼を＿＿＿＿＿＿＿＿＿、友達と来た。

E.　趣味は本を読むことです。　　My hobby is reading books.　　→ AIJ 2 L.1＊

下線に「-ことです」を使って、答えなさい。

1. 私の今学期の目標は、＿＿＿＿＿＿＿＿＿＿＿＿＿＿＿＿＿＿＿＿＿＿＿＿＿。

2. 今年の目標は、＿＿＿＿＿＿＿＿＿＿＿＿＿＿＿＿＿＿＿＿＿＿＿＿＿。

3. 私の将来の夢は、＿＿＿＿＿＿＿＿＿＿＿＿＿＿＿＿＿＿＿＿＿＿＿。

4. この学校の良い点は、＿＿＿＿＿＿＿＿＿＿＿＿＿＿＿＿＿＿＿＿＿＿＿。

F.　Usage of も　　　　　　　　　　　　　　　　　　→ AIJ 1 L.3＊
　　〜も〜も＋ Affirmative predicate　　Both 〜 and 〜　　→ AIJ 1 L.3＊
　　〜も〜も＋ Negative predicate　　　Neither 〜 nor 〜　　→ AIJ 1 L.3＊

（　　）の中に下から正しい助詞を選んで書きなさい。何度使ってもよろしい。

父は一月に東京へ行った。母（　　）一月（　　）東京（　　）行った。

父（　　）一月（　　）大阪（　　）行った。

父（　　）一月（　　）東京（　　）大阪（　　）行った。

父（　　）二月（　　）東京（　　）行った。

父（　　）一月（　　）二月（　　）東京（　　）行った。

父（　　）母（　　）一月（　　）東京（　　）行った。

父（　　）母（　　）一月（　　）北海道（　　）行かなかった。

は　も　へ　へも　に　にも　で　でも

G. おかげさまで、〜	Thanks to you, 〜	→ AIJ 3 L.3 *
両親のおかげで、〜	Thanks to my parents, 〜	
日本語を習ったおかげで、〜	Thanks to having learned Japanese, 〜	

下線のところに感謝する人や事を書きなさい。

1. Your friend's parents made your birthday party very special, so you want to thank them before leaving their house.

　「＿＿＿＿＿＿＿＿＿＿＿＿＿＿＿＿＿＿＿、今日はとても楽しかったです。」

2. You are writing a thank-you letter to your teacher. You want to thank your teacher for teaching you Japanese well, so you can speak Japanese well.

　＿＿＿＿＿＿＿＿＿＿＿＿＿＿＿＿＿＿＿、私は日本語が上手になりました。

3. In a thank-you letter, you thank your teacher for writing a college recommendation, so you can go to college.

　＿＿＿＿＿＿＿＿＿＿＿＿＿＿＿＿＿＿＿、私は大学へ行くことが出来ます。

4. In a Japanese speech, you thank your classmates for your wonderful high school time.

　＿＿＿＿＿＿＿＿＿＿＿＿＿＿＿＿＿＿＿、私は楽しい高校生活が過ごせました。

A. 学部と職業：ペアワーク→クラスワーク

どんな学部に行きたいと思いますか。どんな職業をしたいと思いますか。ベスト１〜３と読み方と英語の訳を空白に書きなさい。そして、クラスで発表しなさい。

ベスト1〜3	学部名	読みがな	英訳	ベスト1〜3	職業	読みがな	英訳
	1. 法学部				1. 医者		
	2. 経済学部				2. 歯医者		
	3. 文学部				3. 獣医	じゅうい	
	4. 理学部				4. 看護婦	かんごふ	
	5. 工学部				5. 弁護士	べんごし	
	6. 農学部	のうがくぶ			6. 会計士		
	7. 教育学部				7. 教師		
	8. 医学部				8. 教授		
	9. 薬学部				9. 建築家	けんちくか	
	10. 美術学部				10. 警官	けいかん	
	11. 音楽学部				11. 消防士	しょうぼうし	
	12. 体育学部				12. ビジネスマン		
	13. 外国語学部				13. コック		
					14. 芸術家		
					15. 銀行家		
					16. エンジニア		
					17.		

B. 大学でどこまで学位を取りたいと思いますか。取りたいと思う学位を全部丸しなさい。

学士号（しごう）　修士号（しゅうしごう）　博士号（はかせごう）　MBA

C. 「プロフィール」について：ペアワーク→クラスワーク

上のプロフィールの例（れい）を見ながら、下の「私のプロフィール」の空白に漢字の読みがな
と個人情報（じょうほう）を書きなさい。

●プロフィール●

氏名：吉島進
出身地：福岡県福岡市
生年月日：１９７７年９月６日
星座：乙女座
身長：177 ㎝
体重：65 ㎏
血液型：A 型
スポーツ：テニス
特技：料理、デッサン
得意な学科：美術、科学、数学
好きな言葉：「感謝の気持ちを忘れずに」
趣味：音楽鑑賞、ダンス

私のプロフィール	読みがな	個人情報
氏名		
出身地		
生年月日		
干支〔えと〕		
星座		
身長（センチ）		
体重（キロ）		
血液型		
スポーツ		
特技		
得意な学科		
好きな言葉		
趣味		

四課

D. 「日本での就職時の面接試験のマナー」について：ペアワーク→クラスワーク

　日本で就職をしたい場合、面接試験があります。面接の時のマナーについて、正しいと思う言葉に○をしなさい。それか、答えなさい。

1. 面接の服装は（清潔　不潔）な服装をする。

2. 面接の時、着て行く服装は（リクルートスーツ　ビジネススーツ）と呼ばれている。

3. 面接の服装は（派手　地味）な方がいい。

4. 面接の服装の色は（グレイや紺色　黒や白　青や黄色）がいい。

5. 面接の時、男性はスーツとタイが（必要だ　必要ではない）。

6. 面接の時、言葉使いは（ていねい語　敬語）を使う。

7. 面接の時、女性はメークを（派手にする　地味にする　全然しない）方がいい。

8. 面接の時、男性の髪型は（長い髪　茶髪　短い髪　坊主頭）がいい。

9. 面接の時、男性はピアスを（していても問題はない　しない方がいい）。

10. 面接の時、入れ墨を（していても問題はない　していれば問題になる）。

11. 面接の時、（明るく元気に　暗く静かに）話す方がいい。

12. ビル・ゲイツ氏は面接試験の時に「あなたは富士山をどう動かしますか。」というような質問したそうです。どう答えますか。

13. 日本の面接のマナーについての意見を述べなさい。

E. 仕事を選ぶ時に何が大事？：ペアワーク→クラスワーク

　仕事を選ぶ時、何が大事ですか。ベスト１〜３を書きなさい。

ベスト１〜３	仕事を選ぶ時、何が大事？
	給料〔きゅうりょう〕がいい仕事
	人やコミュニティーの役〔やく〕に立てる仕事
	情熱〔じょうねつ〕をかけられる仕事
	好きな場所で働ける仕事
	休暇〔きゅうか〕が多い仕事
	健康保険〔けんこうほけん〕や退職金〔たいしょくきん〕やボーナスなどが良い仕事
	転勤がある (or ない) 仕事

F. 人生すごろくゲーム：ペアーかグループワーク

a. ゲームの単語の勉強をしましょう。空白の中に単語の読み方と英訳を書きなさい。

単語	読み方	英訳	単語	読み方	英訳
1. 誕生			21. 成人式		
2. お宮参り	おみやまいり	shrine visit	22. 就職活動		
3. 偶数	ぐうすう		23. 年末		
4. 端午の節句	たんごのせっく	Boy's Day	24. 恋人		
5. 奇数	きすう		25. 結婚		
6. ひな祭り			26. 長男出産		
7. 幼稚園			27. 転職		
8. 入園式			28. 長女出産		
9. 遠足			29. 厄年	やくどし	unlucky year
10. 忘れ物			30. 厄払い	やくばらい	exorcism
11. 祝い			31. 過労	かろう	overwork
12. 卒園式			32. 入院		
13. 転校			33. 退職	たいしょく	
14. 初恋			34. 還暦	かんれき	60th birthday
15. 高校受験			35. 葬式		
16. 橋を渡る			36. 米寿	べいじゅ	88th birthday
17. 活躍			37. 賞金		
18. 準備			38. 一等	いっとう	
19. 予備校			39. すごろく		a child's dice game
20. 合格			40. さいころ		dice

b. ゲームを遊びましょう!　Necessary items: Dice and markers for each player.
  Instructions:
  1) Each player rolls the dice to determine the order of players. Highest score goes first.
  2) Each player rolls the dice and advances accordingly. Read instructions at each spot on which the player lands. Keep track of the amount of money gained/lost at each occasion.
  3) Take turns the goal earns 2,000 yen and the second to reach the goal receives 1,000 yen.
  4) After all players are finished, count up the money each player has earned. The player with the most money wins the game.

人生すごろくゲーム

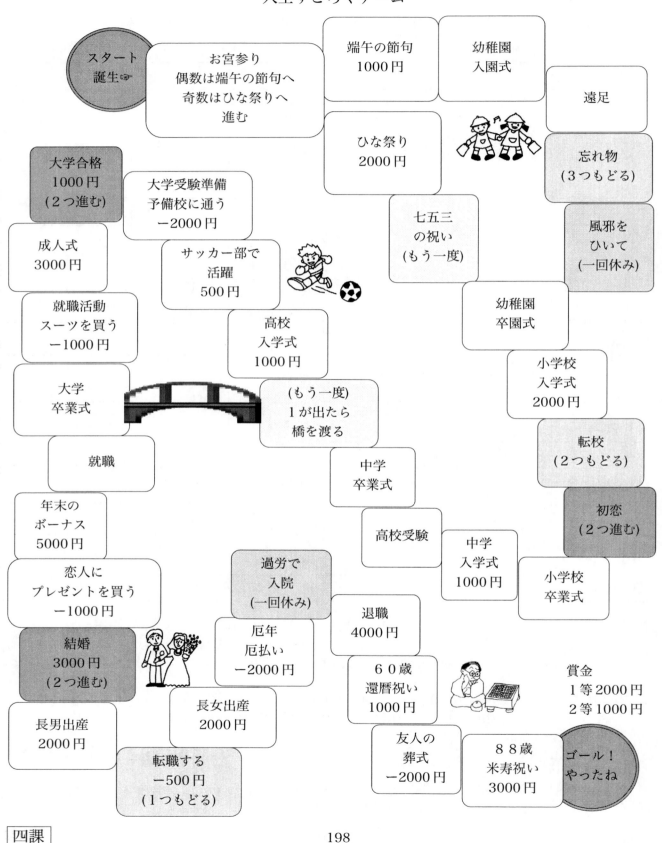

スタート
誕生☞

お宮参り
偶数は端午の節句へ
奇数はひな祭りへ
進む

端午の節句
1000円

幼稚園
入園式

遠足

ひな祭り
2000円

忘れ物
(3つもどる)

大学合格
1000円
(2つ進む)

大学受験準備
予備校に通う
－2000円

七五三
の祝い
(もう一度)

風邪を
ひいて
(一回休み)

成人式
3000円

サッカー部で
活躍
500円

幼稚園
卒園式

就職活動
スーツを買う
－1000円

高校
入学式
1000円

小学校
入学式
2000円

大学
卒業式

(もう一度)
1が出たら
橋を渡る

転校
(2つもどる)

就職

中学
卒業式

初恋
(2つ進む)

年末の
ボーナス
5000円

高校受験

中学
入学式
1000円

小学校
卒業式

過労で
入院
(一回休み)

恋人に
プレゼントを買う
－1000円

退職
4000円

厄年
厄払い
－2000円

結婚
3000円
(2つ進む)

60歳
還暦祝い
1000円

賞金
1等2000円
2等1000円

長女出産
2000円

長男出産
2000円

友人の
葬式
－2000円

88歳
米寿祝い
3000円

ゴール！
やったね

転職する
－500円
(1つもどる)

G. 日本の四季：ペアーワーク→クラスワーク

a. 日本の季節の言葉の読みと英訳と季節を書きなさい。

風物	読み	英訳	季節	風物	読み	英訳	季節
1. 七五三				21. ひな祭り			
2. 引っ越し				22. 遠足			
3. お花見				23. 梅	うめ		
4. バラ				24. 梅雨	つゆ/ばいう		
5. 朝顔				25. こたつ			
6. ひまわり				26. 門松	かどまつ		
7. 獅子舞	ししまい			27. 運動会			
8. 秋祭り				28. 卒業式			
9. 芸術				29. 紅葉	もみじ/こうよう		
10. とんぼ				30. あやめ			
11. 桜				31. あじさい			
12. 海水浴	かいすいよく			32. 羽子板	はごいた		
13. 花火大会				33. お月見			
14. カブト虫				34. 入学式			
15. サンタクロース				35. すいか			
16. クリスマスツリー				36. いちょう			
17. 七夕				37. 風鈴	ふうりん		
18. 鯉のぼり				38. 雪だるま			
19. 読書				39. 初日の出	はつひので		
20. どんぐり				40. 凧揚げ	たこあげ		

四課

b. それぞれの絵は何ですか。前のページのリストから選んで、（　）の中に書きなさい。
　そして、日本の季節についての意見と感想を書きなさい。

四季	季節の行事と風物と花					意見と感想
春	（　　　　）	（　　　　）	（　　　　）	（　　　　）	（　　　　）	
	（　　　　）	（　　　　）	（　　　　）	（　　　　）	（　　　　）	
夏	（　　　　）	（　　　　）	（　　　　）	（　　　　）	（　　　　）	
	（　　　　）	（　　　　）	（　　　　）	（　　　　）	（　　　　）	
秋	（　　　　）	（　　　　）	（　　　　）	（　　　　）	（　　　　）	
	（　　　　）	（　　　　）	（　　　　）	（　　　　）	（　　　　）	
冬	（　　　　）	（　　　　）	（　　　　）	（　　　　）	（　　　　）	
	（　　　　）	（　　　　）	（　　　　）	（　　　　）	（　　　　）	

H. 贈り物の習慣：ペアワーク→クラスワーク

a. 日本にはいろいろな贈り物の習慣があります。（　）の中に下から適当な言葉を選んで書きなさい。

1. だれかのうちを訪問する時、お菓子とかの（　　　　　　　）を持って行く習慣がある。

2. 旅行から帰って来ると、家族や友人に旅行へ行った場所の（　　　　　　）をあげる習慣がある。

3. お世話になった両親やおじいさんおばあさんや会社の上司などに、夏のお盆の頃に、
（　　　　　　　）を、年の暮れに（　　　　　　　）をあげる習慣がある。贈り物は
（　　　　　　　）とかコーヒーなどが多く、（　　　　　　）から直接、自宅へ送って
もらうことが一般的だ。

4. ２月１４日の（　　　　　　）に女性は好きな男性にチョコレートをあげて、一カ月後
の３月１４日には男性が女性に（　　　　　　）として白いチョコレートを送る日がある。
これを（　　　　　　）と言う。

5. 結婚式に（　　　　　）として、お葬式に（　　　　　）として、（　　　　　）を
のし袋に入れてあげる習慣がある。祝う時は（　　　　　　）と白ののし袋で、お葬式
には（　　　　　　）と白ののし袋を使う。

お土産　御中元　現金　ホワイトデー　香典　御歳暮　手土産		
お返し　黒　商品券　赤　バレンタインデー　お祝い　デパート		

b. 日本の贈り物の習慣についての意見、感想を述べなさい。

_____

_____

_____

四課

I. お礼状：ペアワーク→一人ワーク

a. 次のお礼状を読んで、質問に日本語で答えなさい。

　1. ケンさんはどんな将来の夢を持っていますか。

　2. ケンさんは日本語を勉強して、人間としてどう変わったと言っていますか。

　3. ケンさんはなぜ橋本先生にお礼状を書くことにしましたか。

　先生、お元気ですか。私は今年、高校を卒業し、スタンフォード大学に行くことになりました。卒業する前に、先生に一言お礼を申し上げたいです。

　先生のクラスにいた時のことを懐かしく思い出します。先生のクラスにいた時、私はあまりいい生徒ではありませんでしたね。あまり宿題もせずに、勉強もしませんでしたが、先生はいつも私を励ましてくださいました。おかげさまで日本語はだんだんおもしろくなって行きました。今はだいたい日本人と日本語で話せるし、日本の文化が分かるようになりました。日本語を習ったおかげで、*謙虚な人間になったような気がします。カラオケで日本語の歌が歌えるようになったし、日本語のテレビドラマも見るようになりました。そして、戦争体験のプロジェクトで祖父にインタビューした後、その祖父が亡くなって、あの祖父のビデオが貴重な形見になりました。茶道や生け花や書道をしたこともいい経験になりました。今日本人と話せる自信があります。大学へ行っても日本語を続けるつもりです。そして、日本の大学に留学したいです。将来の夢は、地球科学を専攻して、日米両国で仕事をすることです。

　いろいろお世話になりました。教えて下さいまして、ありがとうございました。心より感謝しております。お元気でお過ごし下さい。

　　　　　六月一日

　　橋本町子先生

　　　　　　　　　　　　ケン・スミス

<ruby>謙虚<rt>けんきょ</rt></ruby>
*謙虚

b. 大学の<ruby>推薦状<rt>すいせんじょう</rt></ruby>を書いていただいた先生に日本語でお礼状を書きなさい。

＜4課-1・聞く＞

聞く： Interview

(Narrator) Now you will listen once to a graduate school interview between Ken and a Japanese college professor.

四課

(Narrator) Now answer the questions for this section.

1.   When did Ken study in Japan?
     (A)   When he was in the 11th grade.
     (B)   After he graduated from high school.
     (C)   When he was a junior in college.
     (D)   After he graduated from college.

2.   Which one of the following choices is NOT related to Ken's study of interest?
     (A)   Environment
     (B)   Science
     (C)   Economics
     (D)   City planning

3.   What did Ken study while in Japan?
     (A)   The study of converting sea water to drinking water and city planning on the moon.
     (B)   The study of drinking water and city planning in Japan.
     (C)   The study of civil engineering and city planning on the moon.
     (D)   The study of sea water and environmental consulting.

4.   Why does Ken want to study at a Japanese graduate school?
     (A)   He wants to improve his Japanese.
     (B)   He thinks that Japanese society is more advanced in dealing with environmental issues.
     (C)   He made many friends while he studied in Japan.
     (D)   He wants to pursue a career in international business.

5.   Which one is NOT his dream for the future?
     (A)   He wants to get a job in an environmental consulting firm.
     (B)   He want to earn a higher salary and become rich.
     (C)   He wants to solve environmental problems.
     (D)   He wants to engage in a helpful job.

＜4課 - 2・読む＞

読む: Honda

Read this excerpt taken from a letter by a Japanese teacher to Ken.

　本田宗一郎という人を知っていますか。今の世界のHONDAの創業者です。戦後、彼は貧乏のどん底にあった日本の中から、現代日本を代表する企業を始めました。本田氏は静岡の町工場で仕事を始めました。一番初めに作った物は、「バタバタ」という製品だったそうです。奥さんが買物に行く時、その荷物が重そうなので、自転車にモーターをつけたら楽になると思い、第一号を作りました。それがよく売れたそうです。本田氏はよく工員に「ばかやろう」とどなっていたそうです。しかし、彼のニックネームは「親父さん」で、工場の工員に「親父さん」「親父さん」と呼ばれて、「お父さん」のように慕われていたようです。このお話から、本田氏がこわいけど、温かい人だったことが分かります。

　彼が生前言った言葉がたくさん残されています。君に紹介したいと思います。彼の学歴は小学校だけでした。でも、本田氏は言っています。「僕は学歴がないから、ほかの人に教えてもらうことを全然恥ずかしいと思わなかった。」「人が喜ぶ物を作れば必ず売れる。」「一人では成功出来ない。人と協力出来なければ、何事も成功しない。」「失敗をおそれるな。９９％の失敗から１％の成功が産まれる。」「運も実力のうちだ。」などです。

　自分の能力に挑戦し続け、人をいつも信頼し、人の喜ぶ物を作り続けた彼の人生は、本当にすばらしいと思います。君にもぜひ彼について書かれた本を読んでほしいです。

四課

読む: Honda

(Narrator)   Now answer the questions for this section.

1.   What inspired Mr. Honda to make his first product?
     (A)   His love towards his wife
     (B)   His love towards his product
     (C)   Poverty
     (D)   Speed

2.   What kind of person was Mr. Honda?
     (A)   Mr. Honda started his factory even before World War II.
     (B)   Mr. Honda started his factory in a big city.
     (C)   Mr. Honda yelled at his workers a lot.
     (D)   Mr. Honda was called "Emperor" by his workers.

3.   What was the highest level of education Mr. Honda completed?
     (A)   College
     (B)   High school
     (C)   Junior high school
     (D)   Elementary school

4.   What value did Mr. Honda NOT insist on in his quotes?
     (A)   Make products that please people.
     (B)   Collaborate with people.
     (C)   Don't worry to make a mistake.
     (D)   Make products at a low cost.

5.   What does the teacher want Ken to do in the letter?
     (A)   He wants Ken to read many Japanese books to improve his Japanese.
     (B)   He wants Ken to read books about Mr. Honda to learn from his life.
     (C)   He wants Ken to finish his college degree soon.
     (D)   He wants Ken to become a famous person like Mr. Honda.

＜４課 - 3a・書く＞

Text Chat: Future

Note: In this part of the exam, the student may not move back and forth among the questions.

You will participate in a simulated exchange of text-chat-messages. You will have 90 seconds to write your answer when it is your turn. You should respond as fully and as appropriately as possible.

You will have a conversation about your future plans with Kaori, a student at a Japanese school.

1. Respond. (90 seconds)

    今日はありがとうございます。ところで、進学先の大学はもう決まりましたか。どんな大学ですか。

2. Respond. (90 seconds)

    大学では何を専攻するつもりですか。

3. Describe your plan. (90 seconds)

    大学を卒業したら、大学院にも行って、修士号とか博士号も取る予定ですか。

4. Explain your preference. (90 seconds)

    将来、どんな職業につきたいと希望していますか。

5. State your opinion. (90 seconds)

    いい給料をもらうのと、好きな仕事をするのと、どちらの方が大事だと思いますか。

6. Ask a specific question. (90 seconds)

    私も今年は大学受験の年ですが、何か日本の受験について質問がありますか。

四課

Compare and Contrast:

Thanksgiving, Christmas and New Year's Day in the U.S.

You are writing an article for the student newspaper of your sister school in Japan. Choose two American annual events from Thanksgiving, Christmas and New Year's Day and write an article in which you compare and contrast two of these annual events. Based on your personal experiences, describe at least THREE similarities and differences between the two American annual events. Also state your preference and give reasons for it.

Your article should be 300 to 400 characters or longer. Use the *desu/masu* or *da* (plain) style, but use one style consistently. Also, use *kanji* wherever *kanji* from the AP Japanese *kanji* list is appropriate. You have 20 minutes to write.

【自分の作文のアウトラインを書こう！】

Introduction:

_____

Your two choices:

_____

Three similarities and differences:

   1. _____

   2. _____

   3. _____

Your preference and give reasons:

_____

_____

＜４課 - 3c・書く＞

Cultural Topic Posting: Rites of Life

You are responding to a posting in a Web forum for high school students studying Japanese. The posting asks about rites of life. Select ONE Japanese rite of life, such as weddings, funerals, graduations, etc. Describe in detail at least THREE characteristics of the rite of life as celebrated in Japan. Also, express your opinion or feelings about the rite of life.

Your posting should be 300 to 400 characters or longer. Use the *desu/masu* or *da* (plain) style, but use one style consistently. Also, use *kanji* wherever *kanji* from the AP Japanese *kanji* list is appropriate. You have 20 minutes to write.

【自分の作文のアウトラインを書こう！】

Introduction:

_____

One example:

_____

Three characteristics of the rite of life:

1. _____

2. _____

3. _____

Your opinion and feelings:

_____

_____

四課

Conversation: Birthday Party

You will participate in a simulated conversation. Each time it is your turn to speak, you will have 20 seconds to record. You should respond as fully and as appropriately as possible.

You will have a conversation with Emi who is your friend.

(Emi)

(20 seconds)

(Emi)

(20 seconds)

(Emi)

(20 seconds)

(Emi)

(20 seconds)

15点
20秒×4

Return Telephone Call: Part-time Job

You will participate in a simulated telephone conversation with someone you are calling back after receiving a message. First, you will listen to the voice message. Then the telephone call will begin. Each time it is your turn to speak, you will have 20 seconds to record. You should respond as fully and as appropriately as possible.

(Narrator)   Listen to the voice message.

(Woman)

(Narrator)   Now the telephone call will begin. After the phone is answered, begin with a greeting and then explain why you are calling.

(Woman)   [Telephone] [Rings twice and picks up]

(20 seconds)

(Woman)

(20 seconds)

(Woman)

(20 seconds)

(Woman)

(20 seconds)

School Announcement: Funeral

Directions: Imagine that you are making an announcement in Japanese to an assembly of Japanese students studying English at your school. First, you will see some notes in English about what to include in your announcement. You will have 1 minute to prepare your announcement while you look at the notes. Then you will have 1 minute to record your announcement. Your announcement should have an opening remark, details according to the notes, and a closing remark. Deliver your announcement using complete sentences in *desu/masu* style.

Announcement of your English teacher Mr. Matsui's funeral.
You are invited to the funeral.
The funeral is next Saturday, December 8th, 11:30 a.m. - 1:30 p.m.
The location is the school chapel.
The attire is uniform.
Monetary gifts are not necessary.

Story Narration: Life

Directions: Imagine that you are making an oral presentation to your Japanese class. In your presentation, you will narrate a story. First, you will see pictures depicting the story. You will have 4 minutes to prepare your narration while you look at the pictures. Then you will have 2 minutes to record your narration. Narrate your story using complete sentences in *desu/masu* style.

213

四課

Cultural Perspective Presentation: Japanese Holidays

Directions: Imagine you are making an oral presentation to your Japanese class. First, you will read and hear the topic for your presentation. You will have 4 minutes to prepare your presentation. Then you will have 2 minutes to record your presentation. Your presentation should be as full as possible.

Present your own view or perspective on Japanese holidays. Discuss at least FIVE aspects or examples of the Japanese holidays.

Begin with an appropriate introduction, give details, explain your own view or perspective, and end with a concluding remark.

【Let's take notes!】

1. Begin with an appropriate introduction.

_____

2. Discuss five aspects/examples of the topic.

     1.) _____

     2.) _____

     3.) _____

     4.) _____

     5.) _____

3. Explain your view or perspective.

_____

4. End with a concluding remark.

_____

At the end of this lesson, you are expected to be able to handle the following tasks.

【AP-5課 タスク1：交通】

Discuss dangerous driving in our daily lives. Share an experience of car accident that you have been involved in or have seen. How can we change our lifestyle in order to improve sustainability? Discuss the pros and cons of mass transit systems.

【AP-5課 タスク2：天気と気候】

Predict tomorrow's weather by forecasting information such as average temperatures in centigrade and the probability of rain or other kinds of weather. How can we change our daily lives in order to save energy even in very hot or cold climates?

調べよう！

A. 地方

北海道地方

東北地方

関東地方

中部地方

近畿地方

中国地方

四国地方

九州地方

沖縄地方

（地図：北海道、東北、中部、関東、中国、近畿、四国、九州、沖縄）

B. 梅雨前線、桜前線、紅葉前線

C. 温度：摂氏と華氏

Centigrade ℃ = (Fahrenheit °F － 32) × 5 ÷ 9

Fahrenheit °F = Centigrade ℃ × 9 ÷ 5 + 32

風速：メートルとマイル

D. エコマーク、クールビズ、ウォームビズ

E. OB、二次会

F. バイク　オートバイ　自家用車　軽自動車　中古車　エコ車　ヘルメット　高速道路

[*Kanji* in text font]

1. 背　height　　　　せ　　　背が高〔たか〕い tall (for height)

　　　　　　　　　　　　　背中〔せなか〕 back (body)

2. 低　low,　　　　ひく(い)　低い机 low desk

　　　short　　　　　　　　背〔せ〕が低い short (for height)

　　　(for height)　テイ　最低気温〔さいていきおん〕

　　　　　　　　　　　　　lowest temperature

　　　　　　　　　　　　　低気圧〔ていきあつ〕 low

　　　　　　　　　　　　　(atmospheric) pressure

3. 形　shape　　　　かたち　色〔いろ〕と形 color and shape

　　　　　　　　　　かた/がた　形見〔かたみ〕 memento

　　　　　　　　　　ケイ　三角形〔さんかっけい〕 triangular

4. 急　to hurry　　　いそ(ぐ)　急〔いそ〕げ！Hurry up!

　　　　　　　　　　　　　急がば回れ〔いそがばまわれ〕

　　　　　　　　　　　　　Less haste, more speed.

　　　　　　　　　　キュウ　急に〔きゅうに〕 suddenly

　　　　　　　　　　　　　急行〔きゅうこう〕 express

　　　　　　　　　　　　　特急〔とっきゅう〕 super express

　　　　　　　　　　　　　至急〔しきゅう〕 urgent

　　　　　　　　　　　　　急停車〔きゅうていしゃ〕 sudden stop

217

5. 忙　busy　　　いそが(しい)　忙しい日〔ひ〕a busy day

　　　　　　　　ボウ　　　　多忙〔たぼう〕very busy

6. 側　side　　　ガワ　　　　右側〔みぎがわ〕right side

　　　　　　　　　　　　　　左側〔ひだりがわ〕left side

7. 酒　rice wine,　さけ　　　　酒を飲〔の〕む drink alcohol
　　　alcohol　　シュ　　　　日本酒〔にほんしゅ〕Japanese
　　　　　　　　　　　　　　rice wine

　　　　　　　　　　　　　　飲酒運転〔いんしゅうんてん〕
　　　　　　　　　　　　　　drunken-driving

8. 調　to check,　しら(べる)　大学〔だいがく〕を調べる
　　　to investigate　　　　　investigate colleges
　　　　　　　　チョウ　　　調査〔ちょうさ〕する to check

　　　　　　　　　　　　　　調子〔ちょうし〕がいい
　　　　　　　　　　　　　　in good condition

9. 横　side　　　よこ　　　　木〔き〕の横 beside the tree
　　　　　　　　　　　　　　横山〔よこやま〕さん
　　　　　　　　　　　　　　Yokoyama-san
　　　　　　　　オウ　　　　横断歩道〔おうだんほどう〕
　　　　　　　　　　　　　　pedestrian crossing
　　　　　　　　　　　　　　横転〔おうてん〕turning sideways

10. 橋 bridge　　　　はし　　　　橋を渡る cross the bridge

橋本〔はしもと〕さん

Hashimoto-san

キョウ　　　歩道橋〔ほどうきょう〕pedestrian bridge

11. 飛 to fly　　　　と(ぶ)　　　空〔そら〕を飛ぶ fly through the sky

ヒ　　　　　飛行機〔ひこうき〕airplane

12. 機 machine,　　キ　　　　　飛行機〔ひこうき〕airplane

機械〔きかい〕machine

洗濯機〔せんたくき〕washing machine

掃除機〔そうじき〕vacuum cleaner

皿洗い機〔さらあらいき〕dishwasher

公共交通機関〔こうきょうこうつうきかん〕

public transportation system

opportunity　　　機会〔きかい〕chance

13. 線 line　　　　セン　　　　新幹線〔しんかんせん〕bullet train

山の手線〔やまのてせん〕

Yamanote Line

白線〔はくせん〕white line

車線〔しゃせん〕car lane

下線〔かせん〕underline

点線〔てんせん〕dotted line

14. 便 convenience　ベン　　　便利〔べんり〕convenient

不便〔ふべん〕inconvenient

便所〔べんじょ〕toilet

ビン　　　郵便〔ゆうびん〕mail

郵便箱〔ゆうびんばこ〕mail box

JAL 2 便〔にびん〕JAL Flight #2

たよ(り)　(お)便り letter

15. 利 advantage　リ　　　便利〔べんり〕convenient

利用〔りよう〕する to utilize

16. 配 to distribute　くば(る)　贈り物〔おくりもの〕を配る

deliver the gifts

ハイ/パイ　心配〔しんぱい〕する to worry

配達人〔はいたつにん〕delivery person

17. 写 to copy　シャ　　写真〔しゃしん〕photo

複写〔ふくしゃ〕する to copy

複写機〔ふくしゃき〕copy machine

18. 予 previously　ヨ　　　予習〔よしゅう〕する to preview

天気予報〔てんきよほう〕

weather forecast

予選〔よせん〕primary

予約〔よやく〕する to reserve

予定〔よてい〕plan; schedule

19. 払 to pay　　　　はら(う)　　　お金を払う to pay money

【読みかえの漢字】　　　* Previously introduced.

1. 降　to fall,　　ふ(る)＊　　　雪〔ゆき〕が降る It will snow.
　　　　to get off　お(りる)＊　　車〔くるま〕を降りる to get off a car
　　　　　　　　　コウ　　　　　降水量〔こうすいりょう〕level of precipitation

2. 小　small　　ちい(さい)＊　小さい花〔はな〕small flowers
　　　　　　　　　ショウ＊　　　小学校〔しょうがっこう〕elementary school
　　　　　　　　　コ　　　　　　小型〔こがた〕small size

3. 古　old　　　ふる(い)＊　　古い家〔いえ〕old house
　　　　　　　　　コ　　　　　　中古車〔ちゅうこしゃ〕used car

4. 遅　to be late　おそ(い)＊　　遅くなりました。 Sorry to be late.
　　　　　　　　　チ＊　　　　　遅刻〔ちこく〕tardy
　　　　　　　　　おく(れる)　　クラスに遅れた was late to class

5. 幸　happy　　しあわ(せ)＊　幸せな生活〔せいかつ〕happy (daily) lifestyle
　　　　　　　　　コウ＊　　　　幸福〔こうふく〕な一生〔いっしょう〕happy life
　　　　　　　　　さいわ(い)　　幸い luckily

6. 助　to rescue　たす(ける)＊　助けて！ Help!
　　　　　　　　　ジョ　　　　　助手〔じょしゅ〕assistant

7. 治　to be cured　なお(る)＊　病気〔びょうき〕が治った My illness is cured.
　　　　　　　　　ジ＊　　　　　政治〔せいじ〕politics
　　　　　　　　　チ　　　　　　治療〔ちりょう〕treatment

221　　　　　　　　　　　　　　　　　五課

【読めればいい漢字】

1. 道路	どうろ	road
2. 大丈夫	だいじょうぶ	all right
3. 危ない	あぶない	dangerous
4. 危険	きけん	danger
5. 駐車	ちゅうしゃ	parking
6. 禁止	きんし	prohibition
7. 違反	いはん	violation
8. (天気)予報	(てんき)よほう	(weather) forecast
9. 気候	きこう	climate
10. 明後日	あさって	the day after tomorrow
11. 消す	けす	to turn off
12. 太陽	たいよう	sun
13. 事故	じこ	accident

《Activity A》

1. ほこうしゃ＜歩行者＞　N　pedestrians

歩行者に気をつけて運転する。I pay attention to the pedestrians as I drive.

2. おうだんほどう＜横断歩道＞　N　pedestrian crossing

ほどう＜歩道＞　N　sidewalk

横断歩道を渡ろう。Let's cross at the pedestrian crossing.

3. ちゅうこしゃ＜中古車＞　N　used car

両親に中古車を買ってもらった。I had my parents buy a used car.

4. しゅうり＜修理＞(を)する／します　V3　to repair

車を修理に出している。I sent my car to be repaired.

5. いんしゅうんてん＜飲酒運転＞　N　drunken driving

飲酒運転は本当に危ない。Drunken driving is truly dangerous.

6. いねむり＜居眠り＞(を)する／します　V3　to doze

いねむりうんてん＜居眠り運転＞　N　falling asleep while driving

居眠り運転をして事故を起こしてしまった。I fell asleep while driving and caused an accident.

7. タイヤがパンクする／します　V3　to have a flat tire

学校へ来る途中、タイヤがパンクしてしまった。On the way to school, I got a flat tire.

8. ほうりつ＜法律＞　N　law

法律は守るはずだ。We are supposed to follow the laws.

9. きんし＜禁止＞(を)する／します　V3　to prohibit

ちゅうしゃきんし＜駐車禁止＞　N　No Parking

駐車禁止の所に駐車したら、切符を切られた。When I parked in a no parking zone, I got a ticket.

10. おいこす＜追い越す＞／追い越します　V1　to overtake (e.g. a car)

おいこし＜追い越し＞(を)する／します　V3　to overtake (e.g. a car)

追い越しをする時には、よく隣りの車線を見ること。When you pass a car, watch the next lane well.

11. しょうとつ＜衝突＞(を)する／します　V3　to collide

　　しょうとつじこ＜衝突事故＞　N　collision (accident)

　　しょうめんしょうとつ＜正面衝突＞　N　head-on collision

　　前の車に衝突しそうになった。I almost collided with the car in front.

12. きゅうていしゃ＜急停車＞(を)する／します　V3　to stop suddenly

　　前の車が急停車をしたから、衝突してしまった。Because the car in front of me stopped

　　suddenly, I collided with it.

13. きけん＜危険＞　Na　dangerous

　　道路に危険という標識が出ている。There is a danger sign on the road.

14. のろのろする　V3　to move slowly

　　のろのろうんてん＜のろのろ運転＞(を)する／します　V3　to drive slowly

　　道が混んでいて、毎日のろのろ運転だ。The road is crowded and it is a slow drive every day.

15. じゅうたい＜渋滞＞(を)する／します　V3　to cause congestion (e.g. traffic)

　　交通渋滞はだんだんひどくなっている。The traffic congestion is gradually becoming terrible.

16. いらいらする／します　V3　to become irritated

　　道が渋滞していると、いらいらする。When the streets are congested, I get irritated.

17. (～を)ひく＜轢く＞／轢きます　V1　to run over ～ (with a vehicle)

　　今朝、犬を轢きそうになった。I almost ran over a dog this morning.

18. いはん＜違反＞　N　violation (of law)

　　駐車違反をして切符を切られた。I parked illegally and got a ticket.

19. ばっきん＜罰金＞　N　fine; penalty

　　駐車違反の罰金を払わなくてはいけない。I have to pay a fine for a parking violation.

《Activity B》

20. エコしゃ＜エコ車＞　N　eco-friendly car

　　環境のために皆エコ車を運転しよう。Let's everyone drive an eco-friendly car for the

　　environment.

21. とうもろこし　N　corn (fresh)

　　とうもろこしから出来るエタノール(ethanol)とガソリンで、どちらの方が環境にやさし

　　いですか。Which is better for the environment, ethanol made from corn or gasoline?

《Activity C》

22. こうつうきかん＜交通機関＞　N　transportation facilitiy

こうきょうこうつうきかん＜公共交通機関＞　N　public transportation

日本の公共交通機関はよく発達している。Japan's public transportation is well developed.

23. じかようしゃ＜自家用車＞　N　private automobile

中国にも自家用車の数がだんだん増えているそうだ。I heard that the number of privately

owed cars in China is also gradually increasing.

《Activity D》　No new vocabulary

《Activity E》

24. さいこうきおん＜最高気温＞　N　highest temperature

さいていきおん＜最低気温＞　N　lowest temperature

天気予報によると今日の最高気温は25度で最低気温は18度だそうだ。According to the

weather forecast, today's highest temperature is 25 degrees and the lowest is 18 degrees.

25. こうすいかくりつ＜降水確率＞　N　rainfall probability

こうすいりょう＜降水量＞　N　level of precipitation

明日の降水確率は90％だそうだから、傘を持って行こう。I heard that tomorrow's

probability for rain is 90%, so let's take an umbrella.

《Activity F》

26. せつやく＜節約＞(を)する／します　V3　to save; to economize

水や電気を節約しよう。Let's save water and electricity.

27. (お)ゆをわかす＜(お)湯を沸かす＞／沸かします　V3　to boil (hot) water

お湯を沸かして、コーヒーを飲もう。Let's boil some hot water and drink coffee.

28. (〜を)かわかす＜乾かす＞／乾かします　V1　to dry 〜 [transitive]

☞ (〜が)乾く/乾きます 〜 to dry [intransitive]

洗濯物を乾燥機(dryer)で乾かせば、電気代は高くなる。It you dry laundry using a dryer,

your electricity bill will become expensive.

29. れいぼう＜冷房＞　N　air conditioning

だんぼう＜暖房＞　N　heating

夏は冷房、冬は暖房をつけてしまう。I turn on the air conditioner in summer and the heater in the winter.

《5課‐1・聞く1》

30. こがた＜小型＞　N　small size
　　 ちゅうがた＜中型＞　N　medium size
　　 おおがた＜大型＞　N　large scale
　　 大型台風が来ているそうだ。I heard that a large typhoon is coming.

31. ちかづく＜近づく＞／近づきます　V1　to approach; to get near
　　 台風が沖縄に近づいているそうだ。I heard that a typhoon is approaching Okinawa.

32. ちゅういほう＜注意報＞　N　warning
　　 大雨と強風の注意報が出ている。Heavy rain and strong wind warnings are out.

《5課‐1・聞く2》

33. (〜が)きにいる＜気に入る＞／気に入ります　V1　to be pleased with 〜
　　 私はこの服が気に入っている。I am pleased with this dress.

34. (〜が)おくれる＜遅れる＞／遅れます　V2　to fall behind schedule
　　 事故で学校に遅れてしまった。I was late to school because of an accident.

35. (〜に)ぶつかる／ぶつかります　V1　to collide with 〜
　　 今朝前の車にぶつかりそうになった。I almost bumped the car in front (of me) this morning.

36. さいわい＜幸い＞　Adv　luckily; fortunately
　　 幸い誰も死ななかった。Luckily nobody died.

37. ききいっぱつ＜危機一髪＞　N　by a hair's breadth; critical moment
　　 急ブレーキをかけて、危機一髪で車を止めることが出来た。I used the brake suddenly and was able stop my car within a hair's breadth (of causing an accident).

38. ひやり(or ひやっ)とする／します　V3　to get chilled; to shudder (with fright)
　　 人を轢きそうになって、ひやりとした。I almost ran over a person and shuddered with fright.

39. さんざん＜散々＞　Na　terrible [☞ The 33-year-old female *yakudoshi* (bad luck year) originated from this word.]
　　 キャンプは雨で散々だった。The camping was terrible because of rain.

40. (〜が)つかまる＜捕まる＞／捕まります　V1　to be caught; to be arrested [intransitive]

(〜を)つかまえる＜捕まえる＞／捕まえます　V2　to catch; to arrest [transitive]

泥棒が捕まったそうだ。I heard that the robber was arrested.

《5課‐2・読む》

41. でんしんばしら＜電信柱＞　N　telephone pole

車が電信柱にぶつかった。The car crashed into the telephone pole.

42. そくし＜即死＞　N　instant death

兄はオートバイの事故で亡くなった。即死だった。　My older brother died in a motorcycle accident. It was an instant death.

43. じょしゅせき＜助手席＞　N　assistant driver's seat

友達が助手席に乗って、地図を見ながら道を教えてくれた。My friend rode in the front seat and showed me the way while looking at a map.

44. こっせつ＜骨折＞(を)する／します　V3　to have bone fracture [＝骨を折る]

昨日バスケットをしていて、骨折してしまった。When I was playing basketball yesterday, I broke a bone.

45. じゅうしょう＜重傷＞　N　serious injury

友人は事故で病院に入っているが、重傷らしい。My friend is in the hospital because of an accident and he seems to be seriously injured.

46. しょぞく＜所属＞(を)する／します　V3　to belong to

兄は大学の日本クラブに所属している。My older brother belongs to the Japan Club in college.

47. かんげい＜歓迎＞(を)する／します　V3　to welcome

かんげいかい＜歓迎会＞　N　welcoming party

日本からの留学生のために、この週末に歓迎会を開こう。Let's hold a welcoming party for the foreign students from Japan this weekend.

48. よっぱらう＜酔っぱらう＞／酔っぱらいます　V1　to get drunk

よっぱらい＜酔っぱらい＞　N　drunkard

お酒を飲んで、酔っぱらってしまった。I drank alcohol and got drunk.

49. じじょう＜事情＞　N　circumstances; situation

日本の交通事情を教えて下さい。Please tell me about the Japanese traffic situation.

50. かりめん(きょ)＜仮免(許)＞　N　driver's permit

僕は仮免で運転している。I am driving with a driver's permit.

51. きじ＜記事＞　N　article

私は学校新聞のためにリサイクルについて記事を書いている。I am writing an article for the school newspaper about recycling.

52. じこにあう＜事故に遭う＞／遭います　V1　to be involved in an accident

お年寄りが事故に遭って亡くなった。An elderly person was involved in an accident and died.

53. ちりょう＜治療＞　N　treatment; therapy

ちりょうをうける＜治療を受ける＞／受けます　V2　to be treated

骨折して毎週治療を受けに病院に通っている。I broke a bone and am commuting to the hospital every week for treatment.

54. うで＜腕＞　N　arm

バレーボールの練習をしていた時に、右腕を骨折してしまった。When I was practicing volleyball, I broke my right arm.

55. ギブスをする／します　V3　to have a (plaster) cast

太郎君は腕にギブスをしている。Taro has a cast on his arm.

56. ねぶくろ＜寝袋＞　N　sleeping bag

キャンプに寝袋を持って来なさい。Bring your sleeping bag to camp.

57. まくら＜枕＞　N　pillow

飛行機に乗ると、いつも枕を持って行く。Whenever I ride an airplane, I always take a pillow.

58. きがえ＜着替え＞　　N　　change of clothes

旅行に行く時、着替えを十分持って行く方がいい。When you travel, you should take enough changes of clothes.

《5課‐4d・話す》

59. かみなり＜雷＞　　N　　thunder

かみなりがなる＜雷が鳴る＞／鳴ります　　V1　　thunder cracks

かみなりがおちる＜雷が落ちる＞／落ちます　　V2　　thunder strikes

雷が鳴ると、私は怖くなる。When thunder cracks, I get scared.

60. びちゃびちゃになる／なります　　V1　　to get soaking wet

びちゃびちゃにぬれる＜濡れる＞／濡れます　　V1　　to get soaking wet

傘を持っていなかったから、びちゃびちゃに濡れてしまった。Because I didn't have an umbrella, I got soaking wet.

《5課‐4e・話す》 No new vocabulary

【分かればいい単語】

1. のりかえ＜乗り換え＞　　　　　　N　　transfer
2. ひょうしき＜標識＞　　　　　　　N　　landmark
3. かくち＜各地＞　　　　　　　　　N　　every place
4. せっし＜摂氏＞　　　　　　　　　N　　Centigrade; Celsius
5. かし＜華氏＞　　　　　　　　　　N　　Fahrenheit
6. ～いこう＜～以降＞　　　　　　　Nd　　on and after; hereafter
7. ふうそく＜風速＞　　　　　　　　N　　wind speed
8. しんろ＜進路＞　　　　　　　　　N　　course; route
9. じょうりくする＜上陸する＞　　　V3　　to land

＊ Previously learned.

A.	食べ＋始める	begin/start to eat	→ AIJ 3 L.4＊
	食べ＋終わる	finish eating	
	食べ＋続ける	keep/continue eating	
	食べ＋やすい	is easy to eat	
	食べ＋にくい	is hard/difficult to eat	
	(雨が)降り＋出す	start to rain (suddenly or unexpectedly)	→ AIJ 4 L.3＊
	(雨が)＋止〔や〕む	stop raining	

（　　）の中の言葉を使って、下線のところをこの文法を使って書きなさい。

1. 私は＿＿年前に日本語のクラスを＿＿＿＿＿＿＿＿＿＿＿＿＿＿＿＿＿。（取る）

2. 私は大学でも日本語を＿＿＿＿＿＿＿＿＿＿＿＿＿＿＿つもりです。（勉強する）

3. 単語（は　を）＿＿＿＿＿＿＿＿＿＿＿＿＿＿＿＿。（覚える）

4. ＿＿という漢字（は　を）＿＿＿＿＿＿＿＿＿＿＿＿＿＿。（書く）

5. 私は本を＿＿＿＿＿＿＿＿＿＿＿＿＿＿＿＿＿から、寝る。（読む）

6. 雨が急に＿＿＿＿＿＿＿＿＿＿＿＿＿＿＿、濡れてしまった。（降る）

7. 雨はすぐ＿＿＿＿＿＿＿＿＿＿＿＿＿＿。（止む）

B.	降る/降らない＋でしょう	It probably will/will not rain.	→ AIJ 2 L.7＊
	雨/曇り/晴れ＋でしょう	It probably will be rainy/cloudy/clear.	
	降る/降らない＋だろう＋と思います		→ AIJ 3 L.1＊
		I think it will probably will/will not rain.	
	雨/曇り/晴れ＋だろう＋と思います		
		I think it probably will be rainy/cloudy/clear.	

明日の天気予報を書きなさい。→ ＝ のち　| ＝ 時々

1. ☂　　　　明日は＿＿＿＿＿＿＿＿＿＿＿＿＿＿＿＿＿＿＿＿＿でしょう。

2. ☀ → ☁　明日は＿＿＿＿＿＿＿＿＿＿＿＿＿＿＿＿＿＿＿＿＿でしょう。

3. ☁ | ☂　明日は＿＿＿＿＿＿＿＿＿＿＿＿＿＿＿＿＿＿＿＿＿でしょう。

4. ☁ | ☀ 　　明日は＿＿＿＿＿＿＿＿＿＿＿＿＿＿＿＿＿＿＿＿＿＿と思います。

5. ☂ → ☁ 　　明日は＿＿＿＿＿＿＿＿＿＿＿＿＿＿＿＿＿＿＿＿＿＿と思います。

6. ☂ → ☃ 　　明日は＿＿＿＿＿＿＿＿＿＿＿＿＿＿＿＿＿＿＿＿＿＿と思います。

C. する/しない＋ように＋する　try to make an effort to/not to do　→ AIJ 4 L.3＊

（　）の中の動詞を使い、この文法を使って、文を作りなさい。

1. 日本語のクラスでは日本語を＿＿＿＿＿＿＿＿＿＿＿＿＿＿＿＿＿＿＿。（話す）

2. 先生と出来るだけ英語を＿＿＿＿＿＿＿＿＿＿＿＿＿＿＿＿＿。（話す）

3. 運転しながらケータイを出来るだけ＿＿＿＿＿＿＿＿＿＿＿＿＿＿＿＿＿。（使う）

4. 車を運転する時、食べたり＿＿＿＿＿＿＿＿＿＿＿＿＿＿＿＿＿。（飲む）

5. 道が渋滞（じゅうたい）していても、あまり＿＿＿＿＿＿＿＿＿＿＿＿＿＿＿。（いらいらする）

D. Verb (stem)＋そうになる　almost happens

This construction is used to describe a situation when something is about to happen. The verb is restricted to non-volitional verbs, that is, a verb that expresses something that is beyond human control, such as 風邪を引く "to catch a cold" or おぼれる " to be drowned." Since passive and potential forms are regarded as non-volitional verbs, they can be also used with そうになる. If the verb is a volitional verb, this pattern cannot be used if the subject is the speaker himself/herself.

1. 昨日は雨でぬれて、風邪を<u>引きそうになった</u>。

　　I got wet in the cold rain yesterday and I almost caught a cold. [non-volitional verb]

2. 昨日はもうちょっとで車に<u>ひかれそうになった</u>。

　　Yesterday I almost got run over by a car. [passive = non-volitional verb]

3. やっと日本へ<u>行けそうになった</u>時に、母が病気になってしまった。

　　When I was finally about able to go to Japan, my mother got ill. [potential = non-volitional verb]

X 私がお昼ご飯を食べそうになった時、友達から電話がかかって来た。

　　When I was about to eat my lunch, I received a call from my friend. [volitional verb]

　→ 私がお昼ご飯を食べようとした時、友達から電話がかかって来た。

五課

（　）の中の動詞を使い、この文法を使って、文を作りなさい。そして、英訳しなさい

1. 前の車に＿＿＿＿＿＿＿＿＿＿＿＿＿＿＿＿＿＿＿。（衝突する）

　　英訳：＿＿＿＿＿＿＿＿＿＿＿＿＿＿＿＿＿＿＿＿＿＿＿＿＿＿＿＿＿

2. 今朝、犬を＿＿＿＿＿＿＿＿＿＿＿＿＿＿＿＿＿。（ひく）

　　英訳：＿＿＿＿＿＿＿＿＿＿＿＿＿＿＿＿＿＿＿＿＿＿＿＿＿＿＿＿＿

3. 今朝、前の車に＿＿＿＿＿＿＿＿＿＿＿＿＿＿＿。（ぶつかる）

　　英訳：＿＿＿＿＿＿＿＿＿＿＿＿＿＿＿＿＿＿＿＿＿＿＿＿＿＿＿＿＿

4. 人を＿＿＿＿＿＿＿＿＿＿＿＿＿＿＿、ひやりとした。（ひく）

　　英訳：＿＿＿＿＿＿＿＿＿＿＿＿＿＿＿＿＿＿＿＿＿＿＿＿＿＿＿＿＿

5. ゆうべ悲しい映画を見て、＿＿＿＿＿＿＿＿＿＿＿＿＿＿。（泣く）

　　英訳：＿＿＿＿＿＿＿＿＿＿＿＿＿＿＿＿＿＿＿＿＿＿＿＿＿＿＿＿＿

E.　　Verb (Dic. form)＋ところだった。　　almost happened

　= Verb (Stem form)＋そうになった。　　almost happened

These two patterns have the same meaning of "about to happen." As mentioned in Note D, the verb used in the そうになった pattern is restricted to non-volitional verbs. But するところだった is free of this restriction.

「～そうになった」の部分を「～ところだった」を使って書きかえ、全文を英訳しなさい。

1. 前の車に衝突しそうになった。

　=＿＿＿＿＿＿＿＿＿＿＿＿＿＿＿　英訳：＿＿＿＿＿＿＿＿＿＿＿＿＿＿＿

2. ゆうべ運転していた時に、人をひきそうになった。

　=＿＿＿＿＿＿＿＿＿＿＿＿＿＿＿　英訳：＿＿＿＿＿＿＿＿＿＿＿＿＿＿＿

3. もう少しで車にひかれそうになった。

　=＿＿＿＿＿＿＿＿＿＿＿＿＿＿＿　英訳：＿＿＿＿＿＿＿＿＿＿＿＿＿＿＿

4. 前の車が急に止まったので、事故を起こしそうになった。

　=＿＿＿＿＿＿＿＿＿＿＿＿＿＿＿　英訳：＿＿＿＿＿＿＿＿＿＿＿＿＿＿＿

5. 地震で家が壊れそうになった。

　=＿＿＿＿＿＿＿＿＿＿＿＿＿＿＿　英訳：＿＿＿＿＿＿＿＿＿＿＿＿＿＿＿

A. 交通のマナー：ペアワーク→クラスワーク

交通安全のためにどうすればいいでしょうか。正しい言葉に丸をしなさい。

1. (正しい　違う) 歩行者は横断歩道じゃない道路を渡ってもいい。

2. (正しい　違う) 信号が赤でも、交差点を渡ってもいい。

3. (正しい　違う) スピードを出さない方がいい。

4. (正しい　違う) 中古車でも、よく修理すれば大丈夫だ。

5. (正しい　違う) 飲酒運転は危ない。

6. (正しい　違う) 居眠り運転は危ない。

7. (正しい　違う) 壊れている自動車を運転しても大丈夫。

8. (正しい　違う) パンクしたタイアは修理すべきだ。

9. (正しい　違う) ケータイを使いながら運転するのは、法律で禁止すべきだ。

10. (正しい　違う) 運転している時、前を見なくてもいい。

11. (正しい　違う) 食べたり飲んだりしながら、運転してもいい。

12. (正しい　違う) オートバイを運転する時、ヘルメットをかぶる方がいい。

13. (正しい　違う) オートバイは歩道で乗ってもいい。

14. (正しい　違う) 追い越しする時、隣りの車線を見るべきだ。

15. (正しい　違う) 前の車に衝突してもいい。

16. (正しい　違う) 急停車をすると、危険だ。

17. (正しい　違う) のろのろ運転をすると、ほかの車の迷惑になる。

18. (正しい　違う) 道路が渋滞していて、いらいらしている時も、おこらないようにする。

19. (正しい　違う) 自動車保険があるから、事故を起こしてもいい。

20. (正しい　違う) 警官を見たら、スピードを出して逃げる。

21. (正しい　違う) 人をひかないように、安全運転をする。

22. (正しい　違う) 駐車禁止の標識があっても、自動車を駐車する。

23. (正しい　違う) 駐車違反をして切符をもらっても、罰金を払わない。

B. ゲーム「シャレード」：クラスワーク

クラスを二つのチームに分けて、チーム1とチーム2を作ります。それぞれのチームから二人ずつチームの前に出ます。先生がカードに「～そうになった」か「～ところだった」を使った文をカードに書いて、前の四人に見せます。四人は自分のチームに、ジェスチャーを使って表現します。話してはいけません。チームの生徒は答えを紙に書いて、先生に見せます。速く正しく答えたチームが点をもらいます。さあ、やってみましょう。

C. エコのために：ペアワーク→クラスワーク

環境を守るためにどうすればいいと思いますか。正しいと思うことに✓をして、「～ようにする」を使って書きかえなさい。

1. ＿＿＿ 自転車に乗る。　　　　　　　　　＿＿＿＿＿＿＿＿＿＿＿＿＿＿＿

2. ＿＿＿ 歩く。　　　　　　　　　　　　　＿＿＿＿＿＿＿＿＿＿＿＿＿＿＿

3. ＿＿＿ 自動車に乗る。　　　　　　　　　＿＿＿＿＿＿＿＿＿＿＿＿＿＿＿

4. ＿＿＿ ガソリンをたくさん使う。　　　　＿＿＿＿＿＿＿＿＿＿＿＿＿＿＿

5. ＿＿＿ エコ車に乗る。　　　　　　　　　＿＿＿＿＿＿＿＿＿＿＿＿＿＿＿

6. ＿＿＿ ガソリンをとうもろこしやゴミから作る。　＿＿＿＿＿＿＿＿＿＿＿

7. ＿＿＿ 排気ガスをたくさん出す。　　　　＿＿＿＿＿＿＿＿＿＿＿＿＿＿＿

D. 討論会〔とうろんかい〕「公共交通機関は必要か」：グループワーク→クラスワーク

公共交通機関に賛成意見：

1. 公共交通機関の良い点　＿＿＿＿＿＿＿＿＿＿＿＿＿＿＿＿＿＿＿＿＿＿

2. 自家用車の悪い点　＿＿＿＿＿＿＿＿＿＿＿＿＿＿＿＿＿＿＿＿＿＿＿

3. 公共交通機関が必要だと思う理由

＿＿＿＿＿＿＿＿＿＿＿＿＿＿＿＿＿＿＿＿＿＿＿＿＿＿＿＿＿＿＿＿＿＿＿

公共交通機関に反対意見：

4. 自家用車の良い点　＿＿＿＿＿＿＿＿＿＿＿＿＿＿＿＿＿＿＿＿＿＿＿

5. 公共交通機関の悪い点　＿＿＿＿＿＿＿＿＿＿＿＿＿＿＿＿＿＿＿＿＿

6. 公共交通機関は必要ではないと思う理由

＿＿＿＿＿＿＿＿＿＿＿＿＿＿＿＿＿＿＿＿＿＿＿＿＿＿＿＿＿＿＿＿＿＿＿

E. 車のパーツ：グループワーク→クラスワーク

次の車のパーツは英語で何ですか。

1. ハンドル ＿＿＿＿＿
2. ボディー ＿＿＿＿＿
3. アクセル ＿＿＿＿＿
4. エンジン ＿＿＿＿＿
5. ボンネット ＿＿＿＿＿
6. ウィンカー ＿＿＿＿＿

7. タイヤ ＿＿＿＿＿
8. バックミラー ＿＿＿＿＿
9. トランク ＿＿＿＿＿
10. ライト ＿＿＿＿＿
11. ブレーキ ＿＿＿＿＿
12. メーター ＿＿＿＿＿

13. リヤバンパー ＿＿＿＿＿
14. サイドミラー ＿＿＿＿＿
15. フロントガラス ＿＿＿＿＿
16. ガソリンタンク ＿＿＿＿＿
17. シートベルト ＿＿＿＿＿
18. ナンバープレート ＿＿＿＿＿

F. 交通標識：グループワーク→クラスワーク

次の交通標識は何のためですか。下から正しい言葉を選びなさい。

1. (　　)

2. (　　)

3. (　　)

4. (　　)

5. (　　)

6. (　　)

7. (　　)

8. (　　)

9. (　　)

10. (　　)

11. (　　)

12. (　　)

13. (　　)

14. (　　)

a. 危険	f. 道路工事中	k. 一方通行
b. 通行止め	g. 学校、幼稚園、保育園あり	l. 駐車禁止
c. 強風注意	h. 歩行者専用	m. 横断歩道
d. 動物注意	i. 自転車通行止め	n. 自動車進入禁止
e. 二方向通行	j. 最高速度50キロ	

五課

G. 天気予報：ペアワーク→クラスワーク

今日の天気を見ながら、各地の天気を言いなさい。

→ ＝ のち　｜＝ 時々

各地	きょう	あす	あさって
札幌	⛄→☁	⛄→☁	☁｜⛄
仙台	☁｜⛄	☁	☁｜☂
東京	☀	☀	☁
新潟	⛄	☂｜☁	☁｜☂
名古屋	☁→☀	☁→☀	☁
大阪	☁→☀	☀→☁	☁
神戸	☁→☀	☀→☁	☁
松江	☂→☁	☀→☂	☁｜☂
広島	☁→☀	☀→☁	☁
高松	☁→☀	☀→☁	☁
福岡	☁→☀	☀→☁	☁
那覇	☁	☁	☁｜☂

1. ＿＿＿＿＿は今日＿＿＿雪のち曇り＿＿＿でしょう。

2. 名古屋は今日＿＿＿＿＿＿＿＿＿＿＿＿でしょう。

3. 松江は今日＿＿＿＿＿＿＿＿＿＿＿＿でしょう。

4. 新潟は明日＿＿＿＿＿＿＿＿＿＿＿＿でしょう。

5. 福岡は明日＿＿＿＿＿＿＿＿＿＿＿＿でしょう。

6. 松江は明日＿＿＿＿＿＿＿＿＿＿＿＿でしょう。

7. 札幌は明後日＿＿＿＿＿＿＿＿＿＿＿でしょう。

8. 仙台は明後日＿＿＿＿＿＿＿＿＿＿＿でしょう。

9. 今日私の住んでいる所の天気は

　　　　　　　＿＿＿＿＿＿＿＿＿＿＿でしょう。

H. 天気予報：ペアワーク→クラスワーク

東京の天気予報を見ながら、下の下線に正しい言葉を書きなさい。

東京	12/5 (水)	12/6 (木)	12/7 (金)	12/8 (土)	12/9 (日)	12/10 (月)	12/11 (火)
天気	☀	☀｜☁	☁	☁｜☀	☁｜☀	☀｜☁	☀｜☁
気温	11℃ 4℃	12℃ 4℃	14℃ 7℃	13℃ 8℃	11℃ 6℃	12℃ 6℃	13℃ 6℃
降水確率	0%	10%	40%	20%	30%	20%	20%

Fahrenheit °F ＝ Centigrade °C × 9 ÷ 5 + 32

1. １２月５日水曜日の東京のお天気は＿＿＿＿＿＿＿＿＿＿＿＿でしょう。

2. １２月８日土曜日の＿＿＿＿＿＿＿＿＿＿は摂氏１３度 (＝華氏＿＿＿) でしょう。

3. １２月８日土曜日の＿＿＿＿＿＿＿＿＿＿は摂氏８度 (＝華氏＿＿＿) でしょう。

4. １２月＿＿＿日＿＿＿曜日に東京は雨が降らないでしょう。

五課　　　　　　236

I. 気候とエコ：ペアワーク→クラスワーク

エネルギーを節約するために、生活をどう変えればいいでしょうか。右から正しい言葉を選んで、下線に書きなさい。

1. 暑い日には冷たい＿＿＿＿＿＿を食べる。

2. 暑い夏には、＿＿＿＿＿＿を着る。

3. ビルの＿＿＿＿＿＿をコントロール出来るようにする。

4. トイレや部屋を使っていない時に＿＿＿＿＿＿を消すようにする。

5. ＿＿＿＿＿＿を使わないで、自然に洗濯物を乾かすようにする。

6. ＿＿＿＿＿＿を使わないで、自然にお皿を乾かすようにする。

7. 使っていない時、部屋の暖房や＿＿＿＿＿＿は消しておく。

8. ＿＿＿＿＿＿を使って、シャワーに使うお水をお湯にする。

クールビズ
皿洗い機
電気
ドライヤー
冷房
太陽電池
氷
温度

J. 東西南北：ペアワーク→クラスワーク

（　　　）の中に漢字の読み方を書きなさい。

```
                    (          )
                      北
        (          ) 北西 ＼ ｜ ／ 北東 (          )
( )  西 ――――――――― 東 (          )
        (          ) 南西 ／ ｜ ＼ 南東 (          )
                      南
                    (          )
```

五課

＜5課‐1・聞く1＞

聞く1： Weather Forecast

(Narrator)   Now you will listen twice to a prerecorded message.

聞く1： Weather Forecast

(Narrator) Now answer the questions for this selection.

1. What is the date today?
    (A) Today is Thursday the 4th.
    (B) Today is Friday the 4th.
    (C) Today is Thursday the 8th.
    (D) Today is Friday the 8th.

2. What is today's weather forecast?
    (A) Sunny → cloudy
    (B) Cloudy → rainy → cloudy
    (C) Sunny → cloudy → rainy
    (D) Rainy → cloudy → sunny

3. What is NOT correct about today's weather forecast?
    (A) The highest temperature will be 24°C.
    (B) The lowest temperature will be 19°C.
    (C) The chance of rain is 50%.
    (D) There is a warning of a typhoon.

4. Which description is NOT correct about the typhoon?
    (A) The typhoon is a small scale typhoon.
    (B) The typhoon is the eighth of this year.
    (C) The typhoon is approaching the south of Okinawa.
    (D) The wind speed is 20 kilometers per hour.

5. What will happen to the typhoon?
    (A) The typhoon will land in Shikoku and the Kansai (Kinki) area.
    (B) The typhoon will land in the Kantoo area.
    (C) The typhoon will move away to the Japan Sea.
    (D) The typhoon will move away from Okinawa on Sunday morning.

五課

＜５課 - 1・聞く２＞

聞く２: Driving

(Narrator)   Now you will listen once to a prerecorded message.

聞く 2： Driving

(Narrator)   Now answer the questions for this selection.

1.   What happened to this person today?
    (A)   He got into a big accident.
    (B)   He hit a person with his car.
    (C)   He was hit by a car.
    (D)   He almost got into an accident.

2.   Why did this person going to the university?
    (A)   He had to take his economics exam.
    (B)   He had to turn in his report.
    (C)   The exam started at 9:00 a.m.
    (D)   He had to attend his literature lecture.

3.   What happened to him in the morning while driving his car?
    (A)   A pedestrian started to walk in front of his car.
    (B)   A pedestrian didn't use the pedestrian crossing.
    (C)   The truck in front of him stopped suddenly.
    (D)   He stopped for a pedestrian.

4.   What happened to this person after arriving at the university?
    (A)   The parking lot was full.
    (B)   He could not park his car even on the road.
    (C)   He did not receive a parking violation ticket.
    (D)   He was late to his exam.

5.   What description is correct about the traffic violation this person committed?
    (A)   He has never had a parking violation.
    (B)   He has never driven while drunk.
    (C)   He has never exceeded the speed limit.
    (D)   He once fell asleep while driving.

高三事故死

３月３日午前２時ごろ京都市の国道一号で奈良県奈良市在住Aさん⒅の軽自動車が鴨川手前の電信柱にぶつかった。車はその後、横転し鴨川に転落した。この事故でAさんは即死。助手席に乗っていた友人のB子さんは両足骨折などの重傷を負った。原因は飲酒運転と考えられている。B子さんの話によると、二人は３月1日に奈良市内の高校を卒業したばかりで、翌3月2日

は夕方６時から二人が所属していたバスケット部のOB会歓迎会に出席した。Aさんは先輩のすすめでビールや酒を飲み、その後、二次会のカラオケでもビールやウイスキーを4〜5杯飲んでかなり酔っぱらっていたらしい。カラオケ場からB子さんを家へ送り届ける途中、Aさんはこの事故を起こした。この事故で、歓迎会に参加していた20人全員が明日警察で調べを受ける。

【Post-Activity 1】もしパーティーでお酒が出たら、どうするか。

【Post-Activity 2】インターネットの事故のニュースを読む。

聞く 2：Driving

(Narrator)   Now answer the questions for this selection.

1.   What happened to this person today?
     (A)   He got into a big accident.
     (B)   He hit a person with his car.
     (C)   He was hit by a car.
     (D)   He almost got into an accident.

2.   Why did this person going to the university?
     (A)   He had to take his economics exam.
     (B)   He had to turn in his report.
     (C)   The exam started at 9:00 a.m.
     (D)   He had to attend his literature lecture.

3.   What happened to him in the morning while driving his car?
     (A)   A pedestrian started to walk in front of his car.
     (B)   A pedestrian didn't use the pedestrian crossing.
     (C)   The truck in front of him stopped suddenly.
     (D)   He stopped for a pedestrian.

4.   What happened to this person after arriving at the university?
     (A)   The parking lot was full.
     (B)   He could not park his car even on the road.
     (C)   He did not receive a parking violation ticket.
     (D)   He was late to his exam.

5.   What description is correct about the traffic violation this person committed?
     (A)   He has never had a parking violation.
     (B)   He has never driven while drunk.
     (C)   He has never exceeded the speed limit.
     (D)   He once fell asleep while driving.

五課

高三事故死

3月3日午前2時ごろ京都市の国道一号で奈良県奈良市在住Aさん⒅の軽自動車が鴨川手前の電信柱にぶつかった。車はその後、横転し鴨川に転落した。この事故でAさんは即死。助手席に乗っていた友人のB子さんは両足骨折などの重傷を負った。原因は飲酒運転と考えられている。B子さんの話によると、二人は3月1日に奈良市内の高校を卒業したばかりで、翌3月2日

は夕方6時から二人が所属していたバスケット部のOB会歓迎会に出席した。Aさんは先輩のすすめでビールや酒を飲み、その後、二次会のカラオケでもビールやウイスキーを4～5杯飲んでかなり酔っぱらっていたらしい。カラオケ場からB子さんを家へ送り届ける途中、Aさんはこの事故を起こした。この事故で、歓迎会に参加していた20人全員が明日警察で調べを受ける。

【Post-Activity 1】もしパーティーでお酒が出たら、どうするか。

【Post-Activity 2】インターネットの事故のニュースを読む。

読む: Car Accident

(Narrator)   Now answer the questions for this section.

1.   When and where did this car accident happen?
      (A)   About 2:00 a.m. on March 3rd in Kyoto
      (B)   About 2:00 p.m. on March 3rd in Kyoto
      (C)   About 2:00 a.m. on March 3rd in Nara
      (D)   About 2:00 p.m. on March 3rd in Nara

2.   What happened to the passengers?
      (A)   Persons A and B died.
      (B)   Person A died and Person B broke her two legs.
      (C)   Person A broke two arms and Person B died.
      (D)   Person A broke two legs and Person B died.

3.   What happened to the car?
      (A)   The car hit a tree.
      (B)   The car hit a telephone pole and stopped.
      (C)   The car hit a telephone pole and rolled into the river sideways.
      (D)   The car lost control and jumped into the river from the front.

4.   What activities did the passengers have on the day of the accident?
      (A)   They attended a graduation ceremony.
      (B)   They attended a basketball club welcoming party.
      (C)   They went to a karaoke room with their classmates.
      (D)   They went to a graduation party.

5.   What was the main reason for the accident?
      (A)   speed
      (B)   carelessness
      (C)   sleepiness
      (D)   drunkenness

五課

＜5課 - 3a・書く＞
Text Chat: Driver's License

Note: In this part of the exam, the student may not move back and forth among the questions.

You will participate in a simulated exchange of text-chat-messages. Each time it is your turn to write, you will have 90 seconds. You should respond as fully and as appropriately as possible.

You will have a conversation with Daisuke, a student at a Japanese school, about driver's licenses.

1.   Respond. (90 seconds)

こんにちは。今運転についてアメリカの事情を調べているんですが、御協力を御願いします。あのう、もう運転免許を持っていますか。

2.   Respond. (90 seconds)

アメリカでは運転免許を何歳で取れるんですか。

3.   Describe a specific example. (90 seconds)

だいたい運転免許を取るのにどのくらいの時間とお金がかかるんですか。

4.   Describe a specific example. (90 seconds)

ところで、町を運転すると、いろいろな危ない運転手に出会うと思いますが、今までに見た一番悪い交通事故は、どんなものでしたか。

5.   Describe a situation. (90 seconds)

日本では運転しながらケータイを使うとつかまってしまいますが、そちらでも同じ法律があるんですか。

6.   Ask a specific question. (90 seconds)

どうも有難うございました。日本の交通について何か質問があったらしてください。

五課   244

Compare and Contrast: Two Seasons

You are writing an article for the student newspaper of your sister school in Japan. Write an article in which you compare and contrast two seasons in Japan. Based on your personal experience, describe at least THREE similarities and differences between the two seasons. Also state your preference and give reasons for it.

Your article should be 300 to 400 characters or longer. Use the *desu/masu* or *da* (plain) style, but use one style consistently. Also, use *kanji* wherever *kanji* from the AP Japanese *kanji* list is appropriate. You have 20 minutes to write.

【自分の作文のアウトラインを書こう！】

Introduction:

_____

Three similarities and differences between two seasons in Japan:

1. _____

2. _____

3. _____

Your preference and give reasons:

_____

_____

Cultural Topic Posting: Japanese Transportation

You are responding to a posting in a Web forum for high school students of Japanese. The posting asks about Japanese transportation. Select ONE example of Japanese transportation, such as the electric trains or the bullet train, etc. Describe in detail at least THREE characteristics of Japanese transportation. Also, express your opinion or feelings about Japanese transportation.

Your posting should be 300 to 400 characters or longer. Use the *desu/masu* or *da* (plain) style, but use one style consistently. Also, use *kanji* wherever *kanji* from the AP Japanese *kanji* list is appropriate. You have 20 minutes to write.

【自分の作文のアウトラインを書こう！】

Introduction:

_____

One example:

_____

Three characteristics of Japanese transportation:

1. _____

2. _____

3. _____

Your opinion and feelings:

_____

_____

Conversation: Climate

You will participate in a simulated conversation. Each time it is your turn to speak, you will have 20 seconds to record. You should respond as fully and as appropriately as possible.

You will have a conversation with Mr. Nakata, a Japanese newspaper writer, about the climate.

(Man)

(20 seconds)

(Man)

(20 seconds)

(Man)

(20 seconds)

(Man)

(20 seconds)

＜5課 - 4b・話す＞

15点
20秒 X 4

Return Telephone Call: Traffic Accident

You will participate in a simulated telephone conversation with someone you are calling back after receiving a message. First, you will listen to the voice message. Then the telephone call will begin. Each time it is your turn to speak, you will have 20 seconds to record. You should respond as fully and as appropriately as possible.

(Narrator)   Listen to the voice message.

(Man)

(Narrator)   Now the telephone call will begin. After the phone is answered, begin with a greeting and then explain why you are calling.

(Man)   [Telephone] [Rings twice and picks up]

(20 seconds)

(Man)

(20 seconds)

(Man)

(20 seconds)

(Man)

(20 seconds)

School Announcement: Camping

Directions: Imagine that you are making an announcement in Japanese to an assembly of Japanese students visiting your school. First, you will see some notes in English about what to include in your announcement. You will have 1 minute to prepare your announcement while you look at the notes. Then you will have one minute to record your announcement. Your announcement should have an opening remark, details according to the notes, and a closing remark. Deliver your announcement using complete sentences in *desu/masu* style.

Camping
Date: Friday - Sunday, March 24 - 27
Place: Camp Pacific
Things to bring: sleeping bag, pillow, swim suit, change of clothing
Things not to bring: iPod, cellular phone, camera
Application deadline: Friday, March 3
In case of bad weather: postponed to April 7

＜５課 - 4d・話す＞

Story Narration: Weather

Directions: Imagine that you are making an oral presentation to your Japanese class. In your presentation, you will narrate a story. First, you will see pictures depicting the story. You will have 4 minutes to prepare your narration while you look at the pictures. Then you will have 2 minutes to record your narration. Narrate your story using complete sentences in *desu/masu* style.

＜５課 - 4e・話す＞

Cultural Perspective Presentation: Driving in Japan

Directions: Imagine you are making an oral presentation to your Japanese class. First, you will read and hear the topic for your presentation. You will have 4 minutes to prepare your presentation. Then you will have 2 minutes to record your presentation. Your presentation should be as full as possible.

Present your own view or perspective on driving in Japan. Discuss at least FIVE aspects or examples of driving in Japan.

Begin with an appropriate introduction, give details, explain your own view or perspective, and end with a concluding remark.

【Let's take notes!】

1. Begin with an appropriate introduction.

   _____

2. Discuss five aspects/examples of the topic.

   1.) _____

   2.) _____

   3.) _____

   4.) _____

   5.) _____

3. Explain your view or perspective.

   _____

4. End with a concluding remark.

   _____

At the end of this lesson, you are expected to be able to handle the following tasks.

【AP-6課 タスク１：食物】

Discuss three differences between Japanese cooking and American cooking, and give your preference and opinions. Discuss three characteristics of Japanese table manners such as utensils, tableware, Japanese cooking, etc. State your opinions.

【AP-6課 タスク２：買物】

Discuss three differences between Japanese department stores and American department stores and give your opinions, and preferences regarding various differences.

【AP-6課 タスク３：体と健康】

Discuss one unhealthy practice and one healthy practice of your daily lifestyle. Discuss what you have to be careful about to maintain your health when you are in college. Discuss Americans' health problems related their diet, and discuss your opinions.

調_{しら}べよう！

A. 弁当箱_{べんとうばこ}、マイ箸_{はし}、水筒_{すいとう}

B. 風呂敷_{ふろしき}、包装_{ほうそう}

C. エコバッグ

D. 健康食品_{けんこう}

E. 懐石料理_{かいせき}

F. 癒_{いや}し、指圧_{しあつ}、マッサージ、鍼治療_{はりちりょう}

[*Kanji* in text font]

1. 鼻　nose　　　はな　　　低〔ひく〕い鼻 a short nose

　　　　　　　　　　　　　　　鼻水〔はなみず〕nasal mucus

2. 辞　word,　　　ジ　　　　辞書〔じしょ〕dictionary

　　　to resign　　　　　　辞表〔じひょう〕letter of

　　　　　　　　　　　　　　　resignation

3. 引　to pull,　　　ひ(く)　　ドアを引く pull a door open

　　　to look up (dictionary),　辞書〔じしょ〕を引く

　　　　　　　　　　　　　　　to look up (something) in a dictionary

　　　to catch (a cold)　　風邪〔かぜ〕を引く to catch a cold

4. 暗　dark　　　くら(い)　暗い顔〔かお〕a depressed, gloomy

　　　　　　　　　　　　　　　face

　　　　　　　　アン　　　暗算〔あんざん〕mental arithmetic

5. 品　goods　　　しな　　　品物〔しなもの〕が多い

　　　　　　　　　　　　　　　lots of goods

　　　　　　　　　　　　　　　品川駅〔しながわえき〕

　　　　　　　　　　　　　　　Shinagawa Station

　　　　　　　　ヒン　　　健康食品〔しょくひん〕health foods

　　　　　　　　　　　　　　　上品〔じょうひん〕elegant

6. 注　to pour　チュウ　　　注意〔ちゅうい〕caution; warning

注射〔ちゅうしゃ〕injection

注文〔ちゅうもん〕order; request

7. 残　to remain,　のこ(る)　　残り物〔のこりもの〕left-overs

to leave　のこ(す)　　食べ物〔たべもの〕を残す

(behind)　　　　　　　leave food behind

ザン　　　　残念〔ざんねん〕disappointing

残暑〔ざんしょ〕lingering summer heat

8. 定　to set　テイ　　　予定〔よてい〕a plan

定休日〔ていきゅうび〕day when

a business is regularly closed

指定席〔していせき〕reserved seat

9. 練　to train　レン　　　練習〔れんしゅう〕practice

訓練〔くんれん〕training

10. 短　short (not　みじか(い)　短い髪の毛 short hair

for height)　タン　　　短気〔たんき〕short temper

短大〔たんだい〕a two year college

短所〔たんしょ〕weak point

11. 別 to separate　わか(れる)　彼〔かれ〕と別れた

I separated from my boyfriend.

ベツ　特別〔とくべつ〕special

別々〔べつべつ〕separately

別居〔べっきょ〕する

to live separately

別

12. 指 finger　ゆび　指輪〔ゆびわ〕a ring

親指〔おやゆび〕thumb

中指〔なかゆび〕middle finger

薬指〔くすりゆび〕ring finger

小指〔こゆび〕little finger

シ　指定席〔していせき〕reserved seat

指圧〔しあつ〕finger pressure massage

指

13. 階 floor,
　　-floor　カイ/ガイ　階段〔かいだん〕stairs

地下一階〔ちかいっかい〕

first basement floor

三階〔さんがい〕third floor

14. 婦 lady　フ　主婦〔しゅふ〕housewife

婦人服〔ふじんふく〕women's

wear

看護婦〔かんごふ〕nurse

六課

15. 用 business, 　ヨウ　　　　　用がある have an errand to do
　　　 errand　　　　　　　　　用事〔ようじ〕が多い
　　　　　　　　　　　　　　　There are lots of errands.
　　　　　　　　　　　　　　　急用〔きゅうよう〕urgent business
　　　　　　　　　　　　　　　婦人用〔ふじんよう〕トイレ
　　　　　　　　　　　　　　　women's restroom

16. 絡 to stick to　ラク　　　　　連絡〔れんらく〕する to contact

17. 貸 to lend,　　か(す)　　　　お金を貸す to lend money
　　　 to rent,　　　　　　　　　貸し出し〔かしだし〕lending (out)
　　　 to lease　　　　　　　　　貸家〔かしいえ/かしや〕rental home

18. 付 to include　-つ(き)　　　みそ汁付き with miso soup
　　　　　　　　　　　　　　　included
　　　　　　　　　　フ　　　　　付近〔ふきん〕neighborhood

【読みかえの漢字】　　　　* Previously introduced.

1. 屋　store,　　　ヤ*　　　　　本屋〔ほんや〕bookstore
　　　　　　　　　　　　　　　屋根〔やね〕roof
　　　　 roof　　　　オク　　　　屋上〔おくじょう〕rooftop
2. 頭　head　　　あたま*　　　頭が痛〔いた〕い have a headache
　　　　　　　　　　ズ　　　　　頭痛〔ずつう〕がする have a headache

六課　　　　　　　　258

3. 痛 paiful   いた(い)*   喉が痛〔いた〕い have a sore throat
                ツウ   頭痛〔ずつう〕headache
                            腹痛薬〔ふくつうやく〕medicine for stomachache

4. 都 capital,   ト*   京都〔きょうと〕Kyoto
                            東京都〔とうきょうと〕Tokyo Metropolis
                            都市〔とし〕cities
       convenience ツ   都合〔つごう〕が悪〔わる〕い inconvenient

5. 調 to check   しら(べる)* 大学〔だいがく〕を調べる investigate universities
                チョウ   調味料〔ちょうみりょう〕seasoning
                            調子〔ちょうし〕がいい in good condition

6. 足 foot,   あし*   右足〔みぎあし〕right foot
       enough   た(りる)*   足りない not enough
                ソク   睡眠不足〔すいみんぶそく〕lack of sleep

【読めればいい漢字】

1. 健康   けんこう   health
2. 中華料理   ちゅうかりょうり   Chinese cooking
3. 韓国   かんこく   Korea
4. 化粧室   けしょうしつ   restroom; powder room
5. 紳士用   しんしよう   for gentlemen's use
6. 案内   あんない   information; guidance
7. 材料   ざいりょう   ingredient

《Activity A》 No new vocabulary

《Activity B》

1. ざいりょう＜材料＞　N　ingredient

日本料理は材料として新鮮な魚をよく使う。Japanese cooking often uses fresh fish as an ingredient.

2. ちょうみりょう＜調味料＞　N　seasoning

日本料理は調味料として醤油をよく使う。Japanese cooking often uses soy sauce as a seasoning.

3. しょっき＜食器＞　N　dishes (i.e. plates, bowls, cups, etc.); china

日本料理の食器は1セットが5つで、西洋料理の食器は1セットが6つだ。There are five pieces of china per set in Japan and six in a set in the West.

4. ちゅうかりょうり＜中華料理＞　N　Chinese cooking

中華料理と韓国料理とどちらの方が好きですか。Which do you like better, Chinese cooking or Korean cooking?

5. ゆうきやさい＜有機野菜＞　N　organic vegetables

母は健康のために有機野菜ばかり食べている。My mother is eating only organic vegetables for her health.

6. けんこうしょくひん＜健康食品＞　N　health foods

母は健康食品のお店で野菜や果物を買物する。My mother shops for vegetables and fruits at the health food store.

7. しんせん＜新鮮＞　Na　fresh

母は地元の新鮮な野菜しか食べない。My mother eats only locally grown fresh vegetables.

8. しょうみきげん＜賞味期限＞　N　expiration date

この食物はもう賞味期限が切れている。The expiration date of this food is already past.

9. てんかぶつ＜添加物＞　N　additives

添加物が入っている食物は体に良くないと思う。I think that food with additives is not good for the body.

10. れいとうしょくひん＜冷凍食品＞　N　frozen foods

インスタント食品や冷凍食品より新鮮な食べ物の方を食べる方がいい。It's better to eat fresh food rather than instant food and frozen food.

《Activity C》

11. えいぎょうじかん＜営業時間＞　N　business hours

このレストランの営業時間は午後5時から11時までだ。This restaurant's business hours are from 5:00 p.m. to 11:00 p.m.

12. ていきゅうび＜定休日＞　N　regular day off

多くのレストランは月曜日が定休日で閉まっている。Many restaurants close on Mondays as it is their regular day off.

《Activity D》　No new vocabulary

《Activity E》

13. ねんじゅうむきゅう＜年中無休＞　N　Open year around.

このスーパーは年中無休でいつでも開いている。This supermarket is open year round.

14. おくじょう＜屋上＞　N　rooftop

日本のデパートには屋上に小さな遊園地がある。There are small playgrounds on the rooftops of Japanese department stores.

15. ほうそう＜包装＞　N　wrapping; packing

ほうそう(し)＜包装(紙)＞　N　wrapping (paper)

(〜を)ほうそう＜包装＞する／します　V3　to wrap; to pack

日本のデパートで買物をした時、店員がきれいな包装紙を使ってとても速く包装してくれた。When I shopped in a department store in Japan, the clerk used beautiful wrapping paper and wrapped it quickly (for me).

16. つつむ＜包む＞／包みます　V1　to wrap; to fold

これをほかのと別に包んで下さい。Please wrap this separately from the rest.

17. デパちか＜デパ地下＞　N　basement of department store

日本のデパ地下ではたくさんの食べ物を売っている。In Japan, they sell lots of food in the basement of department stores.

六課

18. しょくりょうひんうりば＜食料品売り場＞　N　food (sales) section

日本のデパ地下は食料品売り場だ。The basements of Japanese department stores are the food sections.

19. ししょく＜試食＞　N　sample tasting

日本のデパートの食料品売り場で試食出来る。You can sample food at the food sections of department stores in Japan.

20. しなもの＜品物＞　N　goods

日本のデパートに行くと、品物がたくさんある。When you go to Japanese department stores, there are many things (to buy).

21. しゅるい＜種類＞　N　kind; variety

日本のお店にはいろいろな種類の鉛筆を売っている。Japanese stores sell various kinds of pencils.

22. ほうふ＜豊富＞　Na　abundant

日本のデパートへ行くと物が豊富だと思う。When I go to department stores in Japan, I think there is an abundance of things (to buy).

《Activity F》

23. せなか＜背中＞　N　(one's) back

背中が痛いんです。My back hurts.

24. はい＜肺＞　N　lung

たばこを吸っていると、肺が黒くなるらしい。When you smoke, it seems that your lungs become dark.

25. にゅうがん＜乳癌＞　N　breast cancer

叔母は乳癌の手術を受けた。My aunt had a breast cancer operation.

26. しんぞうまひ＜心臓麻痺＞　N　heart attack

祖父は心臓麻痺で亡くなった。My grandfather passed away from a heart attack.

27. うつびょう＜鬱病＞　N　depression

鬱病を治療するための薬もある。There are also medications that cure depression.

28. かんじゃ<患者>　N　(a) patient

医者の仕事は患者の病気を治すことだ。A doctor's job is to cure patients' diseases.

29. しょうじょう<症状>　N　symptoms

「病気の症状を説明して下さい。」"Please explain your symptoms."

30. すいみんぶそく<睡眠不足>　N　lack of sleep

「睡眠不足でよく考えられません。」"I cannot think well because of lack of sleep."

31. しょくよく<食欲>　N　appetite

「熱があって、食欲がないんです。」"I have a fever and have no appetite."

32. ずつう<頭痛>　N　headache

「頭痛がひどくて、考えられないんです。」"I cannot think because I have a severe

headache."

33. ほけんしつ<保健室>　N　health center

「気分が悪いんです。保健室へ行ってもいいですか。」"I do not feel good. May I go to the

health center?"

34. ちょうじゅ<長寿>　N　longevity; long life

日本は長寿の国として有名だ。Japan is a country famous for longevity.

《6課‐1・聞く》

35. せきがでる<咳が出る>／出ます　V2　to cough

「ゆうべは咳が出て、寝られなかったんです。」"I coughed (so much) last night, and I could

not sleep."

36. インフルエンザ　N　flu

冬になるとインフルエンザが流行るようだ。When it is winter, it seems that the flu is

common.

37. はれる<腫れる>／腫れます　V2　to swell; to become inflamed

喉が赤く腫れているようだ。Your throat seems to be red and swollen.

38. すいぶん(をとる)<水分(を取る)>／取ります　N　(to take in) water;

moisture; liquid; to hydrate

風邪を引いたら、水分を十分取るように。When you catch a cold, you should take plenty of liquids.

39. えいようがある＜栄養がある＞／あります　V1　nutritious

栄養がある物を食べるように。You should eat something nutritious.

40. (ねつを)さげる＜(熱を)下げる＞／下げます　V2　to lower (fever)

(ねつが)さがる＜(熱が)下がる＞／上げます　V1　(fever) goes down

熱を下げるための薬を飲んだら、熱が本当に下がった。When I took medicine to lower my fever, my fever really went down.

41. こうせいぶっしつ＜抗生物質＞　N　antibiotic

医者から抗生物質を全部飲んでしまうように言われた。I was told by my doctor to finish taking all of the antibiotics.

《6課 - 2・読む》

42. ～のせいで　P+N+P　with ～; because (of) ～ [bad reason, bad cause]

癌の治療のせいで母は髪の毛がなくなった。Because of the cancer treatment, my mother lost her hair.

43. ちゅういぶかく＜注意深く＞　Adv　carefully

ちゅういぶかい＜注意深い＞　A　careful

母は野菜を買う時、新鮮さを注意深く調べる。When my mom buys vegetables, she carefully checks their freshness.

44. けつあつ＜血圧＞　N　blood pressure

こうけつあつ＜高血圧＞　N　high blood pressure

ていけつあつ＜低血圧＞　N　low blood pressure

父は血圧が高くて心臓が弱い。My father has high blood pressure and his heart is weak.

45. えんぶん＜塩分＞　N　salt; saline

父は塩分の少ない食事をしている。My father has meals that are low-salt.

46. しぼう＜脂肪＞　N　fat; grease

アメリカの食事は脂肪が多くて、健康的ではない。American meals are high in fat and they are not healthy.

47. ひまん＜肥満＞　N　obesity

肥満はアメリカの大きな問題の一つだ。Obesity is one of the serious problems in America.

48. （〜を）きにする＜気にする＞／気にします　V3　to care about; to worry about; to be concerned (about)

姉は肥満を気にしている。My older sister is concerned about her weight.

49. けいさん（を）する＜計算（を）する＞／します　V3　to calculate

けいさんき＜計算器＞　N　calculator

姉はカロリーを計算して食事を作る。My older sister calculates calories and prepares meals.

50. ていカロリー＜低カロリー＞　N　low calorie

姉は低カロリーの物しか食べない。My older sister only eats low calorie food.

51. ビタミン　N　vitamin

ビタミンなどのサプリメントを売っている店が増えている。The number of stores which sell supplements like vitamins is increasing.

52. （〜に）こっている＜凝っている＞／凝っています　V1　to be devoted (to)

姉はビタミンなどのサプリメントに凝っている。My sister is particular about supplements like vitamins.

53. じまん（を）する＜自慢（を）する＞／します　V3　to boast

姉は３キロ痩せたと自慢している。My older sister boasts about her 3 kilogram weight loss.

《6課 - 3a・書く》

54. （〜に）かんする＜関する＞／関します　V1　about 〜 [to relate]; is related to

（〜に）かんしてのN＜（〜に）関してのN＞　V1　N about 〜 [=〜についてのN]

健康に関するアンケートに御協力、有難うございます。Thank you for your cooperation on the survey about health.

55. （からだを）きたえる＜（体を）鍛える＞／鍛えます　V2　to strengthen (one's body)

体を鍛えるためにジムに通っている。I go to the gym in order to strengthen my body.

《6課 - 3b・書く》　No new vocabulary

《6課 - 3c・書く》　No new vocabulary

56. くわしい＜詳しい＞　A　detailed

くわしく＜詳しく＞　Adv　in detail

誕生パーティーについてもっと詳しく教えて下さい。Please give me more details about the birthday party.

57. きゅうよう＜急用＞　N　urgent business

「すみません。急用で映画に行けなくなったんです。」"Sorry, I cannot go to the movie because of urgent business (that I must take care of)."

58. つごうが(or の)いい＜都合(or の)いい＞　A　convenient (timewise)

つごうが(or の)わるい＜都合(or の)悪い＞　A　inconvenient (timewise)

「都合のいい日時を教えて下さい。」"Please give me a convenient date and time."

59. きんきゅう＜緊急＞　N　emergency

「緊急連絡カードを出して下さい。」"Please turn in the emergency contact card."

60. アレルギー　N　allergy

「薬のアレルギーがありますか。」"Are you allergic to any medicine?"

【分かればいい単語】

1. デパートあんない＜案内＞　　　　　　　　N　department store information; directory

2. ぶっさんてん＜物産展＞　　　　　　　　　N　product fair

3. ようがし＜洋菓子＞　　　　　　　　　　　N　Western sweets

4. わがし＜和菓子＞　　　　　　　　　　　　N　Japanese sweets

5. おもちゃ　　　　　　　　　　　　　　　　N　toy

6. こうげいひん＜工芸品＞　　　　　　　　　N　crafts

7. ふじんふく＜婦人服＞		N	women's dresses
8. ふじんようけしょうしつ＜婦人用化粧室＞		N	women's restrooms
9. しんしようけしょうしつ＜紳士用化粧室＞		N	men's restrooms
10. しょうてんがい＜商店街＞		N	shopping arcade
11. はなみずがでる＜鼻水が出る＞/出ます		V2	to have a runny nose
12. いきをすって。＜息を吸って。＞/吸います		V1	Inhale.
13. いきをはいて。＜息を吐いて。＞/吐きます		V1	Exhale.
14. しょほうせん＜処方箋＞		N	prescription
15. しあつ＜指圧＞		N	acupressure; *shiatsu*
16. はり(ちりょう)＜鍼(治療)＞		N	acupuncture
17. たんすいかぶつ＜炭水化物＞		N	carbohydrate
18. (お)このみ＜(お)好み＞		N	liking; preference
19. わさび		N	*wasabi* (horseradish)

* Previously learned.

A. せいで   because (with an undesirable result)

The word せい is a dependent noun expressing a cause which brings about an undesirable result beyond speaker's control.

  1. 交通事故<u>のせいで</u>、学校に遅れてしまった。

    I was late to school because of a car accident.

  2. 私が先生にしかられたのは、あなた<u>のせいだ</u>。

    It's because of you that I was scolded by my teacher.

  3. お酒を飲んだ<u>せいで</u>、事故を起こしてしまった。

    I caused a car accident because I drank (alcohol).

Compare: おかげで   because (with a desirable result and appreciation)

                                   → AIJ 3 L.3*

おかげ and せい are similar in that both express a cause. The difference is that おかげ is used when the result is desirable, as せい is used when the result is undesirable. Note also that おかげ implies that the person who attained the result is thankful for the cause.

  4. 先生の<u>おかげで</u>、クラスはとても楽しかったです。

    Thanks (to the teacher), the class was enjoyable.

  5. 日本語を勉強した<u>おかげで</u>、日本へ行ってもあまり困らなかった。

    Because I studied Japanese, I didn't have too many problems in Japan.

Compare: ために "sake; purpose or reason"   → AIJ 4 L.2*

  6. 将来<u>のために</u>、今がんばる。 I will do my best now for the sake of my future.

  7. 両親は子供を育てる<u>ために</u>、朝から晩まで働いている。

    The parents are working from morning until night in order to raise their children.

正しい言葉に○をしなさい。

1. 友達の （おかげで　せいで　ために）宿題を終わることが出来た。

2. 弟の （おかげで　せいで　ために）宿題が出来なかった。

3. 友達が遅く起きた （おかげで　せいで　ために）私も学校に遅れた。

4. 先生の （おかげで　せいで　ために）いい大学に合格出来ました。

5. 私の（おかげで　せいで　ために）祖母は早く起きて私の弁当を作ってくれる。

6. 週末を楽しむ（おかげで　せいで　ために）宿題を全部しておくつもりだ。

7. コーチの（おかげで　せいで　ために）テニスが上手になった。

8. 友達の（おかげで　せいで　ために）誕生ケーキを作るつもりだ。

B.	野菜だけ食べる	eat only vegetables	→ AIJ 2 L.3＊
	野菜しか食べない	eats nothing but vegetables [emphasis]	→ AIJ 3 L.1＊
	野菜ばかり食べる	eat only vegetables (in a good amount)	→ AIJ 3 L.8＊
	食べてばかりいる	is just eating (often and continuously)	

正しい言葉に〇をしなさい。

1. 友達はコンピューターゲーム（だけ　しか　ばかり）している。

2. 姉は変なダイエットをしていて、肉（だけ　しか　ばかり）食べない。

3. 弟はご飯が大好きで、ご飯（だけ　しか　ばかり）食べている。

4. 祖母はあまり食欲がなくて、少し（だけ　しか　ばかり）食べられる。

5. 兄は疲れているようで、寝て（だけ　しか　ばかり）いる。

C.	一日に三度	three times per day	→ AIJ 2 L.6＊
	食後に	after a meal	
	食前に	before a meal	

日本語で何と表現しますか。

1. 医者：「この薬を＿＿＿＿＿＿＿＿＿＿飲みなさい。」(after every meal)

2. 医者：「この抗生物質を＿＿＿＿＿＿＿＿＿＿飲みなさい。」(three times a day)

3. 医者：「この薬を＿＿＿＿＿＿＿＿＿＿飲みなさい。」(before you go to bed)

4. 看護師：「これから、＿＿＿＿＿＿＿＿＿＿来て下さい。」(once a month)

5. 看護師：「この薬は＿＿＿＿＿＿＿＿＿＿飲んで下さい。」(before every meal)

D.「よく寝る<u>ように</u>。」"Sleep well." Advice, suggestion [informal] → AIJ 4 L.8＊

　「よく寝る<u>ように</u>して下さい。」"Please sleep well." Advice, suggestion [polite]

　「よく寝る<u>こと</u>。」"Sleep well." Instruction, direction, resolution [informal]

　　　　　　　　　　　　　　　　　　　　　　　　　　　→ AIJ 4 L.9＊

　「よく寝る<u>こと</u>です。」 "Please sleep well." Instruction, direction, resolution

　　　　　　　　　　　　　　　　　　　　　　　　　　　　　　　[polite]

a. 日本語に訳しなさい。

1. 医者：「水分を十分取る<u>ように</u>。」　　　_____

2. 医者：「少しずつ栄養のある食べ物を食べる<u>ように</u>。」_____

3. 医者：「よく休む<u>こと</u>です。」　　　　_____

4. 医者：「一日に三度食後に飲む<u>ように</u>。」_____

5. 私：「毎日、宿題をする<u>こと</u>。」　　　_____

6. 私：「毎日二十分運動をする<u>こと</u>。」　_____

7. 母：「早く寝る<u>ように</u>しなさい。」　　_____

8. 看護師：「この薬を一日に三度食事の前に飲む<u>ように</u>して下さい。」

　　　　　　　　　　　　　　　　　　　　_____

9. 医者：「元気になるまで学校へ行かない<u>こと</u>です。」_____

E. 食べ過ぎない<u>ようにしている</u>　is trying not to eat too much　→ AIJ 4 L.3＊
　　　　　　　　　　　　　　　　(conscious effort)

(　)の中の言葉を使って、下線に正しい日本語を書きなさい。

1. Your family is trying to practice a healthy lifestyle.

　私の家族は健康的な生活を_____。 （する）

2. You are trying not to eat too many sweets.

　私は甘い物を_____。 （食べ過ぎる）

3. Your mother is trying to eat fresh vegetables and fresh fruits.

　母は新鮮な野菜と新鮮な果物を_____。 （食べる）

六課　　　　　　　　270

4. Your grandmother is trying to walk for half an hour every day.

　祖母は毎日３０分＿＿＿＿＿＿＿＿＿＿＿＿＿＿＿＿＿＿＿＿。（歩く）

5. Your father is trying not to drink too much *sake* and not eat salty foods.

　父はお酒を＿＿＿＿＿＿＿＿＿＿＿＿、塩辛（しおから）い食べ物を＿＿＿＿＿＿＿＿＿＿＿＿＿＿＿＿

　＿＿＿＿＿＿＿＿＿＿。（飲む、食べる）

F.	風邪のようだ	seem to be a cold [formal]	→ AIJ 4 L.3*
	風邪みたいだ	seem to be a cold [informal]	→ AIJ 4 L.8*
	元気そうだ	looks healthy	→ AIJ 2 L.5*
	悪そうだ	looks bad	
	良〔よ〕さそうだ	looks good	
	悪くなさそうだ	does not look bad	
	元気だそうだ	I heard that he/she is healthy.	→ AIJ 3 L.6*

（　）の中の言葉を使って、下線に正しい日本語を書きなさい。

1. A doctor tells the patient that he seems to have caught a bad flu.

　医者：「悪い風邪を＿＿＿＿＿＿＿＿＿＿＿＿＿＿＿＿＿＿＿。」（引く）

2. A doctor tells the patient after an examination that his lungs seem fine.

　医者：「肺（はい）は＿＿＿＿＿＿＿＿＿＿＿＿＿＿＿＿＿＿＿。」（大丈夫）

3. A doctor reports to his patient that the patient seems to have cancer.

　医者：「癌（がん）＿＿＿＿＿＿＿＿＿＿＿＿＿＿＿＿＿＿＿。」

4. Your friend reports to you that your classmate Taro seems to be absent from school tomorrow.

　友達：「太郎は病気で明日学校を＿＿＿＿＿＿＿＿＿＿＿＿＿＿＿。」（休む）

5. A doctor reports to the patient's wife that her husband looks healthy, but he seems to have diabetes.

　医者：「ご主人は＿＿＿＿＿＿＿＿＿＿が、糖尿病（とうにょう）がある＿＿＿＿＿＿＿＿＿＿。」

　（元気、ある）

G.	食べさせてくれる	allow me/us to eat (as a favor)　[causative + くれる]
		→ AIJ 4 L.4* + AIJ 2 L.15*

英語に訳しなさい。

1. 客：「おいしそうですねえ。私にも食べさせて下さい。」　店員：「どうぞ。」
   _____　_____

2. 日本のデパ地下ではいろいろな食べ物を試食させてくれる。
   _____

3. 妹：「友達と映画に行かせて。」　母：「行ってもいいけど、早く帰って来なさいよ。」
   _____　_____

4. 両親は私を大学に行かせてくれるので、感謝している。
   _____

5. 気分が悪かった時、看護師さんが保健室で休ませてくれた。
   _____

H.	病気に関する本	a book about illness	[関する is more formal than ついて]
	病気に関しての本	a book about illness	
	病気に関して	about illness	
	病気についての本	a book about illness	
	病気について	about illness	→ AIJ 2 L.2*

英語に訳しなさい。

1. 「今日は健康に関するアンケートに御協力、有難うございます。」
   _____

2. 子供の食事に関してのレポートを読んで、驚いた。
   _____

3. 日本の指圧や鍼治療に関してもっと知りたいと思う。
   _____

4. 私は日本での体験についてのスピーチを書いた。
   _____

5. 日本のマッサージについてもっと研究するつもりだ。
   _____

A. 日本料理メニュー：ペアワーク→クラスワーク

日本料理レストランのメニューを見て、質問に答えなさい。

日本料理　あじひな

お品書き

一品料理

やっこ豆腐	¥300
納豆	¥350
枝豆	¥400
きゅうり酢の物	¥450
たこ酢の物	¥500
野菜サラダ	¥400
天ぷら盛り合わせ	¥1,000
えび天ぷら	¥1,000
いか天ぷら	¥800
野菜天ぷら	¥700
さしみ盛り合わせ	¥2,000
まぐろ刺身	¥2,500
いか刺身	¥1,000
たこ刺身	¥800
焼き魚	¥1,000
焼き鳥	¥1,000
鳥照焼き	¥800
いか照焼き	¥800
おでん	¥1,000
野菜煮物	¥500
漬物盛り合わせ	¥500
お茶漬け	¥700

うどん、そば

肉うどん	¥800
月見うどん	¥700
きつねうどん	¥700
天ぷらうどん	¥850
なべ焼きうどん	¥1,200
月見そば	¥700
天ぷらそば	¥850
ざるそば	¥700

どんぶり
みそ汁・漬物付き

天丼	¥1,500
親子丼	¥1,200
牛丼	¥1,500
かつ丼	¥1,500
うな丼	¥2,000

デザート

抹茶アイスクリーム	¥500
バニラアイスクリーム	¥500
あんみつ	¥850
ぜんざい	¥850

質問1：

　a. このメニューの中で食べたことがない食物は何ですか。　_____

　b. 食べてみたい食物は何ですか。　_____

　c. なぜ食べてみたいですか。　_____

質問2：

　今日は友達の誕生日です。予算は3,000円です。一品料理とデザートをいくつか注文してみましょう。

注文する料理	値段	
		円
		円
		円
		円
小計		円
税金5％		円
合計		円

質問3：

　日本のレストランとアメリカのレストランの料理を比べてみましょう。違う点を三つ書きなさい。そして、なぜ違うと思いますか。

違う点1：_____

違う点2：_____

違う点3：_____

その理由：_____

B. 野菜と果物：ペアワーク→クラスワーク

a. 下の野菜と果物の名前は何ですか。英語を書きなさい。

   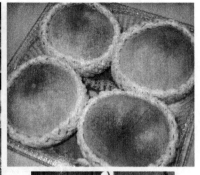

きゅうり	_____	苺〔いちご〕	_____
レタス	_____	りんご	_____
人参〔にんじん〕	_____	梨〔なし〕	_____
玉葱〔たまねぎ〕	_____	みかん	_____
葱〔ねぎ〕	_____	すいか	_____
じゃがいも	_____	桃〔もも〕	_____
れんこん	_____	柿〔かき〕	_____
ごぼう	_____	バナナ	_____
大根〔だいこん〕	_____	ぶどう	_____
なす(び)	_____	レモン	_____
ほうれん草〔そう〕	_____	トマト	_____
キャベツ	_____	枝豆〔えだまめ〕	_____

b. 写真は日本のスーパーで撮られた写真です。何が変だと思いますか。

_____

C. 料理：ペアワーク→クラスワーク

a. 日米の有名な料理のベスト３を書きなさい。そして、日米料理の材料、調味料、料理
   方法、食器の特徴を書きなさい。最後に自分の意見、感想を書きなさい。

国	有名料理3つ	材料の特徴	調味料の特徴	料理の特徴	食器の特徴	意見、感想
日本料理	1. 2. 3.					
アメリカ料理	1. 2. 3.					

b. それぞれの国の有名な料理のベスト３を書きなさい。そして、その国の料理の特徴を
   書きなさい。

国	有名料理1	有名料理2	有名料理3	特徴〔とくちょう〕
中華料理				
韓国料理				
イタリア料理				
（　　　）料理				

c. 次の質問に答えなさい。

1. 健康な体のために有機野菜を食べることは（いい　悪い）。

2. 私の町にある健康食品のスーパーの名前は（　　　　　　　　　　）だ。

3. 地元の野菜や果物は（新鮮だ　古い）。

4. 賞味期限が切れている食物は（食べた方がいい　食べない方がいい）。

5. 食物に入っている添加物は体に（いい　悪い）。

6. インスタント食品は体に（いい　悪い）。

7. 冷凍食品の方が新鮮な食物より体に（いい　悪い）。

8. 残り物を捨てるのはもったいない（から、全部食べる方が体にいい　が、全部食べ
   るのは体に良くない）。

次のレストラン案内を読んで、下の質問に英語で答えなさい。

レストラン東風　国際ホテル内２階　電話：240-0558

新鮮な海鮮と国内産中国野菜をふんだんに体にやさしい、
あっさりとコクのある中華料理
営業時間：11:30〜15:00、17:30〜22:00
席数：テーブル 40（個室５）
セットメニュー料金：季節のおすすめコース 3,150 円、5,250 円、
　　　　　　　　　料理長特選 8,400 円
単品メニュー料金：五目焼きそば 940 円、
　　　　　　　　　カニと卵入りフカヒレスープ 1,200 円、
　　　　　　　　　えびチャーハン 1,300 円
飲物料金：生ビール（中）550 円、ビンビール（中）650 円、酒 600 円、
　　　　　ソフトドリンク（ジュース）330 円
定休日：月曜日
カード利用：UC, VISA, JCB, DC 他
駐車場：５０台（有料）

1. What country's food does this restaurant serve?　_____

2. Where is this restaurant located?　_____

3. What is this restaurant famous for?　_____

4. Are they open for breakfast, lunch and dinner?　_____

5. Are there any private rooms?　_____

6. Is there a seasonal item for less than 5,000 yen?　_____

7. What is the least expensive dish on the menu?　_____

8. What kind of drinks do they sell?　_____

9. On what day is this restaurant closed?　_____

10. Is there free parking?　_____

11. このレストランに行って食べてみたいですか。なぜですか。（日本語で）

_____

E. デパート案内：ペアワーク→クラスワーク

| あじひなデパート　全館のご案内 | ■営業時間　午前10時〜午後8時　年中無休 |
| | ■10階レストラン街営業時間　午前11時〜午後10時 |

凡例：

- 📞 公衆電話
- 🚻 化粧室
- 婦人用化粧室
- 紳士用化粧室
- 家族用化粧室
- ♿ 車いす用化粧室
- ベビーキープ付き化粧室
- ベビーベッド
- ベビーカー貸し出し
- 総合案内所
- 休憩所
- 喫茶
- 🚌 バスのりば

地下街連絡通路 ←

R	屋上プレイランド	化粧室
10階	レストラン街	公衆電話　化粧室　家族用化粧室　車いす用化粧室　ベビーベッド　ベビーキープ付き化粧室　休憩所
9階	手芸/ペット/ビューティー&ヘルシー/京都物産展/贈り物コーナー	公衆電話　化粧室　休憩所
8階	宝石/時計/メガネ/美術/工芸品/呉服/旅行サロン	公衆電話　化粧室　休憩所
7階	インテリア用品(食器・台所用品・寝具・タオルほか) ギフトサロン ブライダルサロン	化粧室　休憩所
6階	ベビー洋品・こども服 おもちゃ	公衆電話　家族用化粧室　婦人用化粧室　車いす用化粧室　ベビーベッド　ベビーキープ付き化粧室　休憩所
5階	婦人服(ミセス)/エレガンスサロン/サイズ/フォーマル	婦人用化粧室　休憩所　喫茶
4階	婦人服(ミッシー・ミセス)/婦人肌着/ナイティー	公衆電話　婦人用化粧室　休憩所　喫茶
3階	バスセンター	バスのりば　婦人用化粧室
2階	婦人靴・婦人服(ミッシーカジュアル)	公衆電話　紳士用化粧室　総合案内所　ベビーカー貸し出し　休憩所　喫茶
1階 正面入口	化粧品/洋品小物/ハンドバッグ/商品券	公衆電話　紳士用化粧室　婦人用化粧室　家族用化粧室　総合案内所　ベビーカー貸し出し　休憩所　喫茶
B1階	和菓子/洋菓子/酒/茶	公衆電話　紳士用化粧室　婦人用化粧室　休憩所　喫茶
B2階	おかず市場/漬物/ベーカリー	公衆電話　紳士用化粧室　婦人用化粧室　休憩所

a. デパート案内を見て英語で答えを書きなさい。

1. What are the business hours of this department store? _____

2. When is this department store closed? _____

3. What are the business hours of the restaurant floor? _____

4. On what floor do they sell the following items?

a. cakes _____階	f. bread _____階	j. handbags _____階
b. toys _____階	g. watches_____階	k. baby clothes _____階
c. kitchen towels _____階	h. wine _____階	l. gift certificates _____階
d. crafts _____階	i. women's formal dresses _____階	

e. casual clothes for young women _____階

5. What public transportation can you get on at the 3rd floor? _____

6. What is on the roof top? _____

7. Where can you find rental baby strollers? _____

8. Where is the handicapped-accessible restroom? _____

9. Where is the coffee shop? _____

b. 日米のデパートの違いを３つ書きなさい。

1. _____

2. _____

3. _____

c. 日米のデパートでどちらの方が好きですか。なぜですか。

_____

_____

d. 日米のデパートを比(くら)べて、自分意見に丸しなさい。

1. （日本　アメリカ）のデパートの方が包装(ほうそう)が上手だ。

2. （日本　アメリカ）のデパートの方が店員のサービスがとても丁寧(ていねい)だ。

3. （日本　アメリカ）のデパートは食料品売り場が地下にあって試食をさせてくれる。

4. （日本　アメリカ）のデパートの方が品物の種類(しゅるい)が豊富(ほうふ)だ。

5. （日本　アメリカ）のデパートの方が駅の近くにあって買物に便利だ。

F. 体と病気の言葉：ペアワーク→クラスワーク

a. 体の部分の復習：体の部分を(　)の中にひらがなで、下線のところに漢字で書きなさい。

1. (　　　　) 髪の毛 hair
2. (　　　　) ___ head
3. (　　　　) ___ face
4. (　　　　) ___ body
5. (　　　　) ___ hand
6. (　　　　) お腹 stomach
7. (　　　　) ___ foot, leg
8. (　　　　) ___ finger, toe

9. (　　　　) ___ ear
10. (　　　　) ___ eye
11. (　　　　) ___ nose
12. (　　　　) ___ mouth
13. (　　　　) 歯 tooth
14. (　　　　) 首 neck
15. (　　　　) 喉 throat
16. (　　　　) 髭 beard, moustache

b. 体の部分：右のリストの中から選びなさい。

1. (　　　　) 背中　　　back
2. (　　　　) 肩　　　　shoulder
3. (　　　　) 膝　　　　knee
4. (　　　　) 肘　　　　elbow
5. (　　　　) 眉(毛)　　eyebrow
6. (　　　　) 睫毛　　　eyelash
7. (　　　　) 唇　　　　lip
8. (　　　　) 頬　　　　cheek
9. (　　　　) 顎　　　　chin
10. (　　　　) 胸　　　　chest
11. (　　　　) お尻　　　backside, buttocks
12. (　　　　) 骨　　　　bone
13. (　　　　) 筋肉　　　muscle
14. (　　　　) 腰　　　　waist
15. (　　　　) 腕　　　　arm

a. ひじ
b. むね
c. まつげ
d. ほお
e. せなか
f. ほね
g. あご
h. おしり
i. かた
j. うで
k. まゆ(げ)
l. こし
m. ひざ
n. きんにく
o. くちびる

c. 体の中の部分：右のリストの中から選びなさい。

1. ( )	脳	brain
2. ( )	心臓	heart
3. ( )	肺	lungs
4. ( )	胃	stomach
5. ( )	大腸	large intestines
6. ( )	肝臓	liver
7. ( )	腎臓	kidney
8. ( )	盲腸	appendix
9. ( )	血管	blood veins
10. ( )	血液	blood
11. ( )	神経	nerves
12. ( )	関節	joints (knee, elbow, etc.)

a. しんぞう
b. い
c. のう
d. はい
e. じんぞう
f. かんぞう
g. だいちょう
h. もうちょう
i. けっかん
j. けつえき
k. かんせつ
l. しんけい

d. 病気の名前：右のリストの中から選びなさい。

1. ( )	癌	cancer
2. ( )	乳癌	breast cancer
3. ( )	脳卒中	stroke
4. ( )	心臓まひ	heart attack
5. ( )	白血病	leukemia
6. ( )	エイズ	AIDS
7. ( )	盲腸	appendix
8. ( )	糖尿病	diabetes
9. ( )	アルツハイマー病	Alzheimer's disease
10. ( )	鬱病	depression
11. ( )	神経痛	neuralgia

a. しんけいつう
b. はっけつびょう
c. うつびょう
d. もうちょう
e. しんぞうまひ
f. がん
g. にゅうがん
h. のうそっちゅう
i. とうにょうびょう
j. アルツハイマーびょう
k. エイズ

★知りたい病気の名前を書きなさい。

英語の病名＿＿＿＿＿＿＿　日本語の病名＿＿＿＿＿＿＿

六課

G. 医者と患者のロールプレイ：ペアワーク→クラスワーク

次のロールプレイをしなさい。

例．＜病院で＞

医者：どうしましたか。

患者：熱があって、喉が痛くて、食欲がないんです。それに、睡眠不足で。

医者：そうですか。たくさん水分をとって、一日に三度食後に薬を飲んで下さい。よく
　　　寝た方がいいです。

患者：はい、分かりました。どうも有難うございました。

医者：では、お大事に。

a．＜病院で＞

患者：Symptoms: High fever, sore throat, no appetite.

医者：Recommendation: Take Tylenol every six hours, drink enough water, sleep
　　　well.

b．＜うちで＞

娘：Symptoms: Stomachache, headache, not enough sleep.

母：Give advice.

c．＜学校の保健室で＞

生徒：Description of current dietary practice: No food, lots of supplements such as
　　　vitamins and calcium, etc., lost too much weight.

看護婦：Make a recommendation.

d．＜カウンセラー室で＞

生徒：Discussion of your problems: You cannot stop drinking alcohol and smoking.

カウンセラー：Give advice.

e．＜病院で＞

姉：Description of your diet: You eat too many sweets such as cake and ice cream,
　　and worry about your weight.

医者：Make a recommendation.

H. 会話「死亡原因〔しぼうげんいん〕と食生活」：ペアワーク→クラスワーク

アメリカ人の死亡原因の一位は何でしょうか。

その理由はどんな食生活が原因でしょうか。

日本は長寿の国として有名ですが、なぜだと思いますか。

＜6課 - 1・聞く＞

聞く： Illness

(Narrator)　Now you will listen once to a conversation.

聞く： Illness

(Narrator)   Now answer the questions for this selection.

1.   What symptom does this patient NOT have?
     (A)   High fever
     (B)   Stomach ache
     (C)   Coughing
     (D)   Headache

2.   What did the doctor NOT check?
     (A)   The patient's chest
     (B)   The patient's back
     (C)   The patient's throat
     (D)   The patient's ears

3.   What did the doctor find out from examining the patient?
     (A)   The patient's lungs are normal.
     (B)   The patient's stomach is normal.
     (C)   The patient's throat is normal.
     (D)   The patient has the flu.

4.   What did the doctor NOT suggest to the patient?
     (A)   To eat well
     (B)   To drink enough liquids
     (C)   To gradually eat nutritious food
     (D)   To rest well

5.   What medicines did the doctor prescribe to the patient?
     (A)   Fever medicine to be taken two times a day after meals.
     (B)   Antibiotics to be taken three times a day before meals.
     (C)   Fever medicine and antibiotics to be taken three times before meals.
     (D)   Fever medicine and antibiotics to be taken three times after meals.

＜6課-2・読む＞

読む：家族の健康

去年、母は乳癌が見つかって手術した。治療のせいで髪の毛がなくなったりしたが、いつも明るく、暗い顔を全然見せなかった。現在は普通の生活が出来るまで元気になった。その後、食事にとても気をつけるようになった。まず、地元の有機野菜しか食べなくなり、町にある健康食品のスーパーで毎日の買い物をしている。買い物に行っても、野菜や果物の新鮮さや賞味期限や添加物などを注意深く調べる。インスタント食品とか冷凍食品は全然食べなくなった。残り物も全然食べない。そして、毎日健康のために歩くようになった。

また父は血圧が高くて心臓が少し弱いので、塩分の少ない食事をしている。好きな漬物などの塩辛い物をあまり食べないようにしている。たばこはかなり前にやめたが、お酒は現在もまだ少し飲んでいる。

来年結婚を予定している姉は肥満を気にして、最近ダイエットを始めた。カロリー計算をして、低カロリーの物ばかり食べている。甘い物が大好きだったのに、おやつもやめた。今ビタミンなどのサプリメントに凝っている。毎日水泳プールに行って、短い間に3キロも痩せたと自慢している。

私の家族のそれぞれ違う健康問題を持っているが、皆で協力して健康な食生活をするようにしている。

六課

読む: Health

(Narrator)　Now answer the questions for this section.

1. What kind of health problem did the mother have?
　　(A)　The mother had breast cancer and had surgery last year.
　　(B)　The mother lost quite a lot of weight and feels weak now.
　　(C)　The mother had a heart attack and recovered.
　　(D)　The mother has bad headaches once in a while.

2. What description is NOT correct about the mother?
　　(A)　The mother can eat any kind of food now.
　　(B)　The mother shops at the health food store only.
　　(C)　The mother checks the freshness, expiration date and additives of food she buys.
　　(D)　The mother quit eating instant foods and frozen foods.

3. What description is NOT correct about the father?
　　(A)　The father has a heart problem.
　　(B)　The father has high blood pressure.
　　(C)　The father is eating salty food.
　　(D)　The father quit smoking, but is drinking a little alcohol.

4. What description is NOT correct about the older sister?
　　(A)　The older sister is on a diet now.
　　(B)　The older sister eats only a little sweets.
　　(C)　The older sister loves to take supplements.
　　(D)　The older sister is happy about losing 3 kg in a short time.

5. What is this family trying to accomplish?
　　(A)　They try to eat together.
　　(B)　They try to eat healthy food.
　　(C)　They try to lose weight.
　　(D)　They try to communicate more effectively.

＜6課 - 3a・書く＞

Text Chat: Health

Note: In this part of the exam, the student may not move back and forth among questions.

You will participate in a simulated exchange of text-chat messages. Each time it is your turn to write, you will have 90 seconds. You should respond as fully and as appropriately as possible.

You will have a conversation with Mari, a student in a Japanese school, about health.

1. Respond. (90 seconds)

   初めまして。今日は健康に関するアンケートに御協力、有難うございます。

2. Respond. (90 seconds)

   何か特別なダイエットをしていますか。

3. Compare. (90 seconds)

   そうですか。では、アメリカ人の食事と日本人の食事と、どちらの方が健康的だと思いますか。なぜですか。

4. Respond. (90 seconds)

   ところで、体をきたえるために、どんな運動をしていますか。

5. State your opinion. (90 seconds)

   そうですか。では、ストレスをなくすために、何をするべきだと思いますか。

6. State your opinion. (90 seconds)

   ありがとうございました。では、東洋の指圧とか鍼治療について、何か質問をお願いします。

六課

Compare and Contrast: Japanese Food and a Western Country's Food

You are writing an article for the student newspaper of your sister school in Japan. Write an article in which you compare and contrast Japanese food and a Western country's food (American, Italian, French, etc.). Based on your personal experience, describe at least THREE similarities and differences between Japanese food and the other country's food. Also state your preference and give reasons for it.

Your article should be 300 to 400 characters or longer. Use the *desu/masu* or *da* (plain) style, but use one style consistently. Also, use *kanji* wherever *kanji* from the AP Japanese *kanji* list are appropriate. You have 20 minutes to write.

【自分の作文のアウトラインを書こう！】

Introduction:

_____

Three similarities and differences:

1. _____

2. _____

3. _____

Your preference and reasons:

_____

_____

＜６課‐3c・書く＞

Cultural Topic Posting: Shopping in Japan

You are responding to a posting in a Web forum for high school students of Japanese. The posting asks about shopping in Japan. Select ONE example of a shopping situation in Japan, such as shopping at a Japanese department store, shopping at a Japanese 100 yen shop, purchases one can shop for in Japan, etc. Describe in detail at least THREE characteristics of that shopping situation in Japan. Also, express your opinion or feelings about shopping in Japan.

Your posting should be 300 to 400 characters or longer. Use the *desu/masu* or *da* (plain) style, but use one style consistently. Also, use *kanji* wherever *kanji* from the AP Japanese *kanji* list are appropriate. You have 20 minutes to write.

【自分の作文のアウトラインを書こう！】

Introduction:

_____

One example:

_____

Three characteristics:

1. _____

2. _____

3. _____

Your opinion and feelings:

_____

_____

六課

＜6課 - 4a・話す＞

Conversation: Birthday Party

You will participate in a simulated conversation. Each time it is your turn to speak, you will have 20 seconds to record. You should respond as fully and as appropriately as possible.

You will have a conversation with Mr. Kimura, a manager at the restaurant, about planning your friend's birthday party.

(Man)

(20 seconds)

(Man)

(20 seconds)

(Man)

(20 seconds)

(Man)

(20 seconds)

＜6課 - 4b・話す＞

Return Telephone Call: Hospital

You will participate in a simulated telephone conversation with someone you are calling back after receiving a message. First, you will listen to the voice message. Then the telephone call will begin. Each time it is your turn to speak, you will have 20 seconds to record. You should respond as fully and as appropriately as possible.

(Narrator)   Listen to the voice message.

(Receptionist)

(Narrator)   Now the telephone call will begin. After the phone is answered, begin with a greeting and then explain why you are calling.

(Receptionist)   [Telephone] [Rings twice and the receptionist answers.]

(20 seconds)

(Receptionist)

(20 seconds)

(Receptionist)

(20 seconds)

(Receptionist)

(20 seconds)

＜ 6 課 - 4c・話す ＞

School Announcement: Emergency Card

Directions: Imagine that you are making an announcement in Japanese to an assembly of Japanese students visiting your school. First, you will see some notes in English about what to include in your announcement. You will have one minute to prepare your announcement while you look at the notes. Then you will have one minute to record your announcement. Your announcement should have an opening remark, details according to the notes, and a closing remark. Deliver your announcement using complete sentences in *desu/masu* style.

Fill in the emergency card.
Any health problems?
Allergy to any medication. Blood type.
Medication you are taking now.
Contact person in Japan and contact's telephone number.
Submit the completed emergency form to the school's health room.
The deadline is March 1st, at 3:30 p.m.

＜6課 - 4b・話す＞

Return Telephone Call: Hospital

You will participate in a simulated telephone conversation with someone you are calling back after receiving a message. First, you will listen to the voice message. Then the telephone call will begin. Each time it is your turn to speak, you will have 20 seconds to record. You should respond as fully and as appropriately as possible.

(Narrator)   Listen to the voice message.

(Receptionist)

(Narrator)   Now the telephone call will begin. After the phone is answered, begin with a greeting and then explain why you are calling.

(Receptionist)   [Telephone] [Rings twice and the receptionist answers.]

(20 seconds)

(Receptionist)

(20 seconds)

(Receptionist)

(20 seconds)

(Receptionist)

(20 seconds)

School Announcement: Emergency Card

Directions: Imagine that you are making an announcement in Japanese to an assembly of Japanese students visiting your school. First, you will see some notes in English about what to include in your announcement. You will have one minute to prepare your announcement while you look at the notes. Then you will have one minute to record your announcement. Your announcement should have an opening remark, details according to the notes, and a closing remark. Deliver your announcement using complete sentences in *desu/masu* style.

Fill in the emergency card.
Any health problems?
Allergy to any medication. Blood type.
Medication you are taking now.
Contact person in Japan and contact's telephone number.
Submit the completed emergency form to the school's health room.
The deadline is March 1st, at 3:30 p.m.

Story Narration: Sushi Bar

Directions: Imagine that you are making an oral presentation to your Japanese class. In your presentation, you will narrate a story. First, you will see pictures depicting the story. You will have 4 minutes to prepare your narration while you look at the pictures. Then you will have 2 minutes to record your narration. Narrate your story using complete sentences in *desu/masu* style.

＜6課 - 4e・話す＞

Cultural Perspective Presentation: Healthy lifestyle of the Japanese

Directions: Imagine you are making an oral presentation to your Japanese class. First, you will read and hear the topic for your presentation. You will have 4 minutes to prepare your presentation. Then you will have 2 minutes to record your presentation. Your presentation should be as complete as possible.

Present your own view or perspective on the healthy lifestyle of the Japanese. Discuss at least FIVE aspects or examples of the healthy lifestyle of the Japanese.

Begin with an appropriate introduction, give details, explain your own view or perspective, and end with a concluding remark.

【Let's take notes!】

1. Begin with an appropriate introduction.

_____

2. Discuss five aspects/examples of the topic.

    1.) _____

    2.) _____

    3.) _____

    4.) _____

    5.) _____

3. Explain your view or perspective.

_____

4. End with a concluding remark.

_____

七課		世界と旅行 World & Travel	

 At the end of this lesson, you are expected to be able to handle the following tasks.

【AP-7課 タスク1：世界】

What kind of global citizen do you want to become? How would you like to incorporate Japan and/or the Japanese language in your life? How would you want to contribute to the global community using the Japanese language?

【AP-7課 タスク2：旅行】

Think about your travel experiences to a foreign country or another state. What did you learn? How did the travel change your way of thinking? What was the biggest difference between the place where you traveled and the place where you live? Describe your inner change. What is significant about travel to another country? If you had a chance to live in Japan, what would you want to experience most? Why?

A. 世界の国名

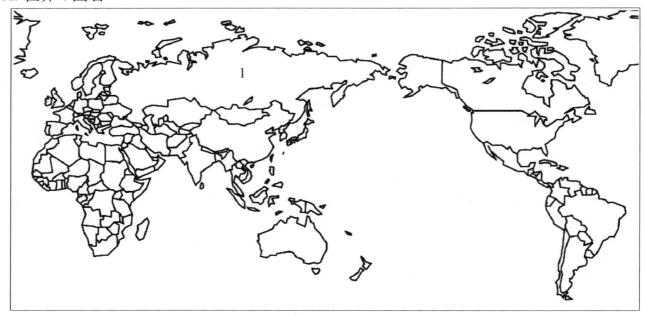

a. 国の番号を地図に書きなさい。そして、国名を英語で書きなさい。

	国名	英語		国名	英語		国名	英語
1	ロシア		11	メキシコ		21	イギリス	
2	中国		12	ブラジル		22	フランス	
3	北朝鮮〔きたちょうせん〕		13	南アフリカ		23	スペイン	
4	韓国		14	エジプト		24	イタリア	
5	フィリピン		15	サウジアラビア		25	ドイツ	
6	インドネシア		16	トルコ		26	スイス	
7	インド		17	イラク		27	オーストリア	
8	オーストラリア		18	イラン		28	デンマーク	
9	ニュージーランド		19	ギリシャ		29	ノルウェー	
10	カナダ		20	オランダ		30	スウェーデン	

b. この日本で作った世界地図とアメリカで作られる世界地図は何が違いますか。

c. オリンピックの５つの輪は五大陸(continent)を表しているそうです。　（　）の中から

　　正しい大陸の名前を選んで下線のところに書きなさい。

青: ＿＿＿＿＿＿＿　黒: ＿＿＿＿＿＿＿　赤: ＿＿＿＿＿＿＿

黄: ＿＿＿＿＿＿＿　緑: ＿＿＿＿＿＿＿

（ヨーロッパ　南北アメリカ　アフリカ　アジア　オセアニア）

B. 調べましょう。

a. 宅急便、クール宅急便

b. 地方の御土産

　　例：もみじまんじゅう（広島）

c. 駅弁

七課

[*Kanji* in text font]

1. 登　to climb　　のぼ(る)　　山〔やま〕を登る to climb a mountain

山登り〔やまのぼり〕mountain climbing

ト　　登山〔とざん〕mountain climbing

登山家〔とざんか〕mountain climber (professional)

トウ　　登場人物〔とうじょうじんぶつ〕characters (in a play or novel)

2. 荷　luggage　　ニ　　荷物〔にもつ〕luggage; baggage

重荷〔おもに〕heavy burden/responsibility

3. 成　to become　　な(る)　　成田空港〔なりたくうこう〕

なり　　Narita Airport

セイ　　平成時代〔へいせいじだい〕Heisei Period (1989 - present)

成人式〔せいじんしき〕Coming of Age Day (2nd Monday of January)

成功〔せいこう〕success

成績〔せいせき〕results; score; grade

4. 際 edge　　きわ/ぎわ　山際〔やまぎわ〕さん Yamagiwa-san

　　　　　　　　サイ　　　国際〔こくさい〕international

　　　　　　　　　　　　　国際空港〔こくさいくうこう〕

　　　　　　　　　　　　　international airport

　　　　　　　　　　　　　国際問題〔こくさいもんだい〕

　　　　　　　　　　　　　international problem

　　　　　　　　　　　　　国際化〔こくさいか〕

　　　　　　　　　　　　　internationalization

5. 打 to hit　　う(つ)　　ボールを打つ to hit a ball

　　　　　　　　ダ　　　　打者〔だしゃ〕batter (baseball)

　　　　　　　　　　　　打撃〔だげき〕batting (baseball)

　　　　　　　　　　　　打率〔だりつ〕batting average

6. 説 to explain　セツ　　説明〔せつめい〕する to explain

　　　　　　　　　　　　小説〔しょうせつ〕novel

　　　　　　　　　　　　解説者〔かいせつしゃ〕commentator

　　　　　　　　ゼツ　　演説〔えんぜつ〕speech; address

　　　　　　　　　　　　(formal)

7. 様 (polite equiv.　さま　御客様〔おきゃくさま〕customers

　　　of さん),　　　　　様々〔さまざま〕various

　　　manner　　　ヨウ　　様子〔ようす〕circumstances;

　　　　　　　　　　　　condition

七課

8. 未　not yet　　　ミ　　　未来〔みらい〕future (distant)

　　　　　　　　　　　　　　　　未知〔みち〕unknown

　[☞ 末　end　　　すえ　　末っ子〔すえっこ〕youngest child

　　　　　　　　　　　　　　　　(in a family)

　　　　　　　　　マツ　　　週末〔しゅうまつ〕weekend]

9. 夫　man,　　　　おっと　私の夫〔おっと〕my husband

　　　(own) husband　フ　　ケネディー夫人〔ふじん〕

　　　　　　　　　　　　　　　　Mrs. Kennedy

　　　　　　　　　フウ　　　夫婦〔ふうふ〕married couple

10. 選 to choose　　えら(ぶ)　選ぶ to choose

　　　　　　　　　　セン　　　選手〔せんしゅ〕(sports) player

　　　　　　　　　　　　　　　選挙〔せんきょ〕election

11. 雑 miscellaneous　ザツ　　雑誌〔ざっし〕magazine

　　　　　　　　　　　　　　　複雑〔ふくざつ〕complicated

　　　　　　　　　　　　　　　雑音〔ざつおん〕noise

　　　　　　　　　　　　　　　雑学〔ざつがく〕miscellaneous

　　　　　　　　　　　　　　　knowledge

12. 現 present　　　ゲン　　　現在〔げんざい〕present time

　　　　　　　　　　　　　　　現代〔げんだい〕modern time

　　　　　　　　　　　　　　　表現〔ひょうげん〕expression

　　　　　　　　　　　　　　　現金〔げんきん〕cash

七課　　　　　　　　　300

13. 係 in charge 　　かか(り)　　　係りの人〔かかりのひと〕

　　　　　　　　　　　　　　　　a person in charge

　　　　　　　　　　ケイ　　　　関係〔かんけい〕 relationship

14. 号 number 　　　ゴウ　　　　番号〔ばんごう〕 number

　　　　　　　　　　　　　　　　３号車〔さんごうしゃ〕 train car #3

　　　　　　　　　　　　　　　　修士号〔しゅうしごう〕 master's degree

　　　　　　　　　　　　　　　　信号〔しんごう〕 traffic light

【読みかえの漢字】　　　　＊ Previously introduced.

1. 写 to copy 　　シャ＊　　　　写真〔しゃしん〕 photo

　　　　　　　　うつ(す)　　　　ノートを写す to copy notes

2. 家 house, 　　いえ＊　　　　私〔わたし〕の家 my house

　　　family, 　　カ＊　　　　　家族〔かぞく〕 family

　　　person 　　　　　　　　　画家〔がか〕 painter (artist)

　　　　　　　　ケ　　　　　　　田中家〔たなかけ〕 Tanaka family

3. 伝 to convey 　　つた(える)＊　伝える to inform

　　　　　　　　　　　　　　　　手伝う〔てつだう〕 to help

　　　　　　　　デン　　　　　　伝言〔でんごん〕 verbal message

　　　　　　　　　　　　　　　　伝統〔でんとう〕 tradition

　　　　　　　　　　　　　　　　伝説〔でんせつ〕 legend

【読めればいい漢字】

1. 宅急便　　　　たっきゅうびん　home delivery service

2. 予約　　　　　よやく　　　　　reservation

3. 通訳	つうやく	interpreter; interpretation
4. 約〜	やく〜	approximately 〜
5. (お)宮	(お)みや	shrine (=神社)
6. - 神宮	- じんぐう	- Shrine
7. (お)城	(お)しろ	castle
8. - 城	- じょう	- Castle
9. 石油	せきゆ	petroleum

《Activity A》

1. しょうご＜正午＞　N　noon

   チェックインは正午で、チェックアウトは午前11時だ。The check-in time is noon and the check-out time is 11:00 a.m.

2. しゅくはく＜宿泊＞　N　lodging

   京都での宿泊は国際ホテルだった。The lodging in Kyoto was the International Hotel.

《Activity B》

3. でむかえ＜出迎え＞　N　meeting; welcome

   (〜を)でむかえる＜出迎える＞／出迎えます　V2　to meet 〜; to greet 〜

   空港で英語の通訳が私達を出迎えてくれた。The English interpreter met us at the airport.

4. しりょう＜資料＞　N　materials; data; records

   しりょうかん＜資料館＞　N　museum; reference library

   原爆資料館へ行って、考え方が変わった。When I went to the atomic bomb museum, my way of thinking changed.

5. しないかんこう＜市内観光＞　N　city tour

   観光バスで市内観光をした。We did a city tour by tour bus.

6. おおさかじょう＜大阪城＞　N　Osaka Castle

   大阪城は豊臣秀吉によって作られた。Osaka Castle was built by Hideyoshi Toyotomi.

7. めいじじんぐう＜明治神宮＞　N　Meiji Shrine (in Tokyo)

   へいあんじんぐう＜平安神宮＞　N　Heian Shrine (in Kyoto)

   平安神宮に大きい鳥居がある。There is a big gateway at the Heian Shrine.

8. かきこうざ＜夏期講座＞　N　summer session

   東京の高校で日本語の夏期講座を受けた。We took a Japanese language class during the summer session at a high school in Tokyo.

9. (しゃかい)けんがく＜(社会)見学＞　N　field trip (to study society)

   けんがく＜見学＞(を)する／します　V3　to visit (for study)

   午後は自動車工場を見学する予定だ。We are scheduled to visit a car factory in the afternoon.

10. しゅうごうばしょ＜集合場所＞　N　meeting place

　　しゅうごうじかん＜集合時間＞　N　meeting time

　　集合場所は学校で、集合時間は午前８時です。The meeting place is school and the meeting time is 8:00 a.m.

11. こくさい＜国際＞　N　international

　　なりたこくさいくうこう＜成田国際空港＞　N　Narita International Airport

　　午後8時30分成田国際空港発の飛行機で帰る。We will return by the airplane that leaves at 8:30 p.m. from the Narita International Airport.

12. こくさいこうりゅう＜国際交流＞　N　international exchange

　　私達の学校は日本の学校とテレビ会議を使って、国際交流をしている。Our school is doing an international teleconference exchange with a school in Japan.

《Activity C》

13. たっきゅうびん＜宅急便＞　N　express (home) delivery

　　空港へ宅急便で重い荷物を送ると便利だ。It's convenient to send heavy baggage to the airport by express delivery service.

《Activity D》

14. うつ＜打つ＞／打ちます　V1　to hit (an object)

　　弟は野球が上手で、よく打つ。My younger brother is good at baseball and hits well.

15. だしゃ＜打者＞　N　hitter

　　弟はいい打者だ。My younger brother is a good hitter.

16. しんきろく＜新記録＞　N　a (new) record

　　雑誌の記事によると、イチローはたくさんの新記録を作ったそうだ。According to the magazine article, Ichiro broke many records.

17. こくさいか＜国際化＞　N　internationalization

　　相撲やサッカーや野球などのスポーツは国際化している。Sports such as sumo, soccer, baseball, etc. are internationalized.

18. （〜に)こうけん＜貢献＞(を)する／します　V3　to contribute (to 〜)

　　将来、社会に貢献出来る人間になりたい。In the future, I want to become a person who can contribute to society.

19. ゆめをかなえる＜夢を叶える＞／叶えます　V2　to realize a dream

    ゆめがかなう＜夢が叶う＞／叶います　V1　a dream comes a reality

    夢を叶えるために、活動を続けている。We are continuing our activities in order to realize our

    dreams.

《Activity E》

20. せいじ＜政治＞　N　politics

    政治について何か意見がありますか。Do you have any opinions about politics?

21. そうりだいじん＜総理大臣＞　N　prime minister

    今、日本の総理大臣は誰ですか。Who is the prime minister of Japan now?

22. とうひょう＜投票＞(を)する／します　V3　to vote

    アメリカでは高校生でも大統領の選挙に投票出来るんですか。Can even high school

    students vote in the presidential elections in America?

23. せんきょ＜選挙＞　N　election

    選挙に出たことがありますか。Have you ever run in an election?

《Activity F》

24. ぼうえき＜貿易＞　N　trade (foreign)

    日本の貿易の約20%はアメリカが相手だそうだ。I understand that approximately 20% of

    Japan's trade is with the U.S.

25. ゆしゅつ＜輸出＞する／します　V3　to export

    ゆしゅつひん＜輸出品＞　N　exported goods

    日本は多くの自動車を外国に輸出している。Japan exports lots of automobiles to foreign

    countries.

26. ゆにゅう＜輸入＞する／します　V3　to import

    ゆにゅうひん＜輸入品＞　N　imported goods

    アメリカは日本から多くの自動車を輸入している。The U.S. imports lots of cars from Japan.

27. せきゆ＜石油＞　N　oil; petroleum

    日本の輸入品の一位は石油だそうだ。I understand that Japan's largest import item is oil.

28. せきたん＜石炭＞　N　coal

石炭から出るCO₂は地球温暖化の一つの原因だ。CO₂ from coal is one of the reasons for global warming.

29. しげん＜資源＞　N　resources

日本は資源が少ないので、資源を輸入しなければならない。Since Japan has (only) a few resources, Japan has to import its (natural) resources.

30. ちゅうとう＜中東＞　N　Middle East

日本はほとんどの石油を中東から輸入している。Japan is importing most of its oil from the Middle East.

31. ますます＜増々＞　Adv　more and more

現在、日本のアジアとの貿易はますます増えている。Japan's trade with Asia is increasing more and more now.

《Activity G》

32. しようりょう＜使用量＞　N　consumption; amount of use

電気などのエネルギーの使用量を25%減らす計画だ。We plans to reduce energy use of electricity and such by 25%.

33. むり＜無理＞　Na　impossible; unreasonable

ガソリンの使用量を半分に減らすのは無理だと思う。I think it's impossible to reduce gasoline usage by half.

《7課‐1・聞く》

34. まわりのひと＜周りの人＞　N　people around (someone)

周りの人を心配させたくない。I don't want to make people around me worry about me.

35. おもいやり＜思いやり＞　N　compassion; empathetic thoughtfulness

平和な社会を作るためには思いやりの心が大事だ。To create a peaceful society, a compassionate spirit is important.

36. (〜を)みおくる＜見送る＞／見送ります　V1　to see (〜) off

友達を空港まで見送った。I saw my friend off at the airport.

37. メモ　N　note

先生の話を聞きながら、メモを取る。I take notes while listening to my teacher's talk.

38. そんざい＜存在＞　N　existence

そんざい＜存在＞する／します　V3　to exist

誰も彼女のメモの存在を知らなかった。Nobody knew her note existed.

39. (〜に)しんぱいをかける＜心配をかける＞／かけます　V2　to cause 〜 worry

＝(〜を)しんぱいさせる＜心配させる＞／させます　V2　to cause 〜 worry

[causative form of 心配する]

両親には心配をかけたくない。I don't want to make my parents worry about me.

40. (〜を)ひろげる＜広げる＞／広げます　V2　to spread 〜; to extend 〜 [trans.]

(〜が)ひろがる＜広がる＞／広がります V1 〜 spread(s); 〜 extend(s) [intrans.]

平和運動を広げよう。Let's spread the peace movement.

41. (〜を)つなげる＜繋げる＞／繋げます　V2　to connect 〜 [trans.]

(〜が)つながる＜繋がる＞／繋がります　V1　〜 connect(s) [intrans.]

小さな思いやりの心が平和へと繋がっていく。A small bit of compassion will lead to peace.

42. (〜を)かくしんしている＜確信している＞／います　V2　to be certain; sure

世界平和が来ることを確信しています。I am sure that world peace will come.

43. みなおす＜見直す＞／見直します　V1　to look at again; to reconsider

人との関係を見直してみて下さい。Please reconsider your relationship with others.

44. みらい＜未来＞　N　(distant) future

明るい未来を作ろう。Let's create a bright future.

45. おりづる＜折り鶴＞　N　folded paper crane

千羽の折り鶴を折ろう。Let's make a thousand folded paper cranes.

46. (〜に)ねがいをこめる＜願いをこめる＞／こめます　V2　with all one's

hopes (for 〜)

明るい未来に願いをこめて、折り鶴を折りましょう。Let's fold the origami cranes with all of

our hopes for a bright future.

《7課 - 2・読む》

47. とざんか＜登山家＞　N　mountain climber (professional)

野口さんは登山家だ。Mr. Noguchi is a mountain climber.

48. ぼうけんか＜冒険家＞　N　adventurer

野口さんは冒険家だった植村さんの本を読んで感動した。Mr. Noguchi read and was moved by a book written by a former adventurer, Mr. Uemura.

49. おちこぼれ＜落ちこぼれ＞　N　dropout

野口さんは子供の時、落ちこぼれだった。When he was a child, Mr. Noguchi was a dropout.

50. たいりょう＜大量＞　N　a large quantity

富士山に大量のゴミが捨てられていた。A large amount of trash was strewn on Mt. Fuji.

51. いちりゅう＜一流＞　N　first-class; top tier

米国の一流大学はだいたい私立だ。The top tier universities in the U.S. are mostly private.

52. えんぜつ＜演説＞　N　speech; address (formal)

ケネディー大統領の演説を聞いた。I listened to the speech by President Kennedy.

53. かけがえのない　A　irreplaceable; precious

このかけがえのない自然を守ろう。Let's protect this irreplaceable nature.

54. じせだい＜次世代＞　N　next generation

この戦争の話を次世代にも伝えたい。I want to pass this war story on to the next generation.

55. （〜を）のこす＜残す＞／残します　V1　to leave behind 〜 [trans.]

（〜が）のこる＜残る＞／残ります　V1　〜 remain(s) [intrans.]

美しい自然を残したい。I want to preserve the natural beauty.

《7課 - 3a, b, c・書く》　No new vocabulary

《7課 - 4a・話す》　No new vocabulary

《7課 - 4b・話す》　No new vocabulary

《7課 - 4c・話す》

56. こくれん＜国連＞　N　United Nations [a short form of こくさいれんごう ＜国際連合＞]

国連は国際問題を解決するために非常に大切だ。The United Nations is extremely important to resolve international problems.

57. こうどう＜講堂＞　N　auditorium

コンサートが講堂であった。There was a concert in the auditorium.

58. (〜に)さんか＜参加＞(を)する　V3　to participate (in 〜)

さんかしゃ＜参加者＞　N　participant(s)

今年のスピーチコンテストに３０人ぐらいの参加者があった。There were about 30 participants in this year's speech contest.

＜8課 - 4d・話す＞

59. たき＜滝＞　N　waterfall

美しい滝の前で女の子に写真を撮ってもらった。We asked a girl to take our photo in front of the beautiful waterfall.

60. ゆめをみる＜夢を見る＞／見ます　V2　to dream 〜

御馳走を食べている夢を見た。I dreamed about eating a feast.

《7課 - 4e・話す》　No new vocabulary

【分かればいい単語】

1. みんしゅとう＜民主党＞　　　　　N　the Democratic Party
2. きょうわとう＜共和党＞　　　　　N　the Republican Party
3. しじする＜支持する＞　　　　　　V3　to support
4. とうせんする＜当選する＞　　　　V3　to be elected
5. らくせんする＜落選する＞　　　　V3　to be defeated (in an election)
6. みんしゅしゅぎ＜民主主義＞　　　N　democracy
7. びょうどう＜平等＞　　　　　　　N　equality
8. カルテ　　　　　　　　　　　　　N　medical records

* Previously learned.

| A. Words related to travel: | → AIJ 4 L.8* |

ひらがなで読み方を、英語でその意味を書きなさい。

言葉	ひらがな	英訳	言葉	ひらがな	英訳
1. 出発時間			13. 神社		
2. 到着時間			14. お宮		
3. 成田空港着			15. 平安神宮		
4. 関西空港発			16. お城		
5. JAL 77 便			17. 大阪城		
6. 新幹線 のぞみ 20 号			18. 朝食		
7. 宿泊			19. 昼食		
8. 国際旅館泊			20. 夕食		
9. 4 泊 5 日			21. 弁当		
10. 市内観光			22. 駅弁		
11. お寺			23. 御土産		
12. 東大寺			24. 予定表		

| B. 大きさ size, 大切さ importance | → AIJ 4 L.3* |

長い is long → 長さ length   静か is quiet → 静かさ quietness

重い is heavy → 重さ weight   大事 is important → 大事さ importance

寒い is cold → 寒さ coldness   ていねい polite → ていねいさ politeness

良い is good → 良さ goodness; good point

Certain いadjectives become nouns when the final い is dropped and replaced with さ. Note that for the adjective いい, the よい form must be used. Certain な adjectives become nouns when さ is added.

右のリストの中から適当な言葉を選んで、下線のところに「-さ」を使って書きなさい。

1. 桜の花の_____は、印象的だった。

2. 富士山の_____は、3,776メートルだそうだ。

3. 新幹線の_____に驚いた。

4. 祖母は癌の_____を誰にも言わなかった。

5. 戦争の映画を見て、平和の_____を感じた。

高い
大切
速い
美しい
苦しい

C. More Transitive verbs and Intransitive verbs   → AIJ 4 L.4＊
   Direct object を ＋ Transitive verb
   Subject が ＋ Intransitive verb

---

a. 正しい自動詞(intransitive verb)「〜が」の後に書きなさい。

	Transitive verb 〜を	(someone) does (something)	Intransitive verb 〜が	(something) does
1.	〜を 見つける	(SO) finds (ST)	〜が	(ST) be found
2.	〜を ふやす	(SO) increases (ST)	〜が	(ST) increases
3.	〜を へらす	(SO) decreases (ST)	〜が	(ST) decreases
4.	〜を 閉める	(SO) closes (ST)	〜が	(ST) closes
5.	〜を 開ける	(SO) opens (ST)	〜が	(ST) opens
6.	〜を 残す	(SO) leaves (ST)	〜が	(ST) remains
7.	〜を 集める	(SO) collects (ST)	〜が	(People) gather
8.	〜を 続ける	(SO) continues (ST)	〜が	(ST) continues
9.	〜を きれいにする	(SO) cleans (ST)	〜が	(ST) becomes clean
10.	〜を つなげる	(SO) connects (ST)	〜が	(ST) be connected
11.	〜を 広げる	(SO) expands (ST)	〜が	(ST) expands
12.	ゆめを かなえる	(SO) realizes a dream	ゆめが	A dream comes reality.

b. 正しい言葉に丸をしなさい。

1. エコ車に乗って、ガソリンの使用料を（a. 減らす　b. 減る）つもりだ。

2. ペットボトルや缶を（a. 集めて　b. 集まって）、リサイクルしよう。

3. よくがんばって希望の大学に合格出来た。夢が（a. 叶えて　b. 叶って）、嬉しい。

4. 明日までにどこの大学へ行くか（a. 決め　b. 決まら）なければならない。

D. Verb (OO form) ＋と　思っている　I think that I will do ～.　→ AIJ 3 L.8＊

This construction is used when the speaker says that he is considering or deciding to do something in the future. The subject doing the action should be the same as the person who is thinking about doing it. Do not confuse this pattern with the Plain Form ＋と思います pattern that is used when expressing opinions.

    Compare: 行くと思う。　　　　　I think (I/he) will go. (Opinion)

            行こうと思っている。　I am thinking of going. (Intention)

＊ Review of the verb OO form.

    Group 1　飲む→飲もう

    Group 2　食べる→食べよう

    Irregular　する→しよう

            来〔く〕る→来〔こ〕よう

（　）の中の言葉を使って、下線のところに正しい日本語を書きなさい。

1. 先生：「どこの大学に＿＿＿＿＿＿＿＿と思っている？」（行く）

  あなた：「＿＿＿＿＿＿＿＿＿＿＿＿＿＿＿と思っています。」

2. 友達：「パーティーに何を＿＿＿＿＿＿＿と思っている？」（持って来る）

  あなた：「＿＿＿＿＿＿＿＿＿＿＿＿＿＿＿と思っているよ。」

3. 友達：「夏に何を＿＿＿＿＿＿＿と思っている？」（する）

  あなた：「＿＿＿＿＿＿＿＿＿＿＿＿＿＿＿と思っているよ。」

E.　何か ＋ Affirmative　　　something ～　　　　　　　　　→ AIJ 2 L.15＊

   何か ＋ Question　　　　　any ～ ?

   1. 何か食べたい。　　　　　　　　　I want to eat something.

   2. 何か冷たい物を食べたい。　　　　I want to eat something cold.

   3. 何か質問がある？　　　　　　　　Do you have any questions?

   4. 何か困っていることがある？　　　Do you have anything troubling you?

日本語で何と表現しますか。

1. You ask your friend if he wants something to drink.

  「＿＿＿＿＿＿＿＿飲みたい？」

2. You suggest to your friend that you have something delicious together.

  「一緒に何か＿＿＿＿＿＿＿＿＿＿＿＿＿＿を食べに行こう。」

3. You want to know if your friend has had any good memories on his trip.

  「旅行で何か＿＿＿＿＿＿＿＿＿＿＿＿＿＿がある？」

4. You tell your friend that you want to give something special to your mother.

  「母の日に、母に何か＿＿＿＿＿＿＿＿＿＿＿＿＿をあげたいんだけどね。」

A. ホテル：ペアワーク→クラスワーク

雑誌に出ているホテル案内です。案内を読んで、質問に答えなさい。

ホテルセンチュリー21 名古屋

名古屋駅南口より徒歩３分。ビジネスに観光に
幅広く御利用いただける本格的なホテルです。
便利で優れた２１世紀という名のホテルです。

シングル	¥9,240〜
ツイン	¥16,170〜
ダブル	\15,015
和室	¥16,170〜
和洋室	¥20,790〜
ロイヤルスイート	\34,650
インペリアルスイート	\57,750

（税*・サービス料込み*)

| チェックイン | 正午 |
| チェックアウト | 午前 11:00 |

●駐車場　３４台（有料）
●名古屋駅南口より徒歩３分

宿泊予約・婚礼・レストラン各種のご案内
ご予約・お問い合わせは (0568)263-3111
http://www.hotelcentury21nagoya.com

税* tax、込み* included

1. Where is this hotel? _____

2. Why is this hotel convenient? _____

3. When traveling alone, which room should you choose? _____

　 How much is this room in dollars? _____

4. Does the price list include tax and a room service fee? _____

5. When are the check-in and the check-out times? _____

6. Is parking free? _____

7. What other facilities does this hotel have? _____

七課

B. 日本旅行：ペアワーク→クラスワーク

これは日本旅行の予定表です。予定表を読んで、質問に英語で答えなさい。

日本旅行予定表

7月11日（火）	12:20	ホノルル発 Jalways 77 便
7月12日（水）	16:05	関西空港着
		英語通訳の出迎え、バスで広島へ（荷物持参）
		夕食：バス内（幕の内弁当）
		宿泊：ニュー広電ホテル
7月13日（木）		朝食：ホテルにて
	08:30	一日観光：宮島（英語ガイド付き）
		昼食：弁当
		夕食：お好み焼き（ホテルグランビアにて）
		宿泊：ニュー広電ホテル
7月14日（金）		＊＊荷物は京都へトラックで搬送＊＊
		朝食：ホテルにて
	08:30	広島平和公園と資料館（英語ガイド付き）
	12:00	広島発　新幹線のぞみ 20 号
		昼食：新幹線で弁当
	13:45	京都着、英語ガイドの出迎え
		市内観光：平安神宮、三十三間堂、清水寺
		夕食：ホテルにて
		宿泊：京都リーガロイヤルホテル
7月15日（土）		朝食：ホテルにて
	08:00	京都観光：二条城、金閣寺、竜安寺（英語ガイド）
		昼食：京料理
		奈良観光：東大寺、鹿公園
		夕食：ステーキハウス
		宿泊：京都リーガロイヤルホテル
7月16日（日）		朝食：ホテルにて
	09:32	京都発　新幹線のぞみ 122 号
	11:53	東京着、バスで慶応高校へ
7月16日（日）～8月3日（木）		：慶応高校にて夏期講座（午前日本語授業、午後社会見学）、国際交流、ホームステイ
8月03日（木）	16:00	慶応高校集合、成田国際空港へバスで
	20:25	成田国際空港発 Jalways76 便
8月03日（木）	08:30	ホノルル空港到着

質問：

1. What airport will you arrive at in Japan? _____

2. Who will meet you at the airport? _____

3. Where you are heading to Hiroshima from the airport, what kind of transportation
   will you take? _____

4. What activity is scheduled on the 13th? _____

5. What will they send to Kyoto by truck on the morning of the 14th? _____

6. Where are you visiting on the morning of the 14th? _____

7. Where are you heading to on the afternoon of the 14th? _____

8. What activity is scheduled on the afternoon of the 14th? _____

9. What two cities are you sightseeing on the 15th? _____

10. Which meal is not Japanese style? _____

11. When are you arriving in Tokyo? _____

12. During your stay at Keio School, what is scheduled in the morning and what in
    the afternoon? _____ _____

13. Where are you staying during the summer program in Tokyo? _____

14. How long is this summer program? _____

15. What airport are you leaving from in Japan? _____

C. 宅急便〔たっきゅうびん〕：ペアワーク→クラスワーク
   宅急便フォームを見て、正しい言葉に丸をしなさい。

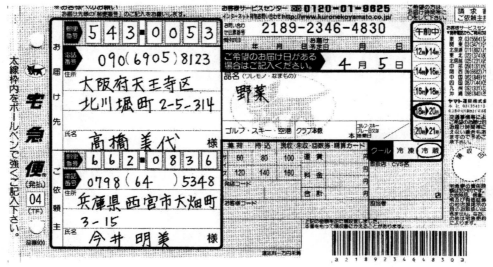

1. (a. Takahashi   b. Imai) is the sender of this package.

2. (a. Takahashi   b. Imai) is the recipient of this package.

3. (a. Fruits   b. Vegetables   c. Fish) are in this package.

4. The requested delivery date of this package is (a. April 5   b. May 4).

5. The requested delivery time of this package is (a. 4:00 p.m - 6:00 p.m.
   b. 6:00 p.m - 8:00 p.m.)

6. The special request made for this package is that it be (a. frozen   b. refrigerated).

D. 有名な日本人：ペアワーク→クラスワーク

次の日本人についての紹介を読んで、後の質問に英語で答えなさい。

イチローはシアトルマリナーズというメジャーリーグで活躍する日本人のプロ野球選手だ。背番号は５１で、右投げ、左打ち、ポジションは外野だ。イチロー選手は、打者として有名だが、打つだけでなく、走るのも、守るのも上手だ。今までにいろいろな新記録を作り、プロ野球の国際化に大きく貢献した。イチロー選手はアメリカに行く前に結婚し、夫婦でアメリカに渡ったそうだ。現在、奥さんと犬と住んでいる。イチロー選手はもっと大きな夢を叶えるために、いつも自分に挑戦している。

1. What team does Ichiro play for? _____

2. Is Ichiro right handed or left handed? _____

3. What is Ichiro's position? _____

4. What is Ichiro famous for? _____

5. When did Ichiro get married? _____

6. Who are the members of Ichiro's immediate family?_____

7. What is Ichiro's attitude toward life? _____

E. 政治〔せいじ〕：ペアワーク→クラスワーク

次の質問に日本語で答えなさい。

1. 今、日本の総理大臣〔そうりだいじん〕は誰ですか。　　　＿＿＿＿＿＿＿＿＿＿＿＿＿＿

2. 日本に大統領〔とうりょう〕がいますか。　　　＿＿＿＿＿＿＿＿＿＿＿＿＿＿

3. アメリカでは何歳から投票〔とうひょう〕出来ますか。　　　＿＿＿＿＿＿＿＿＿＿＿＿＿＿

4. 日本では何歳から投票〔とうひょう〕出来ますか。　　　＿＿＿＿＿＿＿＿＿＿＿＿＿＿

5. 日本はほかの国と関係がいいですか。　　　＿＿＿＿＿＿＿＿＿＿＿＿＿＿

6. アメリカの政治〔せいじ〕についてどんな意見を持っていますか。

＿＿＿＿＿＿＿＿＿＿＿＿＿＿＿＿＿＿＿＿＿＿＿＿＿＿＿＿＿＿＿＿＿＿＿＿＿

F. 貿易〔ぼうえき〕：ペアワーク→クラスワーク

「世界貿易〔ぼうえき〕レポート 2005」を読んで、質問に英語で答えなさい。

　2005 年の世界貿易〔ぼうえき〕レポートによると、日本の貿易〔ぼうえき〕の約 20％は、アメリカを相手にしたものでした。また、貿易〔ぼうえき〕の約半分は、中国、韓国、台湾〔わん〕といったアジアの国々との貿易〔ぼうえき〕であり、近年、アジアとの貿易〔ぼうえき〕はますます増〔ふ〕えています。

　日本の主な輸出品〔ゆ〕は、自動車、半導体〔どう〕*、ビデオカメラ、エンジンなどです。自動車は、約 40％がアメリカに輸出〔ゆ〕されています。そして、日本の主な輸入品〔ゆ〕は、石油、石炭〔たん〕、ガス、半導体〔どう〕*、携帯電話〔けいたい〕、テレビ部品、コンピューターなどです。石油は、サウジアラビアなどの中東から約89％が輸入〔ゆ〕されました。また、衣類〔いるい〕*は、中国から約80％が輸入〔ゆ〕されました。

　日本は資源〔しげん〕が少ない国なので、資源〔しげん〕を輸入〔ゆ〕し、発達したテクノロジーを使って、いい製品を作り、それを輸出〔ゆ〕するというパターンです。日本の一番の輸出〔ゆ〕相手国はアメリカで、一番の輸入〔ゆ〕相手の国は中国でした。

　世界の国々との貿易〔ぼうえき〕なしに、日本の経済〔けいざい〕は成り立ちません。

資料〔し〕:世界貿易機関〔ぼうえき〕(WTO)「世界貿易〔ぼうえき〕レポート 2005」

半導体〔どう〕* semiconductor　　部品* parts
衣類〔いるい〕* clothing [formal, collectible items]; garment

1. What country did Japan export most of its products to in 2005? _____

2. What country did Japan import the most from in 2005? _____

3. What was the top import to Japan in 2005? _____

4. What was the top export from Japan in 2005? _____

5. What is the pattern of trade in Japan?

_____

G. Sustainability：ペアワーク→クラスワーク

今年、校長先生がこんな sustainability の目標を生徒に発表しました。それぞれの目標について、どう思いますか。そして、自分が出来る事を三つ、書きなさい。

	目標	意見	自分が出来る事
目標1	学校で使う電気や水の使用量〔しょうりょう〕を8年間で50%減〔へ〕らす。	(無理　出来る)	1. 2. 3.
目標2	学校で出すゴミ（紙、プラスチック、ガラス、金属〔きんぞく〕）を8年間で50%減〔へ〕らす。	(無理　出来る)	1. 2. 3.
目標3	学校の飲料水の使用量〔しょうりょう〕を8年間で50%減〔へ〕らす。	(無理　出来る)	1. 2. 3.
目標4	学校に入る車の量を8年間で25%減〔へ〕らす。	(無理　出来る)	1. 2. 3.
目標5	100%の生徒が健康な食物を8年間で食べるようにする。	(無理　出来る)	1. 2. 3.

＜7課‐1・聞く＞

聞く： World Peace

(Narrator)   Now you will listen to a speech given by SADAKO's older brother who attended the 9/11 memorial service in New York in 2007. It will be read once.

聞く： World Peace

(Narrator) Now answer the questions for this selection.

1. Why wasn't Sadako's father wearing his wristwatch on his visit to Sadako?
   - (A) He left it at home.
   - (B) He sold it.
   - (C) He lost it.
   - (D) He gave it to Sadako.

2. How did Sadako deal with her disease?
   - (A) She cried in front of her father.
   - (B) She expressed her fears to her father.
   - (C) She complained about her pain to the nurse.
   - (D) She showed her tears only once when her mother was about to leave.

3. How did Sadako deal with her death?
   - (A) She knew she was dying.
   - (B) She was not aware of her imminent death.
   - (C) She could not tell anyone about her death because of fear.
   - (D) She told people around her about her imminent death.

4. What was found under Sadako's bed after she passed away?
   - (A) a letter to her parents
   - (B) her father's watch
   - (C) origami cranes
   - (D) a memo about her white blood cell count

5. What message did Sadako's older brother want to give to the audience?
   - (A) make paper cranes
   - (B) be considerate of others
   - (C) wish for a bright future
   - (D) all of the above

読む: Environment

　野口健さんは登山家です。一九九七年に世界7大陸最高峰の登頂という冒険に成功しました。野口さんが登山家になろうと思ったきっかけはある本でした。その本は冒険家の植村直樹さんが書いた「青春を山にかけて」という本でした。その本は落ちこぼれだった植村さんが山登りを始めて世界的な冒険を成功させ、自信を取り戻すという話です。野口さんも落ちこぼれだったので、この本を読んで、山を登りたくなりました。

　ある日、野口さんは外国人の登山家たちに一緒にゴミ拾いをしないかと誘われました。その時、エベレストに大量のゴミが捨てられていることを知りました。そして、その多くが日本の登山隊のゴミだったと知りました。「日本は経済は一流だけど、マナーは三流だね。」と外国人の登山家に言われました。ほかに富士山にもゴミがたくさんあることを知りました。野口さんはとてもびっくりし、何かをしないといけないと思い、野口さんはゴミ拾いを始めました。そこから、地球を守るという野口さんの次の冒険が始まりました。

　野口さんはエベレストや富士山などでゴミ拾いを始めた時には、手伝ってくれる人があまりいなくて、とても大変でした。野口さんはたくさんの演説をし、だんだんと手伝ってくれる人が集まり、山はだんだんきれいになりました。野口さんは「あきらめないこと、それが冒険だ。」と言っています。かけがえのないこの自然を次世代に残すため、野口さんの活動はこれからも続いていきます。

参考：学習研究社 野口健著「あきらめないこと、それが冒険だ」

読む: Environment

(Narrator)   Now answer the questions for this section.

1.   What kind of child was Mr. Noguchi?
   (A)   He was a good student.
   (B)   He was a school dropout.
   (C)   He loved mountain climbing.
   (D)   He was very self-confident.

2.   What made Mr. Noguchi want to become a mountain climber?
   (A)   He saw pictures of mountains.
   (B)   His father took him to the mountains when he was young.
   (C)   He joined a mountain climbing club in college.
   (D)   He was inspired by a book written by a mountain climber.

3.   Which of the following was NOT mentioned as a motivating factor for
   Mr. Noguchi to pick up trash on Mt. Everest and Mt. Fuji?
   (A)   He saw the news of foreign mountain climbers picking up trash on
         Mt. Everest.
   (B)   He learned about all of the trash that was left behind on Mt. Everest
         by Japanese climbers.
   (C)   Other foreign mountain climbers told him, "the Japanese economy is
         first class, but Japanese manners are third class."
   (D)   He learned that there was lots of trash on Mt. Fuji.

4.   How did Mr. Noguchi recruit people to pick up trash on Mt. Everest and
   Mt. Fuji?
   (A)   He put an advertisement in the newspaper and asked for
         cooperation from the public.
   (B)   He started a trash pick-up club at the college where he teaches.
   (C)   He gave speeches at many places.
   (D)   He made a web page and asked people for their cooperation.

5.   What is Mr. Noguchi's definition of "adventure"?
   (A)   Don't give up picking up trash.
   (B)   Recruit more people to pick up trash.
   (C)   Climb Mt. Fuji and pick up trash.
   (D)   Do trash pick-up campaigns through the media.

＜７課‐3a・書く＞

Text Chat: Trip in Japan

You will participate in a simulated exchange of text-chat messages. Each time it is your turn to write, you will have 90 seconds. You should respond as fully and as appropriately as possible.

You will have a conversation with Mika Nonaka, your host mother in Tokyo for this summer, about your plans.

1.   Respond. (90 seconds)

初めまして。日本行きも、もうすぐですね。

2.   Respond. (90 seconds)

日本に来た時に私達家族と一緒に旅行しませんか。旅行は好きですか。

3.   State your opinion. (90 seconds)

じゃ、日本で行ってみたい所はどこですか。なぜですか。

4.   Give your preference. (90 seconds)

そうですか。ホテルと旅館とどっちの方が好きですか。

5.   Give a specific example. (90 seconds)

以前、旅行をして、何か困った経験とかありますか。

6.   Respond. (90 seconds)

じゃ、会えるのを楽しみにしていますね。日本の旅行について何か質問がありますか。

Compare and Contrast: Japan and America

You are writing an article for the student newspaper of your sister school in Japan. Write an article in which you compare and contrast Japan and America as countries with respect to such things as history, people, geography, culture, etc. Based on your personal experience, describe at least THREE similarities and differences between Japan and America. Also state your preference and give reasons for it.

Your article should be 300 to 400 characters or longer. Use the *desu/masu* or *da* (plain) style, but use one style consistently. Also, use *kanji* wherever *kanji* from the AP Japanese *kanji* list is appropriate. You have 20 minutes to write.

【自分の作文のアウトラインを書こう！】

Introduction:

_____

Three similarities and differences:

1. _____

2. _____

3. _____

Your preference and give reasons:

_____

_____

15点
20分

Cultural Topic Posting: Famous historical Japanese person

You are responding to a posting in a Web forum for high school students of Japanese. The posting asks about a historically famous Japanese person. Select ONE example of a famous historical Japanese person. Describe in detail at least THREE characteristics of this Japanese person. Also, express your opinion or feelings about this person.

Your article should be 300 to 400 characters or longer. Use the *desu/masu* or *da* (plain) style, but use one style consistently. Also, use *kanji* wherever *kanji* from the AP Japanese *kanji* list is appropriate. You have 20 minutes to write.

【自分の作文のアウトラインを書こう！】

Introduction:

_____

One example:

_____

Three characteristics of the example:

1. _____
2. _____
3. _____

Your opinion or feelings:

_____

_____

＜7課 - 4a・話す＞

Conversation: Elections

You will participate in a simulated conversation. Each time it is your turn to speak, you will have 20 seconds to record. You should respond as fully and as appropriately as possible.

You will have a conversation with Mr. Ito, a Japanese newspaper reporter from the Nihon Shinbun, about the election system.

(Man)

(20 seconds)

(Man)

(20 seconds)

(Man)

(20 seconds)

(Man)

(20 seconds)

＜ 7 課 - 4b・話す＞

Return Telephone Call: Speech Contest

You will participate in a simulated telephone conversation with someone you are calling back after receiving a message. First, you will listen to the voice message. Then the telephone call will begin. Each time it is your turn to speak, you will have 20 seconds to record. You should respond as fully and as appropriately as possible.

(Narrator)   Listen to the voice message.

(Boy)

(Narrator)   Now the telephone call will begin. After the phone is answered, begin with a greeting and then explain why you are calling.

(Boy)   [Telephone] [Rings twice and the boy picks it up]

(20 seconds)

(Boy)

(20 seconds)

(Boy)

(20 seconds)

(Boy)

(20 seconds)

School Announcement: Model U.N.

Directions: Imagine that you are making an announcement in Japanese to an assembly of Japanese students visiting your school. First, you will see some notes in English about what to include in your announcement. You will have 1 minute to prepare your announcement while you look at the notes. Then you will have 1 minute to record your announcement. Your announcement should have an opening remark, details according to the notes, and a closing remark. Deliver your announcement using complete sentences in *desu/masu* style.

Model U.N.
Date: Friday, May 1st, at 4:00 p.m.
Location: The school auditorium
Topic: Global warming
Participants: Two students each from 15 high schools in the state
Open to public
Two students are needed to represent Japan.
Contact me asap.

＜７課 - 4d・話す＞

10点
4分＋2分

Story Narration: Travel

Directions: Imagine that you are making an oral presentation to your Japanese class. In your presentation, you will narrate a story. First, you will see pictures depicting the story. You will have 4 minutes to prepare your narration while you look at the pictures. Then you will have 2 minutes to record your narration. Narrate your story using complete sentences in *desu/masu* style.

七課

＜7課 - 4e・話す＞

Cultural Perspective Presentation: Japan Trip

Directions: Imagine you are making an oral presentation to your Japanese class. First, you will read and hear the topic for your presentation. You will have 4 minutes to prepare your presentation. Then you will have 2 minutes to record your presentation. Your presentation should be as complete as possible.

Present your own view or perspective on Japan trip. Discuss at least FIVE aspects or examples of Japan trip.

Begin with an appropriate introduction, give details, explain your own view or perspective, and end with a concluding remark.

【Let's take notes!】

1. Begin with an appropriate introduction.

   _____

2. Discuss five aspects/examples of the topic.

   1.) _____

   2.) _____

   3.) _____

   4.) _____

   5.) _____

3. Explain your view or perspective.

   _____

4. End with a concluding remark.

   _____

スクリプトと聴解問題と読解問題の答

Script & Listening and Reading Answers

This corner provides the following for each lesson, so that you can check your own work and identify any areas that need more practice.

1. 聴解問題のスクリプトと答　　　Listening Script & Answers

2. 読解問題の答　　　　　　　　　Reading Answers

3. 会話問題のスクリプト　　　　　Conversation Script

4. 留守番電話問題のスクリプト　　Return Telephone Call Script

＜1課‐1・聞く＞
聞く：Movie Star Interview

5点

(Narrator) Now you will listen once to an interview.

(Woman) 初めまして。今日は渡部健二さんをスタジオに御迎えしております。今日はお忙しいところ、ありがとうございます。では、まず渡部さんはどんなお子さんだったんですか。

(Man) そうですね。僕の父は不動産の仕事をしていて、母は郵便局で働いていたんです。僕は一人っ子で、けっこう甘やかされて育てられたみたいです。中学1年の時、母が突然癌で亡くなったんです。優しい母でした。僕は母によく似ていると言われてました。その後、近所に住んでいた祖母が僕をよく世話してくれたんですが、その頃寂しくて、いろいろな問題を起こしてました。高校1年の時、父が再婚してから、もっと孤独な気持ちが強くなって、たばこはもちろん、麻薬も使い出したんです。もちろん学校は退学させられました。その時、僕をいつも心配してくれた友人達がいて、有り難かったです。彼らはいつもリハビリの病院にも見舞いに来てくれて、僕は立ち直ることが出来たんです。友情の大切さを感じました。友人には今も感謝してます。家族も本当に良くしてくれましたが、大人になってやっと感謝する事が出来るようになりました。父には随分迷惑をかけたんじゃないかな。

(Woman) 俳優になられたのは、何がきっかけだったんですか。

(Man) 高校を卒業したころ、友人が誕生日のパーティーにさそってくれたんですよ。そして、その友人のお父さんが映画監督で、パーティーが終わった後、俳優になることを勧められたんですよ。本当に偶然なんです。でも、今は俳優の仕事に情熱をかけています。

(Woman) そうですか。今日は貴重なお話をどうも有難うございました。では、増々ご活躍なさってください。

スクリプトと答
332

聞く： Movie Star Interview

(Narrator)　Now answer the questions for this selection.

1. What kind of family did he have?
   - (A) His mother was a movie star.
   - (B) His father worked at the post office.
   - (C) He had no siblings. ＊
   - (D) He didn't have his grandparents.

2. What happened to his family?
   - (A) His mother died in a car accident.
   - (B) His parents separated.
   - (C) His parents divorced.
   - (D) His father remarried. ＊

3. Who helped him the most when he was going through his drug rehabilitation?
   - (A) his mother
   - (B) his grandmother
   - (C) his father
   - (D) his friends ＊

4. What was the major reason for his recovery from drug abuse?
   - (A) religion
   - (B) friendship ＊
   - (C) drug rehabilitation program
   - (D) career

5. Who recommended him for an acting job?
   - (A) himself
   - (B) his father
   - (C) his friend's father ＊
   - (D) his teacher

スクリプトと答

読む: Movie Review

1. How old was Aya when she became ill?
   (A) 5
   (B) 10
   (C) 15 ＊
   (D) 25

2. Even though Aya gradually could not do what she normally did, what thing could she still do?
   (A) walk
   (B) talk
   (C) think ＊
   (D) write

3. What made Aya write her journal?
   (A) She enjoyed writing.
   (B) Her mother advised her to. ＊
   (C) Her friend encouraged her.
   (D) Her teacher advised her to.

4. How did Aya's life change the writer's life?
   (A) The writer decided to make more friends.
   (B) The writer decided to write a journal.
   (C) The writer decided to write thank-you cards to her family and friends.
   (D) The writer decided to live every moment fully. ＊

5. Who in particular wanted to show this drama to children?
   (A) parents ＊
   (B) teachers
   (C) students
   (D) Department of Education

＜１課 - 4a・話す＞

Conversation: Daily Life

You will participate in a simulated conversation. Each time it is your turn to speak, you will have 20 seconds to record. You should respond as fully and as appropriately as possible.

You will have a conversation with Taro, your Japanese friend, about your daily life.

(Taro)　　　　　あのさ、今このアンケートに答えてくれない？明日英語のクラスで発表<ruby>発表<rt>びょう</rt></ruby>しなきゃいけないんだ。

(20 seconds)

(Taro)　　　　　一番目の質問だけど、今情熱<ruby><rt>じょうねつ</rt></ruby>をかけてやっている趣味ってある？

(20 seconds)

(Taro)　　　　　そう？じゃ、二番目の質問。問題とか悩<ruby>悩<rt>なや</rt></ruby>みとかあったら、親か友達のどちらに相談<ruby><rt>そうだん</rt></ruby>する？

(20 seconds)

(Taro)　　　　　そう？今日はアンケートに答えてくれてありがとう。これを明日、英語で発表<ruby><rt>びょう</rt></ruby>しなきゃいけないんだ。出来るかなあ。

(20 seconds)

スクリプトと答

＜１課 - 4b・話す＞

15点
20秒Ｘ４

Return Telephone Call: Concert

You will participate in a simulated telephone conversation with someone you are calling back after receiving a message. First, you will listen to the voice message. Then the telephone call will begin. Each time it is your turn to speak, you will have 20 seconds to record. You should respond as fully and as appropriately as possible.

(Narrator)   Listen to the voice message.

(Female speaker) もしもし、由美だけど、行きたい行きたいって言っていたあの
コンサートの招待券がね、ラジオ局のクイズに当たったのよ。
至急、電話して。

(Narrator)   Now the telephone call will begin. After the phone is
answered, begin with a greeting and then explain why you
are calling.

(Female speaker) [Telephone] [Rings twice and picks up] はい、由美ですが。

(20 seconds)

(Female speaker) ところが、この招待券は今晩８時のなの。一緒に行ける？

(20 seconds)

(Female speaker) でもね、ちょっと問題があって、この招待券を今日午後４時まで
に放送局へ取りに行かなくちゃいけないのよ。私、今日忙しくて
時間ないし、どうしよう。

(20 seconds)

(Female speaker) じゃ、いつもの所で６時に待ち合わせようね。ああ、今からドキ
ドキしちゃう。

(20 seconds)

＜２課‐１・聞く＞

聞く： Earthquake

(Narrator)　Now you will listen once to a report.

(Woman)　神戸では１９９５年１月１７日に、震度７．２の大きな地震が起きました。この地震による被害はひどく、多くの建物や道路が壊れ、地震後、火事も発生し、多くの家が焼かれました。この地震による死亡者数は約５３００人でした。幸い、津波は発生しませんでしたが、地震後、多くの人達が学校の体育館などに避難したりしました。そして、多くの人達が家をなくしました。この神戸地震の時に、たくさんの若者のボランティアが全国から集まり、救助活動を手伝いました。また全国の人々からいろいろな物やお金が寄付されました。日本は地震や台風や火山噴火などの自然災害が多い国ですから、いつもトランジスターラジオとか懐中電灯とか飲み水とかの準備をしておくことが大事かと思います。

スクリプトと答

聞く: Earthquake

(Narrator)　Now answer the questions for this selection.

1.　When did the Kobe earthquake happen?
(A)　January 19th, 1995
(B)　February 17th, 1995
(C)　January 17th, 1995 *
(D)　January 19th, 1985

2.　How big was the Kobe earthquake?
(A)　Magnitude 7.0
(B)　Magnitude 7.2 *
(C)　Magnitude 8.0
(D)　Magnitude 8.2

3.　What damage did NOT occur in the Kobe earthquake?
(A)　Lots of buildings and roads were destroyed.
(B)　Lost of houses were burned.
(C)　Almost 5,300 people died.
(D)　Lots of houses were destroyed by a tidal wave. *

4.　What did NOT happen after the Kobe earthquake?
(A)　Lots of people evacuated to school gyms.
(B)　Lots of young volunteers went to Kobe to assist with the rescues.
(C)　Lots of young volunteers were from the Tokyo area. *
(D)　Lots of people donated things and money to people in Kobe.

5.　What is the purpose of this announcement?
(A)　Asking people to evacuate for the coming disaster.
(B)　Explaining the effects of the disaster and how to prepare for the coming disaster. *
(C)　Explaining the importance of community service and encouraging people to participate in it.
(D)　Reporting the damage from the earthquakes in Japan in general.

読む: Totoro

(Narrator)　Now answer the questions for this selection.

1.　What are the writer's thoughts about "Totoro"?
　　(A)　This is one of her favorite stories. ＊
　　(B)　There are many things she did not understand.
　　(C)　There are some parts that need improvement.
　　(D)　This must be shown to both children and adults.

2.　Who is the most adventurous in this story?
　　(A)　Totoro
　　(B)　Mei ＊
　　(C)　Satsuki
　　(D)　father

3.　What is NOT a correct description of Totoro?
　　(A)　Totoro existed even before human beings. ＊
　　(B)　Totoro eats leaves.
　　(C)　Totoro lives in a forest.
　　(D)　Totoro is usually invisible to people.

4.　What is a correct description of Totoro?
　　(A)　Totoro sleeps at night.
　　(B)　Totoro likes to play a violin.
　　(C)　Totoro can fly. ＊
　　(D)　Big Totoro is youngest.

5.　What is the author's opinion about the animator's intention in creating "Totoro"?
　　(A)　To respect nature ＊
　　(B)　To respect animals
　　(C)　To take care of children
　　(D)　To promote family values

スクリプトと答

＜２課 - 4a・話す＞

Conversation: Visiting Town

You will participate in a simulated conversation. Each time it is your turn to speak, you will have 20 seconds to record. You should respond as fully and as appropriately as possible.

You will have a conversation about staying at your house next week with Yuko, your Japanese host family's daughter who is an 8th grader,

| (Girl) | もしもし、優子です。おひさしぶり。一年ぶりね。元気？ |

(20 seconds)

| (Girl) | 来週、そちらでお世話になりますが、よろしく御願いします。 |

(20 seconds)

| (Girl) | 今、荷物を準備しているんだけど、どんな服を持って行ったらいいのか困ってるの。何を持って行ったらいいのかな？温度は何度ぐらい？ |

(20 seconds)

| (Girl) | 何か日本からほしい物ない？お母さんがお土産に何がいいかなって困ってるから、ほしい物教えて。遠慮しないで。 |

(20 seconds)

スクリプトと答

＜2課‐4b・話す＞

Return Telephone Call: I got lost!

15点
20秒×4

You will participate in a simulated telephone conversation with someone you are calling back after receiving a message from the caller. First, you will listen to the voice message. Then the telephone call will begin. Each time it is your turn to speak, you will have 20 seconds to record. You should respond as fully and as appropriately as possible.

(Narrator)   Listen to the voice message.

(Girl)   もしもし、私、優子。私迷子になっちゃったみたいで、おうちにどう帰ったらいいか分かんないで困ってるんだけど、至急電話してくれる？

(Narrator)   Now the telephone call will begin. After the phone is answered, begin with a greeting and then explain why you are calling.

(Girl)   [Telephone] [Rings twice and picks up] もしもし、優子ですが。

(20 seconds)

(Girl)   お昼すぎにショッピングモールへバスで行って、いろいろなお店を見ていたんだけど、バス乗り場が分かんなくなっちゃったの。英語も出来ないし。

(20 seconds)

(Girl)   今、ブルーベリーというレストランが見える所にいるんだけど、私がどこにいるか分かる？

(20 seconds)

(Girl)   じゃ、ここで待っているから、すぐ迎えに来てね。助かった。ありがとう。

(20 seconds)

スクリプトと答

＜3課‑1・聞く＞
聞く：School Uniform Debate

5点

(Narrator) Now you will listen once to a school debate between Ken and Mari.

(Man) それでは、これから制服についての討論会を始めたいと思います。今日は、留学生のケンさんとこの学校の卒業生のまりさんに討論をしてもらいます。まず、まりさんのご意見を御願いします。

(Mari) 私は制服に反対です。皆が同じ服を着ていると、一人一人の個性もなくなります。制服ではおシャレも出来ません。それに、毎日同じ服だと、飽きてしまいます。

(Man) それでは、ケンさん、どうぞ。

(Ken) 僕は制服に賛成です。制服を着ているとどこの学校か分かりやすくて、見た目がきれいです。私服だと、だらしなく見えます。

(Mari) でも、制服は不潔だと思います。汗をかいて、気持ちが悪いです。だって、毎日洗濯しませんから。

(Ken) 制服があれば、毎朝何を着るか迷わなくていいです。それに、制服は学生の時にだけ着られるので、青春の思い出になると思います。この学校の制服を着たくて、この学校を選んだ人もいるそうですよ。

(Mari) そうね、この学校のセーラー服って可愛くていいですよね！

(Ken) そうですね。ここの制服なら、悪くないと思います。

(Man) 今日はどうもいいご意見を有難うございました。

聞く: School Uniform Debate

(Narrator) Now answer the questions for this selection.

1. What kind of students are Ken and Mari?
(A) 　Both Ken and Mari graduated from this school.
(B) 　Both Ken and Mari are students at this school now.
(C) 　Ken is a study abroad student and Mari graduated from this school. *
(D) 　Both Ken and Mari are study abroad students.

2. What is Mari's opinion about school uniforms?
(A) 　Mari is for uniforms.
(B) 　Mari thinks that students can have individuality with uniforms.
(C) 　Mari thinks that students can dress up with uniforms.
(D) 　Mari thinks that students will get tired of uniforms. *

3. What is Ken's opinion about school uniforms?
(A) 　Ken does not like uniforms.
(B) 　Ken thinks people cannot tell student's schools by their uniforms.
(C) 　Ken thinks uniforms look good. *
(D) 　Ken thinks that students who wear their own clothes look good.

4. Which statement by Ken and Mari is NOT correct?
(A) 　Ken thinks that students don't have to worry about what to wear in the morning with uniforms.
(B) 　Ken thinks wearing uniforms will become a memory of their youth.
(C) 　Mari thinks uniforms become unsanitary from perspiration.
(D) 　Ken thinks that students do not like uniforms. *

5. What is Ken's and Mari's opinions about school uniforms?
(A) 　Both Ken and Mari generally like uniforms.
(B) 　Neither Ken nor Mari like uniforms.
(C) 　Only Ken likes uniforms. *
(D) 　Only Mari likes uniforms.

スクリプトと答

読む: Robot

(Narrator)   Now answer the questions for this selection.

1.   What is the problem Japan has faced in recent years?
    (A)   Decreased number of children
    (B)   Increased number of elderly people
    (C)   Both (A) and (B) ＊
    (D)   None of the above

2.   What role will the immigrants from Southeast Asia play in Japan?
    (A)   They will help to care for children.
    (B)   They will help to build robots.
    (C)   They will help to care for elderly people. ＊
    (D)   They will help Japanese with domestic work.

3.   The author is describing the possible capabilities of robots. Which one was NOT mentioned in this passage?
    (A)   Speaking and listening to a person
    (B)   Laundry
    (C)   Repairing ＊
    (D)   Cooking

4.   Where does the author think robots will be sold in the future?
    (A)   Electric goods shop ＊
    (B)   Computer shop
    (C)   Robot shop
    (D)   Department store

5.   What opinion does the author have about robots?
    (A)   Robots will help with the problems that Japan will face in the future. ＊
    (B)   Robots will expand the problems that Japan will face in the future.
    (C)   Robots will not replace people.
    (D)   Robots will help only rich people who can afford them.

＜3課 - 4a・話す＞

Conversation: Media

| 15点 |
| 20秒 × 4 |

You will participate in a simulated conversation. Each time it is your turn to speak, you will have 20 seconds to record. You should respond as fully and as appropriately as possible.

You will have a conversation with a person who conducts a survey for a TV station about media.

(Interviewer)　　初めまして。テレビ番組についてアンケートを行っています。
ご協力お願いします。

(20 seconds)

(Interviewer)　　まず、視聴率を調べているんですが、一番好きなテレビ番組の名前と
曜日と時間を教えて下さい。

(20 seconds)

(Interviewer)　　どんなコマーシャルがお好きですか。具体的に教えて下さい。

(20 seconds)

(Interviewer)　　そうですか。テレビ番組について何かご希望がありますか。

(20 seconds)

スクリプトと答

＜3課 - 4b・話す＞

Return Telephone Call: Game Machine

You will participate in a simulated telephone conversation with someone you are calling back after receiving a message. First, you will listen to the voice message. Then the telephone call will begin. Each time it is your turn to speak, you will have 20 seconds to record. You should respond as fully and as appropriately as possible.

(Narrator)	Listen to the voice message.
(Boy)	もしもし、山村だけど、君のゲーム器、返すの忘れちゃった。至急、電話して。
(Narrator)	Now the telephone call will begin. After the phone is answered, begin with a greeting and then explain why you are calling.
(Boy)	[Telephone] [Rings twice and you pick it up] もしもし、山村ですが。
(20 seconds)	
(Boy)	実は、ちょっと遊んでたら、動かなくなっちゃったんだよ。
(20 seconds)	
(Boy)	本当にごめん。どうやって返したらいい？
(20 seconds)	
(Boy)	分かった。じゃ、そうする。
(20 seconds)	

＜４課 - １・聞く＞

聞く : Interview

(Narrator)　Now you will listen once to a graduate school interview between Ken and a Japanese college professor.

(Professor)　東洋大学の松田です。よろしく。

(Ken)　ケンスミスと申します。どうぞよろしくお願いいたします。

(Professor)　大学での経歴について話して下さい。

(Ken)　僕はスタンフォード大学に合格して、地球科学を専攻ました。大学３年の時に、日本に留学しました。その時に、インターンとして、日本の企業で研修する機会がありました。僕は大松組という建築会社に送られました。その会社ではいろいろな研究をしていました。例えば、海の水をどうやって飲料水に変えられるかとか、月にどんな都市が作れるかとか、非常に興味深かったです。

(Professor)　それはいい経験でしたねえ。大学院では何を研究したいんですか。

(Ken)　スタンフォード大学を卒業した後、東洋大学の大学院に進み、都市計画で修士号を取りたいと思っています。

(Professor)　なぜアメリカの大学院へ行かないで、日本の大学院に入りたいんですか。

(Ken)　日本の環境問題の取り組みは進んでいると思うので、学ぶ事がたくさんあると思います。

(Professor)　将来、どんな仕事を希望してますか。

(Ken)　環境問題のコンサルタント会社に就職して、社会の環境問題を解決したいです。給料はそんなに良くないかも知れませんが、やりがいのある仕事だと思っています。社会の役に立つ仕事をすることが、僕の夢です。

スクリプトと答

聞く： Interview

(Narrator) Now answer the questions for this section.

1.　When did Ken study in Japan?
(A)　When he was in the 11th grade.
(B)　After he graduated from high school.
(C)　When he was a junior in college. ＊
(D)　After he graduated from college.

2.　Which one of the following choices is NOT related to Ken's study of interest?
(A)　Environment
(B)　Science
(C)　Economics ＊
(D)　City planning

3.　What did Ken study while in Japan?
(A)　The study of converting sea water to drinking water and city planning on the moon. ＊
(B)　The study of drinking water and city planning in Japan.
(C)　The study of civil engineering and city planning on the moon.
(D)　The study of sea water and environmental consulting.

4.　Why does Ken want to study at a Japanese graduate school?
(A)　He wants to improve his Japanese.
(B)　He thinks that Japanese society is more advanced in dealing with environmental issues. ＊
(C)　He made many friends while he studied in Japan.
(D)　He wants to pursue a career in international business.

5. Which one is NOT his dream for the future?
(A)　He wants to get a job in an environmental consulting firm.
(B)　He want to earn a higher salary and become rich. ＊
(C)　He wants to solve environmental problems.
(D)　He wants to engage in a helpful job.

読む: Honda

1. What inspired Mr. Honda to make his first product?
    (A) His love towards his wife ＊
    (B) His love towards his product
    (C) Poverty
    (D) Speed

2. What kind of person was Mr. Honda?
    (A) Mr. Honda started his factory even before World War II.
    (B) Mr. Honda started his factory in a big city.
    (C) Mr. Honda yelled at his workers a lot. ＊
    (D) Mr. Honda was called "Emperor" by his workers.

3. What was the highest level of education Mr. Honda completed?
    (A) College
    (B) High school
    (C) Junior high school
    (D) Elementary school＊

4. What value did Mr. Honda NOT insist on in his quotes?
    (A) Make products that please people.
    (B) Collaborate with people.
    (C) Don't worry to make a mistake.
    (D) Make products at a low cost. ＊

5. What does the teacher want Ken to do?
    (A) He wants Ken to read many Japanese books to improve his Japanese.
    (B) He wants Ken to read books about Mr. Honda to learn from his life. ＊
    (C) He wants Ken to study more to challenge himself further.
    (D) He wants Ken to become a resourceful person.

スクリプトと答

＜4課‐4a・話す＞

Conversation: Birthday Party

15点
20秒×4

You will participate in a simulated conversation. Each time it is your turn to speak, you will have 20 seconds to record. You should respond as fully and as appropriately as possible.

You will have a conversation with Emi who is your friend.

(Emi) 今度の金曜日、マイクの誕生日だから、私達仲間で小さなパーティーして、祝ってあげない？

(20 seconds)

(Emi) 私、バースデーケーキとろうそくとマッチ、持って来るね。
何を持って来てくれる？

(20 seconds)

(Emi) プレゼント、何にしようかなあ。マイク、何をあげたら喜ぶかなあ。

(20 seconds)

(Emi) パーティーについて、ほかに何か決めなきゃいけないことある？

(20 seconds)

＜4課 - 4b・話す＞

15点
20秒 X 4

Return Telephone Call: Part-time Job

You will participate in a simulated telephone conversation with someone you are calling back after receiving a message. First, you will listen to the voice message. Then the telephone call will begin. Each time it is your turn to speak, you will have 20 seconds to record. You should respond as fully and as appropriately as possible.

(Narrator)　　Listen to the voice message.

(Woman)　　もしもし、スマイリーシャツの山田ですが、うちの会社でアルバイトをしたいそうですね。電話して下さい。

(Narrator)　　Now the telephone call will begin. After the phone is answered, begin with a greeting and then explain why you are calling.

(Woman)　　[Telephone] [Rings twice and picks up] もしもし、山田ですが。

(20 seconds)

(Woman)　　うちの店は日本人観光客が多いんですよ。前に何か日本語を使ったアルバイトの経験がありますか。

(20 seconds)

(Woman)　　私達は週末に働いてくれる人をさがしているんですが、働ける曜日と時間を教えて下さい。

(20 seconds)

(Woman)　　仕事について何か質問がありますか。

(20 seconds)

スクリプトと答

＜５課-１・聞く１＞

聞く１：Weather Forecast

(Narrator)　Now you will listen twice to a prerecorded message.

(Woman)　今日４日金曜日の天気予報を御知らせします。今朝は晴れていますが、御昼過ぎごろから曇るでしょう。そして、夕方６時以降、雨が降り出すでしょう。今日の最高気温は２４℃、最低気温は１７℃、降水確率は５０％です。大型の台風９号が沖縄の南に近づいています。最大風速が20キロの大型の台風ですが、雨も風もだんだん強くなるでしょう。台風は日曜日の夜には、進路を北東に変え、四国、近畿地方に上陸するおそれがあります。四国、近畿地方には強風大雨注意報が出ていますので、お気をつけ下さい。では、これで今日の天気予報を終わります。

(Narrator)　Now listen again.

(Woman)　今日４日金曜日の天気予報を御知らせします。今朝は晴れていますが、御昼過ぎごろから曇るでしょう。そして、夕方６時以降、雨が降り出すでしょう。今日の最高気温は２４℃、最低気温は１７℃、降水確率は５０％です。大型の台風９号が沖縄の南に近づいています。最大風速が20キロの大型の台風ですが、雨も風もだんだん強くなるでしょう。台風は日曜日の夜には、進路を北東に変え、四国、近畿地方に上陸するおそれがあります。四国、近畿地方には強風大雨注意報が出ていますので、お気をつけ下さい。では、これで今日の天気予報を終わります。

スクリプトと答　　　352

聞く1： Weather Forecast

(Narrator)   Now answer the questions for this selection.

1.   What is the date today?
     (A)   Today is Thursday the 4th.
     (B)   Today is Friday the 4th. ＊
     (C)   Today is Thursday the 8th.
     (D)   Today is Friday the 8th.

2.   What is today's weather forecast?
     (A)   Sunny → cloudy
     (B)   Cloudy → rainy → cloudy
     (C)   Sunny → cloudy → rainy ＊
     (D)   Rainy → cloudy → sunny

3.   What is NOT correct about today's weather forecast?
     (A)   The highest temperature will be 24℃.
     (B)   The lowest temperature will be 19℃. ＊
     (C)   The chance of rain is 50%.
     (D)   There is a warning of a typhoon.

4.   Which description is NOT correct about the typhoon?
     (A)   The typhoon is a small scale typhoon.
     (B)   The typhoon is the eighth of this year. ＊
     (C)   The typhoon is approaching the south of Okinawa.
     (D)   The wind speed is 20 kilometers per hour.

5.   What will happen to the typhoon?
     (A)   The typhoon will land in Shikoku and the Kansai (Kinki) area. ＊
     (B)   The typhoon will land in the Kantoo area.
     (C)   The typhoon will move away to the Japan Sea.
     (D)   The typhoon will move away from Okinawa on Sunday morning.

スクリプトと答

＜５課‐１・聞く２＞

5点

聞く２：Driving

(Narrator)　Now you will listen once to a prerecorded message.

(Man)　先週、両親から中古車だけど、形も色も気に入っている車を買ってもらったんだ。毎日運転を楽しんでいたんだけど、今朝ね、車を運転していて、危なく事故を起こすところだった。今日午前９時から文学の試験があったから遅れると困るし、道路がラッシュで混んでいたし、イライラしていたんだよ。前のトラックが横断歩道を渡り始めた歩行者に急に止まったんで、僕はそのトラックにぶつかりそうになったんだよ。幸い、衝突しなくて良かったんだけどね、危機一髪だった。ひやっとしたよ。大学に着いたら、これまた駐車場がいっぱいでね。また大変。試験には間に合ったんだけど、車を道に停めたら、今度は駐車違反の切符を貼られてたよ。今日はさんざんな一日だった。僕はスピード違反で一度捕まったことはあるけど、飲酒運転とか居眠り運転はしたことがないから、僕の車に安心して乗って。

聞く2：Driving

(Narrator) Now answer the questions for this selection.

1.   What happened to this person today?
      (A)   He got into a big accident.
      (B)   He hit a person with his car.
      (C)   He was hit by a car.
      (D)   He almost got into an accident. ＊

2.   Why did this person going to the university?
      (A)   He had to take his economics exam.
      (B)   He had to turn in his report.
      (C)   The exam started at 9:00 a.m. ＊
      (D)   He had to attend his literature lecture.

3.   What happened to him in the morning while driving his car?
      (A)   A pedestrian started to walk in front of his car.
      (B)   A pedestrian didn't use the pedestrian crossing.
      (C)   The truck in front of him stopped suddenly. ＊
      (D)   He stopped for a pedestrian.

4.   What happened to this person after arriving at the university?
      (A)   The parking lot was full. ＊
      (B)   He could not park his car even on the road.
      (C)   He did not receive a parking violation ticket.
      (D)   He was late to his exam.

5.   What description is correct about the traffic violation this person
      committed?
      (A)   He has never had a parking violation.
      (B)   He has never driven while drunk. ＊
      (C)   He has never exceeded the speed limit.
      (D)   He once fell asleep while driving.

スクリプトと答

読む: Car Accident

1.   When and where did this car accident happen?
   (A)   About 2:00 a.m. on March 3rd in Kyoto ＊
   (B)   About 2:00 p.m. on March 3rd in Kyoto
   (C)   About 2:00 a.m. on March 3rd in Nara
   (D)   About 2:00 p.m. on March 3rd in Nara

2.   What happened to the passengers?
   (A)   Persons A and B died.
   (B)   Person A died and Person B broke her two legs. ＊
   (C)   Person A broke two arms and Person B died.
   (D)   Person A broke two legs and Person B died.

3.   What happened to the car?
   (A)   The car hit a tree.
   (B)   The car hit a telephone pole and stopped.
   (C)   The car hit a telephone pole and rolled into the river sideways. ＊
   (D)   The car lost control and jumped into the river from the front.

4.   What activities did the passengers have on the day of the accident?
   (A)   They attended a graduation ceremony.
   (B)   They attended a basketball club welcoming party. ＊
   (C)   They went to a karaoke room with their classmates.
   (D)   They went to a graduation party.

5.   What was the main reason for the accident?
   (A)   speed
   (B)   carelessness
   (C)   sleepiness
   (D)   drunkenness ＊

＜５課 - 4a・話す＞

15点
20秒×4

Conversation: Climate

You will participate in a simulated conversation. Each time it is your turn to speak, you will have 20 seconds to record. You should respond as fully and as appropriately as possible.

You will have a conversation with Mr. Nakata, a Japanese newspaper writer, about the climate.

(Man) 初めまして。山岡高校新聞部の中田です。今日は世界のいろいろな所の気候について記事を書いています。どうぞ御協力を御願いします。

(20 seconds)

(Man) そちらの一年の気候はどうですか。教えて下さい。

(20 seconds)

(Man) 一年で一番過ごしやすい季節はいつですか。

(20 seconds)

(Man) 今日は御協力ありがとうございました。日本の気候について、何か質問がありますか。

(20 seconds)

スクリプトと答

＜5課 - 4b・話す＞

15点
20秒×4

Return Telephone Call: Traffic Accident

You will participate in a simulated telephone conversation with someone you are calling back after receiving a message. First, you will listen to the voice message. Then the telephone call will begin. Each time it is your turn to speak, you will have 20 seconds to record. You should respond as fully and as appropriately as possible.

(Narrator)   Listen to the voice message.

(Man)   もしもし、ケンだけど、至急電話してくれる？実は、今病院にいるんだ。交通事故に遭って、治療を受けたところなんだけど、ちょっと手伝ってほしいんだ。

(Narrator)   Now the telephone call will begin. After the phone is answered, begin with a greeting and then explain why you are calling.

(Man)   [Telephone] [Rings twice and picks up]　もしもし、ケンです。

(20 seconds)

(Man)   あまり心配いらないよ。ひどい怪我じゃないから。でも、左の腕にギブスをしているよ。

(20 seconds)

(Man)   歩けるけど、うちに一人で帰る自信がないんだ。ちょっと手伝ってくれないかい。

(20 seconds)

(Man)   ありがとう。助かるよ。じゃ、病院の待合室で待ってるね。

(20 seconds)

＜6課‐1・聞く＞

聞く： Illness

5点

(Narrator)　Now you will listen once to a conversation.

(Ken)　すみません、お願いします。

(Doctor)　どうしましたか。

(Ken)　熱が３９度もあって、咳が出て、頭痛もして、鼻水が出て、つらいんです。それに、右側の耳が少し痛くて。

(Doctor)　風邪を引いたようだね。ちょっと胸と背中を調べてみよう。セーターだけ脱いで。まず、こちらを向いて。はい、息を吸って。はい、息を吐いて。肺の方は大丈夫そうだ。しかし、インフルエンザもはやっていることだし、喉を調べておこう。口を開けて。あ〜。ちょっと赤く腫れているなあ。

(Ken)　食欲もないんですよ。

(Doctor)　まあ、それだけ熱があると、食欲はなくなるもんだ。しかし、水分は十分とるように。そして、少しずつ栄養のある物を食べるように。そして、よく休むことだ。２種類の薬の処方箋をあげよう。ひとつは、熱を下げる薬。もうひとつは、抗生物質だ。一日に３度食後に飲むように。では、お大事に。

(Ken)　どうもありがとうございました。

スクリプトと答

聞く：Illness

(Narrator)　Now answer the questions for this selection.

1.　What symptom does this patient NOT have?
(A)　High fever
(B)　Stomach ache ＊
(C)　Frequent coughing
(D)　Headache

2.　What did the doctor NOT check?
(A)　The patient's chest
(B)　The patient's back
(C)　The patient's throat
(D)　The patient's ears ＊

3.　What did the doctor find out from examining the patient?
(A)　The patient's lungs are normal. ＊
(B)　The patient's stomach is normal.
(C)　The patient's throat is normal.
(D)　The patient has the flu.

4.　What did the doctor NOT suggest to the patient?
(A)　To eat well ＊
(B)　To drink enough liquids
(C)　To gradually eat nutritious food
(D)　To rest well

5.　What medicines did the doctor prescribe to the patient?
(A)　Fever medicine to be taken two times a day after meals.
(B)　Antibiotics to be taken three times a day before meals.
(C)　Fever medicine and antibiotics to be taken three times before meals.
(D)　Fever medicine and antibiotics to be taken three times after meals. ＊

読む: Health

1. What kind of health problem did the mother have?
   (A) The mother had breast cancer and had surgery last year. *
   (B) The mother lost quite a lot of weight and feels weak now.
   (C) The mother had a heart attack and recovered.
   (D) The mother has bad headaches once in a while.

2. What description is NOT correct about the mother?
   (A) The mother can eat any kind of food now. *
   (B) The mother shops at the health food store only.
   (C) The mother checks the freshness, expiration date and additives of food she buys.
   (D) The mother quit eating instant foods and frozen foods.

3. What description is NOT correct about the father?
   (A) The father has a heart problem.
   (B) The father has high blood pressure.
   (C) The father is eating salty food. *
   (D) The father quit smoking, but is drinking a little alcohol.

4. What description is NOT correct about the older sister?
   (A) The older sister is on a diet now.
   (B) The older sister eats only a little sweets. *
   (C) The older sister loves to take supplements.
   (D) The older sister is happy about losing 3 kg in a short time.

5. What is this family trying to accomplish?
   (A) They try to eat together.
   (B) They try to eat healthy food. *
   (C) They try to lose weight.
   (D) They try to communicate more effectively.

　　　　　　　　　　　　　　　スクリプトと答

＜6課 - 4a・話す＞

Conversation: Birthday Party

You will participate in a simulated conversation. Each time it is your turn to speak, you will have 20 seconds to record. You should respond as fully and as appropriately as possible.

You will have a conversation with Mr. Kimura, a manager at the restaurant, about planning your friend's birthday party.

(Man) 　　　　初めまして。東京レストランの木村です。どうぞよろしく。

(20 seconds)

(Man) 　　　　誕生日のパーティーについてもう少し詳しく教えて下さい。

(20 seconds)

(Man) 　　　　そうですか。食べ物は和食と洋食とどちらにしましょうか。お友達の好みは？

(20 seconds)

(Man) 　　　　分かりました。何か値段についてご質問がありますか。

(20 seconds)

＜6課 - 4b・話す＞

Return Telephone Call: Hospital

15点
20秒 X 4

You will participate in a simulated telephone conversation with someone whose call you are returning. First, you will listen to the voice message. Then the telephone call will begin. Each time it is your turn to speak, you will have 20 seconds to record. You should respond as fully and as appropriately as possible.

(Narrator)   Listen to the voice message.

(Receptionist)   もしもし、山本病院です。すみません。今日４時のご予約ですが、山本先生は急用で病院の方に来られなくなりました。お電話下さい。

(Narrator)   Now the telephone call will begin. After the phone is answered, begin with a greeting and then explain why you are calling.

(Receptionist)   [Telephone] [Rings twice and the receptionist answers.]
もしもし、山本病院ですが。

(20 seconds)

(Receptionist)   お電話有難うございます。少し症状を教えて下さいませんか。

(20 seconds)

(Receptionist)   分かりました。明日か明後日でもよろしいですか。都合のいい日時を教えて下さい。

(20 seconds)

(Receptionist)   分かりました。では、お大事に。

(20 seconds)

スクリプトと答

＜7課‐1・聞く＞

聞く：World Peace

5点

(Narrator) Now you will listen to a speech given by SADAKO's older brother who attended the 9/11 memorial service in New York in 2007. It will be read once.

　今日はお呼びいただき、皆様とお会いできましたことを感謝いたします。ＳＡＤＡＫＯが白血病で入院したとき、佐々木家はとても経済的に苦しんでいました。ある日父は自分のしていた時計をお金に替えました。父が病院に見舞いに来た時、ベッドの中のＳＡＤＡＫＯは、腕時計がない父の手に気づきました。ＳＡＤＡＫＯは父に分からないように泣きました。痛さも怖さも苦しさも死ぬまで本心を見せませんでした。ＳＡＤＡＫＯは、家族にも、周りの人にも心配させてはいけないという、思いやりの心を持っていたのです。

　ＳＡＤＡＫＯがお母さんをエレベーターまで見送ってドアが閉まろうとした時、「お母ちゃん」と言って流した涙が人に見せた最初で最後の涙でした。ＳＡＤＡＫＯの死後、ベッドの下から一枚のメモが見つかりました。そのメモの存在は誰も知りませんでした。変わっていく白血球の数を先生のカルテから書き写していたのです。ＳＡＤＡＫＯはもうすぐ死ぬことを知っていました。しかし、周りに心配をかけないように誰にも言いませんでした。それはＳＡＤＡＫＯが見せた、心配かけたくないという、思いやりの心がそうさせたのです。

　ＳＡＤＡＫＯが残した「小さな思いやりの心」を周りにつなげ、広げれば、小さな平和がやがて大きな平和へとつながっていくことを確信しています。どうかもう一度自分の周りを見直してみてください。「小さな思いやりの心」を千羽の折りづるに願ったＳＡＤＡＫＯ、もし少しでも「思いやりの心」が皆さんの心の中にあったら、ＳＡＤＡＫＯの折りづるを思い出して、そして明るい未来に願いをこめて、折りづるを折ってください！

　　　　　　　　　　　　　　　ＳＡＤＡＫＯの兄　Masahiro Sasaki

聞く: World Peace

(Narrator)   Now answer the questions for this selection.

1.   Why wasn't Sadako's father wearing his wristwatch on his visit to
     Sadako?
     (A)   He left it at home.
     (B)   He sold it. *
     (C)   He lost it.
     (D)   He gave it to Sadako.

2.   How did Sadako deal with her disease?
     (A)   She cried in front of her father.
     (B)   She expressed her fears to her father.
     (C)   She complained about her pain to the nurse.
     (D)   She showed her tears only once when her mother was about to
           leave. *

3.   How did Sadako deal with her death?
     (A)   She knew she was dying. *
     (B)   She was not aware of her imminent death.
     (C)   She could not tell anyone about her death because of fear.
     (D)   She told people around her about her imminent death.

4.   What was found under Sadako's bed after she passed away.
     (A)   a letter to her parents
     (B)   her father's watch
     (C)   origami cranes
     (D)   a memo about her white blood cell count *

5.   What message did Sadako's older brother want to give to the
     audience?
     (A)   make paper cranes
     (B)   be considerate of others
     (C)   wish for a bright future
     (D)   all of the above *

スクリプトと答

1.　What kind of child was Mr. Noguchi?
(A)　He was a good student.
(B)　He was a school dropout. ＊
(C)　He loved mountain climbing.
(D)　He was very self-confident.

2.　What made Mr. Noguchi want to become a mountain climber?
(A)　He saw pictures of mountains.
(B)　His father took him to the mountains when he was young.
(C)　He joined a mountain climbing club in college.
(D)　He was inspired by a book written by a mountain climber. ＊

3.　Which of the following was NOT mentioned as a motivating factor for Mr. Noguchi to pick up trash on Mt. Everest and Mt. Fuji?
(A)　He saw the news of foreign mountain climbers picking up trash on Mt. Everest. ＊
(B)　He learned about all of the trash that was left behind on Mt. Everest by Japanese climbers.
(C)　Other foreign mountain climbers told him "The Japanese economy is first class, but Japanese manners are third class."
(D)　He learned that there was lots of trash on Mt. Fuji.

4.　How did Mr. Noguchi recruit people to pick up trash on Mt. Everest and Mt. Fuji?
(A)　He put an advertisement in the newspaper and asked for cooperation from the public.
(B)　He started a trash pick-up club at the college where he teaches.
(C)　He gave speeches at many places. ＊
(D)　He made a web page and asked people for their cooperation.

5.　What is Mr. Noguchi's definition of "adventure"?
(A)　Don't give up picking up trash. ＊
(B)　Recruit more people to pick up trash.
(C)　Climb Mt. Fuji and pick up trash.
(D)　Do trash pick-up campaigns through the media.

＜７課 - 4a・話す＞

Conversation: Elections

15点
20秒 X 4

You will participate in a simulated conversation. Each time it is your turn to speak, you will have 20 seconds to record. You should respond as fully and as appropriately as possible.

You will have a conversation with Mr. Ito, a Japanese newspaper reporter from the Nihon Shinbun, about the election system.

(Man)　　　初めまして。日本新聞の伊藤です。今日は御協力有難うございます。

(20 seconds)

(Man)　　　アメリカでは高校生でも大統領の選挙に投票出来るんですか。

(20 seconds)

(Man)　　　そうですか。政治についてどんな御意見がありますか。

(20 seconds)

(Man)　　　そうですか。有難うございました。日本の政治について質問して下さい。

(20 seconds)

スクリプトと答

＜7課 - 4b・話す＞

Return Telephone Call: Speech Contest

15点
20秒 X 4

You will participate in a simulated telephone conversation with someone you are calling back after receiving a message. First, you will listen to the voice message. Then the telephone call will begin. Each time it is your turn to speak, you will have 20 seconds to record. You should respond as fully and as appropriately as possible.

(Narrator)	Listen to the voice message.
(Boy)	もしもし、ケンだけど、今日スピーチコンテストがあっただろう？結果を知らせたいから、すぐ電話して。
(Narrator)	Now the telephone call will begin. After the phone is answered, begin with a greeting and then explain why you are calling.
(Boy)	[Telephone] [Rings twice and the boy picks it up] もしもし、ケンですが。
(20 seconds)	
(Boy)	実はね、僕、一位になったんだよ。そして、日本旅行の賞をもらったんだ。
(20 seconds)	
(Boy)	でも、先生と一緒に行かなくちゃいけないんだ。どうしよう？
(20 seconds)	
(Boy)	そうだね。大丈夫だよね。
(20 seconds)	

<書く Text Chat アドバイス>

【Knowledge/skills】
- Interpersonal communication
- Informing; describing; explaining; expressing preference; elaborating; justifying opinion; requesting; inviting; suggesting

【Format】
- 6 questions X 90 seconds, 30 points, 10 minutes total

【Speech style】
When you communicate with someone you don't know well, use the polite です/ます form. When you communicate with someone superior to you, use the honorific form, although it is not required by the AP exam. When you communicate with someone close to you, use the informal form, although it is not commonly required on the AP exam.

【Suggestion】
1. Each answer counts as five points, which means each response matters. Elaborate and answer throughly. Do not leave any section unanswered.
2. When you introduce yourself, it is polite and natural to say どうぞよろしく お願いします after giving your name.
3. At the closing of the entire conversation, show appreciation to the person with whom you are having a text chat. If you enjoyed the conversation, say 楽しかったです。If you want to offer encouragement to your partner, say がんばって下さい。

<書く Compare & Contrast アドバイス>

【Knowledge/skills】
・Presentational communication
・Comparing; contrasting; describing; justifying opinion

【Format】
・1 question, 15 points, 20 minutes
・300 - 400 characters

【Speech style】
Use です/ます form or だ form consistently.

【Outline sample structure】
1. Opening:

これから、AとBをくらべてみます。AとBは違うことも同じこともあります。

2. Three similarities and/or differences between A and B:

まず 一つ目の違うことは、Aは〜ですが、Bは〜です。

二つ目の違うことは、〜。

そして、三つ目の違うことは、〜。

or しかし、一つの同じことは、AもBも〜。

3. Your preference and reasons:

（結論として）私はAの方がBより好きです。

なぜなら、(reason) からです。

【Comparative patterns】

1. Between A and B, I like A more than B.　AとBで、Aの方がBより好きです。

2. I don't like B as much as A.　BはAほど好きではありません。

3. Among A, B and C, I like A most.　AとBとCで、Aが一番好きです。

4. Among fruits, I like oranges the most. 果物の中で、オレンジが一番好きです。

【Suggestion】

1. First, plan your outline.

2. Use the AP *kanji*.

3. Proofread well, especially for *kanji*. Check that you have not chosen the wrong *kanji*.

アドバイス　　　　　　　370

<書く Cultural Topic Posting アドバイス>

【Knowledge/skills】
- Presentational communication
- Describing and expressing opinions about a Japanese cultural practice or product

【Format】
- 1 question, 15 points, 20 minutes
- 300 - 400 characters

【Speech style】
Use です/ます form or だ form consistently.

【Outline sample structure】
1. Introduction:

    これから、〜について述(の)べたいと思います。

2. One example:

    (Topic) の中にいろいろありますが、私は (one example) について、述(の)べたいと
    思います。

3. Three characteristics of the example:

    まず (or 最初に or 一番目に)、

    次に (or 二番目に)、

    そして、最後に (or 三番目に)、

4. Your opinion and feelings:

    結論(けつろん)として、私は〜と思います。

【Suggestion】
1. First, plan your outline.
2. Use the AP *kanji*.
3. Proofread well, especially for *kanji*.

アドバイス

<話す Conversation アドバイス>

【Knowledge/skills】
- Interpersonal communication
- Participates in conversation by responding appropriately

【Format】
- 4 questions X 20 seconds, 15 points, 3 minutes total

【Speech style】
Immediately decide on which speech style you should use, which is dependent on the person to whom you are speaking.

【Responding appropriately to expressions】
1. 日本人：「ご協力お願いします。」
   答え：「はい、分かりました。何でも聞いて下さい。協力します。」
2. 日本人：「がんばってください。」
   答え：「はい、がんばります。」

【Polite style and informal style】
1. "Let me see..."
   Polite style: そうですねえ。。。
   Informal style (male): そうだねえ。。。
   Informal style (female): そうねえ。。。
2. "have to decide..."
   Polite style: 決めなければなりません
   Informal style: 決めなくちゃ

【Suggestion】
1. Begin with a cheerful greeting.
2. After introducing yourself, say どうぞよろしくお願いします。
3. Carry on a polite conversation.
4. At the end, close your conversation with a word of appreciation and a polite closing remark.
   Ex. どうも有難うございました。
5. When you don't know much about the topic asked, you may answer
   「topic についてよく知りませんから、私は答えられません。」

6. 「分かりません」and 「もう一度言って下さい」 do not count as correct answers.
7. Listen to the questions carefully. Take notes. If you don't understand the question, repeat back the question. At minimum, say 「そうですねえ...」

【Suggestions for improving your listening skills】
1. Practice engaging in impromptu conversations.
2. Listen to Japanese radio programs, Japanese songs, watch Japanese TV programs, Japanese movies, anime, etc.

アドバイス

<話す Return Telephone Call アドバイス>

15点
20秒 X 4

【Knowledge/skills】
· Interpersonal communication
· Participates in a conversation by responding appropriately

【Format】
· 4 questions X 20 seconds, 15 points, 3 minutes total

【Speech style】
Immediately decide on which speech style you will use, which should be dependent on the person to whom you are speaking.

【Sample structure】
1. After listening to the telephone message:
   [Polite form]
   もしもし、(your last name) です。留守番電話を聞きましたが、_____
   (Repeat the message) そうですね。[Respond with your reaction to the situation.]
   [Informal form]
   もしもし、(your first name) だけど。留守番電話を聞いたけど、_____
   (Repeat the message) だって。[Respond with your reaction to the situation.]

【Helpful Expressions】
1. When congratulating someone, say;
   [Polite form] おめでとうございます。[Informal form] おめでとう。
2. When you hear good news, say;
   [Polite form] それは良かったですねえ。[Informal form] それは良かったねえ。
3. When you hear disappointing news, say;
   [Polite form] それは残念でしたねえ。[Informal form] それは残念だったねえ。
4. When you hear about some physical problem, say;
   [Polite form] 大丈夫ですか。[Informal form] 大丈夫？
5. When you hear about sad news such as death or serious illness, say;
   [Polite form] お気のどくに。[Informal form] 気のどくに。
6. When you want to express pity, say;
   [Polite form] Not applicable. [Informal form] かわいそう。

アドバイス   374

【Suggestions】
1. Begin with a cheerful greeting.
2. After introducing yourself, say どうぞよろしくお願いします。
3. Carry on a polite conversation.
4. At the end, close your talk with a word of appreciation and an appropriate remark.

[Polite form]　　　　　　　　　[Informal form]

どうも有難うございました。　　どうも有難う。

では、また。　　　　　　　　　じゃ、またね。

また後で電話します。　　　　　また後で電話するね。

失礼します。　　　　　　　　　じゃね。

アドバイス

<話す School Announcement アドバイス> | 10点
1分+1分 |

【Knowledge/skills】
・Presentational communication
・Informing

【Format】
・1 question, 10 points, 1 minute to prepare & 1 minute to record

【Speech style】
For public speaking, use the polite です/ます style.

【Structure】
1. Opening remark:
   こんにちは、皆さん。これから、(topic) についてのお知らせをします。
2. Information
3. Closing remark:
   では、どうぞよろしくお願いいたします。以上です。

【Helpful word list】
1. Welcome, everyone. →ようこそ、皆さん。
2. 〜月 (ex. 4月、9月)
3. 〜日 (ex. 1日、10日, etc.)
4. 〜曜日
5. 午前、午後、〜時、〜分
6. 4:00 p.m. on Saturday, March 10th →三月十日土曜日の午後4時
7. Place で Event があります。
   There is a basketball game at the gym. 体育館でバスケットの試合があります。
8. Meeting time →集合時間〔しゅうごうじかん〕or 集まる時間
9. Meeting place →集合場所〔しゅうごうばしょ〕or 集まる場所
10. Departure time →出発時間〔しゅっぱつじかん〕
11. Arrival time →到着時間〔とうちゃくじかん〕
12. Be on time. →時間を守って下さい。
13. Things you may bring are 〜. →持って来てもいい物は〜です。
14. Things you may not bring are 〜. →持って来てはいけない物は〜です。

15. RSVP →出席〔しゅっせき〕か欠席〔けっせき〕を知らせて下さい。

16. Please contact. →連絡〔れんらく〕してください。

17. by April 15 →4月15日までに

18. deadline →締め切り〔しめきり〕

19. valuables→貴重品〔きちょうひん〕

20. Please turn in. →提出〔ていしゅつ〕して下さい。or 出して下さい。

21. That's all. →以上〔いじょう〕です。

【Suggestion】
Speak clearly, loudly, cheerfully, pleasantly and politely.

アドバイス

＜話す Story Narration アドバイス＞

【Knowledge/skills】
・ Presentational communication
・ Narrating a story as depicted by a series of pictures

【Format】
・ 1 question, 10 points, 4 minutes to prepare and 2 minutes to record

【Speech style】
For story narrations, use the polite です/ます style.

【Helpful Sentence Structures】
1. Command forms
   a. Command form
      お父さんが「早く決めろ。」と言いました。Father said, "Decide soon."
   b. Negative command form
      お父さんが「走るな。」と言いました。Father said, "Don't run."
   c. Polite command form
      お母さんが「早く決めなさい。」と言いました。Mother said, "Decide soon."
   d. Negative polite command form
      お母さんが「走らないで or 走ってはだめ。」と言いました。
      Mother said, "Don't run."
2. Quotations
   a. Direct quotation
      お母さんが「早く決めなさい。」と言いました。Mother said "Decide soon."
   b. Indirect quotation
      お母さんが早く決めるように言いました。Mother said to decide soon.
   c. Question word in direct quotation
      何を食べようかと考えています。He is thinking about what to eat.
3. Complex sentences
   a. 音楽を聞きながら、お皿を洗っています。
      She is washing dishes while listening to music.
   b. 食べた後、買い物に行きました。After eating, she went shopping.
   c. 起きて、シャワーをあびています。He woke up and is taking a shower.
   d. 寝る前に、歯をみがいています。She is brushing her teeth before she goes to bed.

アドバイス   378

e. 寝る時に、本を読みます。Before she goes to bed, she reads a book.

f. お母さんが料理をしている間に、お父さんは掃除をしています。
   While mother is cooking, father is cleaning.

g. 夕食を食べてから、宿題をしました。After eating dinner, she did her homework.

h. お母さんは子供がまだ寝ているのを見ました。Mother saw her child still sleeping.

i. 何度じゃんけんしても、決まりません。Even though they did jankenpo many
   times, it was undecided.

4. Conditional

a. 右にまがると、大きいデパートがあります。
   When you turn right, there is a large department store.

b. 早く終わったら、買い物に行きましょう。
   If we finish early, let's go shopping.

c. 雨が降らなければ、ピクニックをします。
   If and only if it does not rain, we will have a picnic.

5. Stative conditions

a. ドアが開いています。The door is open.

b. ドアが閉まっています。The door is closed.

c. テレビがついています。The TV is on.

d. テレビが消えています。The TV is off.

e. 絵がかべにかけてあります。A painting has been hung on the wall.

f. お花がかざってあります。Flowers have been decorated.

6. Compare:

a. 電気がついています。The lights are on.

b. 電気がつけてあります。The lights have been turned on.

c. 電気をつけています。(Someone) is turning on the lights.

【Suggestions】

1. Narrate a story; do not write a skit.

2. Use past tense.

3. Express yourself dramatically.

4. Speak clearly and loudly.

5. Use a confident tone of voice.

アドバイス

＜話す Cultural Perspective Presentation アドバイス＞

10点
4分＋2分

【Knowledge/skills】
・ Presentational communication
・ Describing and expressing your opinion about a Japanese cultural practice or product

【Format】
・ 1 question, 10 points, 4 minutes to prepare and 2 minutes to record

【Speech style】
Use polite です/ます style.

【Sample structure】
1. Begin with an appropriate introduction.
　　これから、(topic) について話します。

2. Discuss five aspects of the topic.
　　1.) まず or 第一に、
　　2.) 次に or 第二に、
　　3.) 第三に、
　　4.) 第四に、
　　5.) 第五に、

3. Explain your view or perspective.
　　私の考えとして、〜と思います。

4. End with a concluding remark.
　　最後に、〜。　以上です。

【Helpful words】
1. Conjunction words
　　a. それから、：Then,
　　b. そのうえ、：Besides, moreover
　　c. しかも、：Besides, moreover
　　d. それとも、：Or
　　e. ですから、：Therefore,
　　f. しかし、：However,
　　g. 一般的〔いっぱんてき〕に言って、：Generally speaking,
　　h. たとえば：For instance,
　　i. なぜなら、〜からです。：That's because 〜

2. Uncertainty
   a. 日本人は魚をよく食べる<u>ようです</u>。Japanese seem to eat a lot of fish.
   b. 日本人は魚をよく食べる<u>らしいです</u>。Japanese seem to eat a lot of fish.
   c. 日本人は魚をよく食べる<u>かもしれない</u>。Japanese might eat a lot of fish.
   d. 日本人は魚をよく食べる<u>にちがいありません</u>。Japanese must eat a lot of fish.
   e. 日本人は魚をよく食べ<u>そうです</u>。It seems Japanese eat a lot of fish.
   f. 日本人は魚をよく食べる<u>そうです</u>。I heard that Japanese eat a lot of fish.

【Suggestions】
1. Learn about Japanese culture with accuracy and details.
2. Observe and think critically about reasons for Japanese cultural behavior.
3. If you are not sure about aspects of Japanese culture you are discussing, use grammar forms that express uncertainty.

アドバイス

アドベンチャー日本語１と２の漢字

Ⅰ	一 いち, ひと(つ)	二 に, ふた(つ)	三 さん, みっ(つ)	四 し, よ, よん, よっ(つ)	五 ご, いつ(つ)			
	六 ろく, むっ(つ)	七 しち, なの, なな(つ)	八 はち, よう, やっ(つ)	九 きゅう, く, ここの(つ)	十 じゅう, じっ, じゅっ, とお			
	月 がつ, げつ	日 にち, ひ, [び], か	火 か	水 みず, すい	木 き, もく	金 かね, きん	土 ど	
Ⅱ 2 課	口 くち, [ぐち]	目 め	人 ひと, にん, じん	本 もと ほん, [ぽん], [ぼん]	今 いま, こん	年 とし, ねん	私 わたし, わたくし	曜 よう
Ⅱ 3 課	上 うえ	下 した, くだ(さい)	大 おお(きい), たい, だい	小 ちい(さい), しょう	夕 ゆう	何 なに, なん	中 なか, ちゅう	外 そと, がい
Ⅱ 4 課	行 い(く), こう	来 き(ます), く(る), こ(ない), らい	子 こ	車 くるま, しゃ	学 がく, [がっ]	校 こう	見 み(る)	良 よ(い)	食 た(べる), しょく
Ⅱ 5 課	川 かわ, [がわ]	山 やま, さん	出 で(る), だ(す)	先 せん	生 う(まれる), せい	父 ちち, とう	母 はは, かあ	毎 まい	書 か(く), しょ
Ⅱ 6 課	手 て	耳 みみ	門 もん	聞 き(く), ぶん	女 おんな	好 す(き)	田 た, [だ]	男 おとこ	
Ⅱ 7 課	言 い(う)	語 ご	寺 てら, [でら], じ	時 とき, じ	間 あいだ, かん	分 わ(かる), ふん, [ぶん], [ぷん]	正 ただ(しい), しょう	家 いえ, か	々 [repeat]

第9課	白 しろ, はく	百 ひゃく, [びゃく], [ぴゃく]	千 せん, [ぜん]	万 まん	方 かた, ほう	玉 たま, [だま]	国 くに, [ぐに] こく, [ごく]	安 やす(い)	高 たか(い), こう	
第10課	牛 うし, ぎゅう	半 はん	*手 て, しゅ	友 とも	帰 かえ(る)	待 ま(つ)	持 も(つ)	米 こめ	番 ばん	事 こと, [ごと], じ
第11課	雨 あめ	電 でん	天 てん	気 き	会 あ(う), かい	話 はな(す), はなし, [ばなし], わ	売 う(る)	読 よ(む)		
第13課	右 みぎ	左 ひだり	入 い(れる), はい(る), [いり]	物 もの, ぶつ	名 な, めい	前 まえ, ぜん	戸 と, [ど]	所 ところ, [どころ] しょ	近 ちか(い)	
第14課	立 た(つ), りつ	作 つく(る), さく	肉 にく	魚 さかな	多 おお(い), た	少 すく(ない), すこ(し)	古 ふる(い)	新 あたら(しい), しん	*生 う(まれる), せい, なま	
第15課	才 さい	心 こころ, しん	思 おも(う)	休 やす(み)	買 か(う)	早 はや(い)	自 じ	犬 いぬ	太 ふと(る)	屋 や

* Previously introduced.

AIJ漢字

アドベンチャー日本語３の漢字

Ⅲ 1課	漢 かん	字 じ	姉 あね, ねえ	妹 いもうと	兄 あに, にい	弟 おとうと	朝 あさ, ちょう	昼 ひる, ちゅう
	明 あか(るい)	去 きょ	銀 ぎん	仕 し	*父 ちち, とう, ふ	*母 はは, かあ, ぼ	*先 せん, さき	家族 かぞく
	友達 ともだち	質問 しつもん	答え こたえ	宿題 しゅくだい	試験 しけん	昨日 きのう		
Ⅲ 2課	公 こう	文 ぶん	化 か, け	花 はな	海 うみ, かい	旅 りょ	教 おし(える), きょう	室 しつ
	後 うし(ろ), あと, ご	午 ご	着 き(る), つ(く)	知 し(る)	*私 わたし, わたくし, し	*男 おとこ, だん	*女 おんな, じょ	*子 こ, し
	*入 はい(る), い(れる), いり, にゅう	*行 い(く), こう, ぎょう	生徒 せいと	問題 もんだい	教科書 きょうかしょ	公園 こうえん	一度 いちど	図書館 としょかん
Ⅲ 3課	春 はる	夏 なつ	秋 あき	冬 ふゆ	雪 ゆき	元 げん	飲 の(む)	体 からだ, たい
	音 おと, おん	楽 たの(しい), らく, がく	糸 いと	紙 かみ, [がみ]	*生 う(まれる), なま, せい, しょう	世話 せわ	生活 せいかつ	体育 たいいく
	様 さま	変 へん	大変 たいへん					

＊ Previously introduced.

Underlined *kanji* are for recognition only.

III 4課	英 えい	草 くさ	林 はやし, [ばやし]	森 もり	台 たい, [だい]	始 はじ(める)	終 お(わる)	使 つか(う)
	勉 べん	強 つよ(い), きょう	回 かい	週 しゅう	*近 ちか(い), きん	*間 あいだ, かん, ま	本当 ほんとう	最近 さいきん
	違う ちがう	辞書 じしょ	〜君 -くん	週末 しゅうまつ				
III 6課	映 えい	画 が, かく	歌 うた, か	晩 ばん	夜 よる	黒 くろ, こく	茶 ちゃ, さ	飯 はん
	足 あし	長 なが(い), ちょう	走 はし(る)	起 お(きる)	寝 ね(る)	有名 ゆうめい	番組 ばんぐみ	女性 じょせい
	男性 だんせい	曲 きょく	子供 こども	選手 せんしゅ	彼 かれ	彼女 かのじょ		
III 7課	東 ひがし, とう	西 にし, せい	洋 よう	和 わ	部 ぶ, へ	美 うつく(しい), び	広 ひろ(い)	内 うち, ない
	主 しゅ	住 す(む), じゅう	開 あ(ける)	閉 し(める)	*生 う(まれる), なま, せい, しょう, い(ける)	*上 あ(がる), うえ, じょう	*下 お(りる), した, くだ(さい), へ	*正 せい, ただ(しい), しょう
	*寝 ね(る), しん	〜階 -かい, [-がい]	〜的 -てき	全部 ぜんぶ	座る すわる	正座 せいざ		

＊ Previously introduced.

Underlined *kanji* are for recognition only.

AIJ漢字

III 8課	竹 たけ	鳥 とり, ちょう	色 いろ	赤 あか	青 あお	黄 き	風 かぜ, ふう,[ふ]	味 あじ, み
	料 りょう	理 り	由 ゆう	重 おも(い)	*自 し,[じ]	自然 しぜん	焼く やく	苦手 にがて
	丸 まる	三角 さんかく	四角 しかく	弁当 べんとう	最～ さい～			
III 9課	北 きた, ほく,[ほっ]	南 みなみ	京 きょう	駅 えき	乗 の(る)	地 ち	鉄 てつ	図 ず, と
	道 みち, とう,[どう]	歩 ある(く), ほ,[ぽ]	動 うご(く), どう	働 はたら(く)	円 えん	*明 あか(るい), めい	*売 う(る), ばい	～線 －せん
	橋 はし,[ばし]	病院 びょういん	新幹線 しんかんせん	中央線 ちゅうおうせん				

* Previously introduced.

Underlined *kanji* are for recognition only.

アドベンチャー日本語4の漢字

IV 1課	社 しゃ,[じゃ]	員 いん	店 みせ, てん	客 きゃく	島 しま,[じま]	座 すわ(る), ざ	取 と(る)	卒 そつ
	業 ぎょう	同 おな(じ)	悪 わる(い)	両 りょう	全 ぜん	有 ゆう	当 とう	*少 すく(ない), すこ(し), しょう
	～歳 ～さい	言葉 ことば	失礼 しつれい	御～ ご～, お～	願い ねがい	写真 しゃしん	横浜 よこはま	
IV 2課	世 せ, せい	親 おや, しん	病 びょう	院 いん	医 い	者 しゃ	死 し(ぬ)	亡 な(くなる)
	忘 わす(れる)	育 そだ(てる), いく	降 ふ(る), お(りる)	困 こま(る)	末 すえ, まつ	族 ぞく	達 たち, [だち]	*男 おとこ, だん, なん
	*生 う(まれる), い(ける), い(きる), なま, せい, しょう	試合 しあい	結婚 けっこん	時代 じだい	太郎 たろう	次郎 じろう	子供 こども	忙 いそが(しい)
IV 3課	村 むら, そん	町 まち, ちょう	船 ふね, せん	州 しゅう	界 かい	第 だい	次 つぎ, じ	戦 たたか((う), せん
	争 そう	合 あ(う), あい	止 と(まる), や(む)	平 へい, ひら	不 ふ	活 かつ	送 おく(る)	*米 こめ, べい
	*地 ち, じ	日系人 にっけいじん	祖父 そふ	祖母 そぼ	畑 はたけ	汽車 きしゃ	単語 たんご	

＊ Previously introduced.

Underlined *kanji* are for recognition only.

AIJ漢字

IV 4課	洗 あら(う), せん	市 し	以 い	庭 にわ	軍 ぐん	連 つ(れる)	運 うん	都 と
	空 そら,[ぞら], から,くう	暑 あつ(い)	寒 さむ(い)	泣 な(く)	笑 わら(う)	薬 くすり, やく	館 かん	*口 くち, こう
	*火 ひ, か	*赤 あか, か	押 お(す)	引 ひ(く)	皆 みな(さん), みんな	和子 かずこ	普通 ふつう	急行 きゅうこう
IV 6課	石 いし, せき	園 えん	絵 え	葉 は,[ば]	度 ど	代 だい	然 ぜん	意 い
	最 もっと(も), さい	切 き(る), [きっ], せつ	習 なら(う), しゅう	続 つづ(く), つづ(ける)	苦 く, くる(しい), にが(い)	痛 いた(い)	静 しず(か)	的 てき
	*後 うし(ろ), あと, ご, のち	*庭 にわ, てい	*回 かい, まわ(す)	江戸 えど	刀 かたな	畳 たたみ, -じょう	僕 ぼく	数 かず, すう
IV 7課	神 かみ, しん, [じん]	仏 ぶつ, [ぶっ]	顔 かお	頭 あたま	幸 しあわ(せ), こう	福 ふく	建 た(てる), けん	考 かんが(える)
	助 たす(ける)	変 か(える), か(わる), へん	喜 よろこ(ぶ)	嬉 うれ(しい)	悲 かな(しい)	愛 あい	恋 こい, れん	*米 こめ, べい, まい
	*者 もの, しゃ	松 まつ	井 い	仲 なか	甘 あま(い)	野菜 やさい	果物 くだもの	協力 きょうりょく

＊ Previously introduced.

Underlined *kanji* are for recognition only.

AIJ漢字

388

IV 8課	宗 しゅう	原 はら, [ばら], げん	窓 まど	服 ふく	港 みなと, こう	晴 は(れ)	雲 くも	曇 くも(り)
	交 こう	通 かよ(う), とお(る), つう	泊 と(まる), はく, [ぱく]	発 はつ, [はっ], [ぱつ]	感 かん	関 せき, [ぜき], かん	特 とく, [とっ]	*着 き(る), つ(く), ちゃく
	*色 いろ, しき	富士山 ふじさん, ふじやま	成田 なりた	新宿 しんじゅく	奈良 なら	大阪 おおさか	歴史 れきし	風呂 ふろ
	到着 とうちゃく	飛行機 ひこうき	席 せき					
IV 9課	受 う(ける)	池 いけ, ち	箱 はこ, [ばこ]	冷 つめ(たい), れい	場 ば, じょう	野 の, や	球 たま, きゅう	問 もん
	題 だい	若 わか(い)	寄 よ(る), き	無 む	集 あつ(める), あつ(まる)	決 き(める), けつ, [けっ]	信 しん(じる), しん	*有 あり, ゆう
	*空 そら, くう, あ(き), から	*分 わ(かる), わ(ける), ふん, [ぷん], [ぶん]	*合 あ(う), あい, ごう	缶 かん	袋 ふくろ, [ぶくろ]	猫 ねこ	牛乳 ぎゅうにゅう	置 お(く)

✶ Previously introduced.

Underlined *kanji* are for recognition only.

AIJ漢字

アドベンチャー日本語上級の漢字

上級 1課	初 はじ(め), はつ, しょ	単 たん	試 し	験 けん	昨 さく	皆 みな, みんな	力 ちから, りょく	歳 とし, さい, せい
	局 きょく	記 き	転 てん	枚 まい	遅 おそ(い), ち	難 むずか(しい), -がた(い), なん	泳 およ(ぐ), えい	落 お(ちる), お(とす), らく
	治 なお(す), じ	*集 あつ(める), あつ(まる), しゅう	*音 おと, おん, ね	*待 ま(つ), まち, たい	*当 あ(たる), あ(てる), とう	*止 と(まる), と(める), し	趣味 しゅみ	一緒 いっしょ
	成績 せいせき	風邪 かぜ	将来 しょうらい	自己 紹介 じこしょうかい	誰 だれ	感謝 かんしゃ	目標 もくひょう	
上級 2課	向 む(ける), む(く), む(かう), こう	置 お(く)	祭 まつ(り)	温 あたた(かい), おん	暖 あたた(かい), だん	熱 あつ(い), ねつ	速 はや(い), そく	氷 こおり, ひょう
	工 こう	伝 つた(える), でん	昔 むかし	身 しん	宿 やど, しゅく, じゅく	答 こた(え), とう	期 き	点 てん
	数 かず, かぞ(える), すう	*南 みなみ, なん	*地 ち, じ	*元 げん, がん, もと	*間 あいだ, かん, げん	*色 いろ, しき	*好 す(き), こう	*重 おも(い), じゅう
	*中 なか, ちゅう, じゅう	嫌い きらい	観光地 かんこうち	御土産 おみやげ				

＊ Previously introduced.
Underlined *kanji* are for recognition only.

AIJ漢字

上級 3課	制 せい	服 ふく	進 すす(む), しん	相 あい, そう	願 ねが(う), がん	面 めん	接 せつ	必 かなら(ず), ひつ
	要 い(る), よう	術 じゅつ	組 くみ, ぐみ	個 こ	実 じつ	留 りゅう, る	遠 とお(い), えん	反 はん
	対 たい	遊 あそ(ぶ), ゆう	*足 あし, たり(る)	*行 い(く), こう, ぎょう, おこな(う)	*青 あお, せい	*春 はる, しゅん	合格 ごうかく	相談 そうだん
	その他 そのた	掃除 そうじ	洗濯 せんたく	返す かえす	郵便局 ゆうびんきょく			
上級 4課	法 ほう	経 けい	商 しょう	計 けい	授 じゅ	科 か	究 きゅう	専 せん
	結 むす(ぶ), けつ	婚 こん	式 しき	季 き	節 せつ, ぶし	贈 おく(る), ぞう	失 しつ	礼 れい
	非 ひ	表 おもて, ひょう	*飲 の(む), いん	*学 まな(ぶ), がく	*重 おも(い), じゅう, ちょう	専攻 せんこう	希望 きぼう	職業 しょくぎょう
	給料 きゅうりょう	教師 きょうし	氏名 しめい	得意 とくい	習慣 しゅうかん	祝う いわう	経済 けいざい	研究 けんきゅう
	非常口 ひじょうぐち							

＊ Previously introduced.
Underlined *kanji* are for recognition only.

AIJ漢字

上級 5課	背 せ	低 ひく(い), てい	形 かたち, かた/がた, けい	急 いそ(ぐ), きゅう	忙 いそが(しい), ぼう	側 がわ	酒 さけ, しゅ	調 しら(べる), ちょう
	横 よこ, おう	橋 はし, きょう	飛 と(ぶ), ひ	機 き	線 せん	便 べん, びん, たよ(り)	利 り	配 くば(る), はい/ばい
	写 しゃ	予 よ	払 はら(う)	*降 ふ(る), お(りる), こう	*小 ちい(さい), しょう, こ	*古 ふる(い), しょう, こ	*遅 おそ(い), おく(れる), ち	*幸 しあわ(せ), さいわ(い), こう
	*助 たす(ける), じょ	*治 なお(る), じ,ち	道路 どうろ	大丈夫 だいじょうぶ	危ない あぶない	危険 きけん	駐車 ちゅうしゃ	禁止 きんし
	違反 いはん	予報 よほう	気候 きこう	明後日 あさって	消す けす	太陽 たいよう	事故 じこ	
上級 6課	鼻 はな	辞 じ	引 ひ(く)	暗 くら(い), あん	品 しな, ひん	注 ちゅう	残 のこ(る), のこ(す), ざん	定 てい
	練 れん	短 みじか(い), たん	別 わか(れる), べつ	指 ゆび, し	階 かい/がい	婦 ふ	用 よう	絡 らく
	貸 か(す)	付 -つ(き), ふ	*屋 や, おく	*頭 あたま, ず	*痛 いた(い), つう	*都 と, つ	*調 しら(べる), ちょう	*足 た(りる), あし, そく
	健康 けんこう	中華 ちゅうか	韓国 かんこく	化粧室 けしょうしつ	紳士用 しんしよう	案内 あんない	材料 ざいりょう	

上級 7課	登 のぼ(る), と, とう	荷 に	成 な(る), なり. せい	際 きわ, ぎわ, さい	打 う(つ), だ	説 せつ, ぜつ	様 さま, よう	未 み
	夫 おっと, ふ, ふう	選 えら(ぶ), せん	雑 ざつ	現 げん	係 かか(り), けい	号 ごう	*写 うつ(す), しゃ	*家 いえ, か, け
	*伝 つた(える), でん	宅急便 たっきゅうびん	予約 よやく	通訳 つうやく	約～ やく～	(お)宮 (お)みや	-神宮 -じんぐう	(お)城 (お)しろ
	-城 -じょう	石油 せきゆ	雑誌 ざっし					

Verb Conjugations:

	NAI form informal, neg., nonpast	MASU form formal, nonpast	Dic. form informal, nonpast	BA form conditional	OO form informal, volitional	TE form	TA form informal, past
I. Group 1 Verbs							
み	のまない nomanai	のみます nomimasu	のむ nomu	のめば nomeba	のもう nomoo	のんで nonde	のんだ nonda
に	しなない shinanai	しにます shinimasu	しぬ shinu	しねば shineba	しのう shinoo	しんで shinde	しんだ shinda
び	あそばない asobanai	あそびます asobimasu	あそぶ asobu	あそべば asobeba	あそぼう asoboo	あそんで asonde	あそんだ asonda
い	かわない kawanai	かいます kaimasu	かう kau	かえば kaeba	かおう kaoo	かって katte	かった katta
ち	またない matanai	まちます machimasu	まつ matsu	まてば mateba	まとう matoo	まって matte	まった matta
り	かえらない kaeranai	かえります kaerimasu	かえる kaeru	かえれば kaereba	かえろう kaeroo	かえって kaette	かえった kaetta
	*ない * nai	あります arimasu	ある aru	あれば areba		あって atte	あった atta
き	かかない kakanai	かきます kakimasu	かく kaku	かけば kakeba	かこう kakoo	かいて kaite	かいた kaita
	いかない ikanai	いきます ikimasu	いく iku	いけば ikeba	いこう ikoo	*いって * itte	*いった * itta
ぎ	およがない oyoganai	およぎます oyogimasu	およぐ oyogu	およげば oyogeba	およごう oyogoo	およいで oyoide	およいだ oyoida
し	はなさない hanasanai	はなします hanashimasu	はなす hanasu	はなせば hanaseba	はなそう hanasoo	はなして hanashite	はなした hanashita
II. Group 2 Verbs							
-e	たべない tabenai	たべます tabemasu	たべる taberu	たべれば tabereba	たべよう tabeyoo	たべて tabete	たべた tabeta
□	みない minai	みます mimasu	みる miru	みれば mireba	みよう miyoo	みて mite	みた mita
Special verbs: おきます get up; happen, かります borrow, おります get off; go down, できます can do, -すぎます too ~, (シャワーを)あびます take a shower, いきます to live, おちます to fall, かんじます to feel							
III. Group 3 Irregular verbs							
する (do)	しない shinai	します shimasu	する suru	すれば sureba	しよう shiyoo	して shite	した shita
くる (come)	こない konai	きます kimasu	くる kuru	くれば kureba	こよう koyoo	きて kite	きた kita

＊Exceptional form.

動詞変化   394

	NAKATTA form informal, neg., past	(Honorific-Passive)	Causative Permissive	Polite Command	Neg. Command	Potential (Group 2 verb)	Command
I. Group 1 Verbs							
み	のまなかった nomanakatta	のまれる nomareru	のませる nomaseru	のみなさい nominasai	のむな nomuna	のめる nomeru	のめ nome
に	しななかった shinanakatta	しなれる shinareru	しなせる shinaseru	しになさい shininasai	しぬな shinuna	しねる shineru	しね shine
び	あそばなかった asobanakatta	あそばれる asobareru	あそばせる asobaseru	あそびなさい asobinasai	あそぶな asobuna	あそべる asoberu	あそべ asobe
い	かわなかった kawanakatta	かわれる kawareru	かわせる kawaseru	かいなさい kainasai	かうな kauna	かえる kaeru	かえ kae
ち	またなかった matanakatta	またれる matareru	またせる mataseru	まちなさい machinasai	まつな matsuna	まてる materu	まて mate
り	かえらなかった kaeranakatta ＊なかった * nakatta	かえられる kaerareru	かえらせる kaeraseru	かえりなさい kaerinasai	かえるな kaeruna	かえれる kaereru	かえれ kaere
き	かかなかった kakanakatta いかなかった ikanakatta	かかれる kakareru いかれる ikareru	かかせる kakaseru いかせる ikaseru	かきなさい kakinasai いきなさい ikinasai	かくな kakuna いくな ikuna	かける kakeru いける ikeru	かけ kake いけ ike
ぎ	およがなかった oyoganakatta	およがれる oyogareru	およがせる oyogaseru	およぎなさい oyoginasai	およぐな oyoguna	およげる oyogeru	およげ oyoge
し	はなさなかった hanasanakatta	はなされる hanasareru	はなさせる hanasaseru	はなしなさい hanashinasai	はなすな hanasuna	はなせる hanaseru	はなせ hanase
II. Group 2 Verbs							
-e	たべなかった tabenakatta	たべられる taberareru	たべさせる tabesaseru	たべなさい tabenasai	たべるな taberuna	たべられる taberareru	たべろ tabero
□	みなかった minakatta	みられる mirareru	みさせる misaseru	みなさい minasai	みるな miruna	みられる mirareru	みろ miro
Special verbs: おきます get up; happen, かります borrow, おります get off; go down, できます can do, -すぎます too ~, (シャワーを)あびます take a shower, いきます to live, おちます to fall, かんじます to feel							
III. Group 3 Irregular verbs							
する (do)	しなかった shinakatta	される sareru	させる saseru	しなさい shinasai	するな suruna	できる dekiru	しろ shiro
くる (come)	こなかった konakatta	こられる korareru	こさせる kosaseru	きなさい kinasai	くるな kuruna	こられる korareru	こい koi

＊Exceptional form.

動詞変化

REFERENCES

Japanese Language and Culture Course Description, College Board AP, May 2007

Makino, Seiichi and Tsutsui, Michio. *A Dictionary of Basic Japanese Grammar.* Tokyo: The Japan Times 1998

Makino, Seiichi and Tsutsui, Michio. *A Dictionary of Intermediate Japanese Grammar.* Tokyo: The Japan Times 1998

The Modern Reader's Japanese-English Character Dictionary, Tokyo: Tuttle Publishing 1962

「小学生のための漢字をおぼえる辞典」川嶋優　旺文社 1975 Tokyo

マイロク先生の地球一よく分かる！温暖化問題　www.team-6.net/-6sensei/

「となりのトトロ」徳間書店 Tokyo 1988

「あきらめないこと、それが冒険だ―エベレストに登るのも冒険、ゴミ拾いも冒険！」野口健著　学習研究社、２００７年発行

野口健著「あきらめないこと、それが冒険だ」学習研究社 Tokyo, 2006

on task ?

No

CH

F

B